BLACK BILLY

From the warm paradise of Sa'moa to the freezing cold wastes of Desolation Island in the heart of the Southern Ocean and north to the Bering Sea. Join William Henry Smith and his family in this true story of cannibalism, kidnapping, shipwreck and heartache as they travel the oceans of the world in the oldest whaling ship afloat, the Marie Laure.

First edition

Text, cover, editing and design copyright Kim McDermott

All rights reserved

No part of this publication may be reproduced or transmitted or utilized in any form or by any means, electronic, mechanical, photocopying or otherwise, without the prior permission of the author.

ISBN 978-0-646-71222-2

Apologies

Normally this part of a book is reserved for the introduction of the narrative by the author but this author feels he must apologise to descendants of William and others (my family) for not being able to locate all of the information required to write an absolute true and factual account of the life of 'Black Billy' and his family. Tragically, Lack of records, deliberate obstruction and facts lost to us in the mists of time and death, prevented an accuracy a story of this nature deserves and for any unintended inaccuracies, I humbly apologise.

The great deal of credit for the accurate information we did manage to glean from among the myriad of misleading documents, must go to Mary Ann Smith (granna) who my mum lived with from the time she was three years old until her marriage in 1950 and to whom she imparted a lifetime of firsthand knowledge, instructing that it should be passed on. To cousin Dotty, (Dorothy Armstrong) who scaled the obstacles of ignorance, racism and fear of exposure, to research William (all without the use of computers and modern search engines) and passed on this research, with the words, 'for Christ's sake Kim, put this information together and tell the story!'

To all other descendants of William's, including Glenn and Allana Smith, some of whom I've met and others I have yet to meet, I hope you enjoy the story of a more remarkable man than I could ever hope to portray. Thank you.

Black Billy

Chapter one

Year: 1936

Place: Henry Street, Strahan,

Tasmania.

'Waaaaaackeee!' her resonant, tuneful tones drifted across the grassy paddock as the old woman moved from the back door of the clapboard paling house and shuffled around the wooden tank stand towards the rickety paling fence, sad dark eyes within the folds of olive skin moving slowly from right to left as they scanned the lush green paddocks between the house across the road and the unpainted clapboard sheds and trees that lined the creek wending its way between them.

Save for the gentle hum of bees as they moved among the myriad of yellow buttercups that stood out from the green carpet of grass and the darker green leaves of the giant laurel tree that over hung the creek at the bridge, there was only stony silence.

She moved to the low fence, one calloused hand resting on the wooden rail whilst the other unconsciously moved into the gap created by the broken off paling top, and firmly gripped the side of another of the grey, weather beaten fence palings.

'Waaaaaaackie!' She called again, this time with just a hint of desperation in her voice. She had nodded off in the warmth of the old kitchen as she shelled the bowl of broad beans that would be her and the girl's evening meal, and she felt slightly disoriented and more than a little guilty at not checking on the child earlier. Still, it had only been less than an hour since her granddaughter had set off across the narrow dusty road towards the creek, intent on supplementing the evening meal with a fine passel of native Galaxia, or tiddlies as the fish were known locally.

'Or probably even an eel!' The little girl had exclaimed over her shoulder as she pushed the gate closed behind her and waved absently to the old lady before kneeling down at the first pat of cow or horse dung that dotted the grassy verges of the road. The old woman watched as the girl expertly flicked the whole cow pat on to its back with one deft movement of her wrist, before plunging her fingers deep into the soft cow shit pat and drawing out a fat, juicy worm to adorn the tiny brown hook at the end of the cotton thread of her home made fishing line.

The old lady stared after the girl as the latter made her way through the barbed wire fence at the far side of the road, cotton dress hanging limp over her skinny frame as she gingerly lifted the strands of wire apart and slid her bare feet and legs through the gap, one at a time, before running off to disappear beneath the low hanging branches of the dark green laurel tree.

It was at this point the old woman again stared. Willing the familiar face of her beloved granddaughter to appear from the spread of laurel branches and long grass and make her way towards her. In the gloom of shadow beneath the laurel's branches she knew the dogs at their kennels would be moving about frenetically, each vying for the attentions of the girl if she were at the water's edge nearby.

There was no movement.

The old woman fought down the panic beginning to rise and stepped back, pulling the wooden gate open as she did and stepped through. She turned her head to the right and from her position outside the fence, she could see across to the far paddocks of her neighbor, John Henry. She pursed her lips at the sight of John Henry's red bull grazing lazily in the centre of the paddock, the bull was useful as a secret breeder with her own jersey cow, but the animal hated children and would certainly be showing signs of agitation if the child was anywhere near. Besides, her granddaughter knew this and would not dare attempt to cross the paddock when the bull was present.

She switched her attention to the paddock beyond the small barn on the far side of the creek and lifted her left hand to shield her eyes from the glare of the afternoon sun. At the sight of the horse grazing peacefully near the creeks far edge, she felt the fear rise in her chest. The agonizing memories of losing her daughter to a moment's inattention all those years ago, had all sorts of vivid and terrible thoughts racing through the old woman's mind.

As if sensing her fear and attempting in its own way to calm the old woman, the old horse lifted his head and shook it violently, dislodging the dozens of annoying march flies from their blood sucking feast and scattering them into the air in a cloud of buzzing wings before settling on the animal's neck and ears almost immediately.

Resigned to the flies being part of the price of a warm summer's day, the horse gave up his shaking and looked tiredly in the direction of the old woman, holding her eyes for a few long seconds as if admonishing her for her inattentiveness, before turning his head and staring intently at a spot near the creek that was obscured from the old woman's view by a rise in the paddock floor.

The woman followed the animal's gaze and noticed the tiniest movement just above the line of the grassy hump near the creeks edge. She hardly dared allow the relief to push the fear away lest her faith in the old horse be proved wrong. Just because old Frosty could see something, didn't mean her granddaughter was safe. She felt her voice catch as she called again, becoming sharper and more authoritive, in the direction of the movement.

'Wacky!' Her voice had no sooner stopped echoing across the paddock than she noticed the movement become more violent, a thin black line against the background of bracken and blackberry bushes as it waved in the air, the tip flicking about like some demented dragonfly being pushed higher and higher above the grassy hump, almost vertically, into the air. She strained her eyes to identify the object and her shoulders slumped with relief as she recognized the hook and worm clumped against the tip of the slender fishing pole climbing higher and higher as the carrier ascended the far side of the small knoll from the creeks edge towards the paddock.

'Coming Granna.' The words struck the old woman's ears like a warm, comforting wave and relief flooded over her. She felt like rushing to the child and gathering her into her ample frame, all the while telling her how much she loved her, but here in the road, she was in full view of neighbours who no doubt would be witnessing these events unfold and it simply wouldn't do for her to be showing weakness to those who might use it against her in some petty way. She simply cocked her head sideways, and pretended to admonish the child for not replying sooner as she herded the girl roughly towards the gate.

Once behind the fence, however, the mood changed dramatically as the girl unraveled the eight tiddlies from the whalebone fern. Placing her thumb on top of the fishes' head and wrapping her other fingers against its belly, she reverently lifted each fish clear of the stem of the fern via its mouth and gills until each had been lined up proudly on the small Huon Pine board her grandmother had placed on the tank stand just for this purpose. All the while her dramatic descriptions of the ones that got away and the battles with those that didn't, were met with cries of gosh and wonder from the old woman.

With the fish lined in a row, the little girl turned to her grandmother and grinned evilly as the old woman drew the sharpened knife from that secret place where all much-needed things are stored until required, beneath her massive, stained apron, and commenced to gut and clean the evenings meal. The girl watched in awe as the knife blade flicked back and forth across the fish carcasses, the grey blade worn to less than a quarter of its original width by years of meticulous honing with stone and steel, the thin silver edge of the concave curve of the blade sending glints of sunlight into her eyes as the tiny strings of innards and scales seemed to fly effortlessly from each carcass.

As the final piece of fish gut landed at the feet of the appreciative old tom cat, a skillet appeared in the old woman's left hand as if by magic and the fish were skillfully flicked from the wooden board into the thin film of dripping coating the bottom of the pan.

The girl seemed never to tire of this ritual and laughed out loud, bringing an indulging smile from the old woman before she turned the pan out in front of her with an exaggerated flourish and lead the way back inside the house, leaving the cat to cast aimlessly about in the forlorn hope of more choice tidbits.

'When's grandfather due home?' The girl asked as the two sat at the kitchen table eating the fish and beans supper. The question came out of a constant flow of chatter that had not let up since the girl had walked in the gate and the old woman replied patiently as she always did when the conversation between the two seemed to dry up.

'Not long now.' She answered quietly. 'Just a month or two.'

Harry Doherty, her husband, had left for the Huon Pine forests of the Gordon River about a month ago and seeing as how each trip lasted about three months, she knew she shouldn't expect him for yet another two. She smiled and stared patiently at the little girl as the chatter began again. She cleared the few dishes away and ushered the girl into the tiny lounge room where each undressed, and using the water from the China bowl sparingly, washed up and redressed for bed.

This done, the old woman gathered up the girl on to her knee and held her close. The girl loved these times. With grandfather away in the river, it was just her and Granna and although she loved her grandfather, she much preferred the company of her grandmother, who would regale her with tales of sailing ships and adventures that fascinated her. She could barely believe that this woman who lived in such straightened circumstances had travelled so extensively and seen so much of the world. She didn't notice the darker shade of her grandmother's skin, or the derogatory manner in which some others spoke down to her, but she was fully aware of the sadness behind the beautiful dark eyes of her beloved Granna and questioned repeatedly the reason for the sad smile and long periods of silence, when it appeared the old woman was away in a world of her own, wan smile playing on her lips as if once again riding the wild seas of the Southern Ocean and south pacific. That is, if the stories were true!

With darkness not far off, the old woman hushed the girl from demanding more stories and led her along the short passage to her bed room. At the door of her room, the inevitable request was made as it was made every night her husband was away. The words would come almost in a whisper, 'Can I sleep with you tonight, Granna?'

The old woman would tut tut and admonish the child for not having the courage to sleep alone but secretly she would be so glad of the request. She loved this child so much, peering into the room where only two years before, she had prayed beside her bed, begging the lord not to allow the scarlet fever that wracked her tiny body to take her from them, vowing never to let any harm come to her if he should let her live.

As the memory of her promise surfaced, as it did each time she entered the girl's room, the old woman would lovingly press the girl's cheek against her own hip and gently lead her away from the room full of bad memories to her own room, where she would watch in the darkness as the child's eyes closed in sleep.

This night however, it was different. The summer evening was drawn out into a long twilight, and the fingers of light reaching into the room through the dusty window panes and between the heavy floral curtains, cast a pinkish glow that filled the room and together with the summer heat, cast aside all weariness, staving off sleep and bringing to the surface a thousand memories of years past. The old woman reveled in these times, times where she could lay in an ethereal world of half dreams, half memories, escaping to times of childhood freedom and a world so far away.

She could feel herself drifting off to sleep and felt she was imagining the sleeping child raising her right arm and pointing towards the top of the wardrobe. The child's words jolted her from her past.

'What's in that box, Granna?'

Startled, the old woman came awake, slightly annoyed at being dragged away from fond memories of a long distant past but when her eyes settled on the object of the child's attention she smiled, for here was the proof that it was all real. These reveries were not dreams, nor were they figments of her imaginings as her husband and other members of her family would have her believe. But as she stared at the box, other memories of the past came to her, terrible memories of heartache and suffering foisted on herself and others for no other reason than the colour of their skin.

She stared at the box for a couple of moments, realising she had never shown its contents to anyone since the death of her daughter closed that chapter of her life all those years ago. Now a lifetime and a world away from past events, she found it hard to believe they had actually occurred. She gently turned the blankets away from her and slowly swung her legs over the side of the bed. She knew it was time to confront her demons and pass on the stories of the past as her ancestors had done before her.

She reached up with both hands and gently tapped the box from side to side. Each time she tapped it, the box would move towards her and she continued knocking it back and forth with her fingers until she could grasp each side with her hands. Lifting the box down from its lofty perch, she was surprised at how heavy it was, not like she remembered it at all. When she had been a young girl the box had seemed huge, the triangles of all types of inlaid wood gleaming with polish as the work box sat in pride of place at the captain's table. She recalled her father explaining each piece of timber and recounting where each piece came from and the adventures that accompanied it as her tiny finger traced his gigantic thumb across the surface of the box as if traversing the face of the world, as indeed it was. Then, as she grew older, the box, on the rare occasion she saw it, seemed smaller, almost insignificant. Pushed to the back of his cluttered desk and reduced to nothing more than a glorified candle holder and only through sheer oversight being saved from the yearly burning of all things useless. She shook her head sadly at the reminder of how foolish she and her siblings had been to ignore the very part of their heritage that had survived to prove the story.

She motioned the girl to follow her and the young one needed no encouraging as she sensed an important part of her life beginning to unfold. On countless occasions, she had stared at the square, dark shape atop the wardrobe, gathering the courage to ask her grandmother its purpose, but too soon the darkness would obliterate the shape from her sight and too often sleep would erase the questions from her mind.

The old lady opened the curtains after she had placed the Ditty Box on the dresser and she smiled as the hands of her granddaughter moved gently across the surface of the lid, knowing it was far beyond time to relate the story of their heritage and with her own children grown and scattered, the only audience left to care was this skinny, fair haired child who, unlike all her other children, seemed enchanted by this small piece of history.

Her attention turned from the child to the work box. All edges of the box had been covered with strips of blackwood and inside these, thirty-two triangles of assorted timbers, timbers such as the prized bird's eye Huon pine, blackwood, oak and mahogany, dominated the lid. The sides were also inlaid with the rare timbers, although some had been split and gouged, the corners broken away by many of the violent acts of man and nature the Ditty Box had obviously been subjected to.

Both back and front of the lid had five triangles inlaid between strips of Huon Pine and each end of the lid held four of the polished pieces. Eight large triangles faced the back and front of the box as did each end, the sheen of each piece reflecting the light from the window, giving the appearance of a highly polished and well kept surface. The old woman knew this could not be further from the truth and she smiled sadly as she counted at least four scorch marks where successive candles had either fallen over or, left unattended, had burned down to etch their mark deep into the surface. She could still feel the runs of candle wax along the sides of the box as her shaking hands turned the small brass key and lifted the lid.

The girl's wide eyes of anticipation turned to a frown of disappointment at the sight of one central open compartment with three smaller compartments down each side. In one or two of the compartments a button and thread stared forlornly back at them, otherwise the box was empty. The girl lifted her head and stared questioningly up at her grandmother. The old lady smiled her sad smile, and placing each thumb and forefinger against the two thin edges of the outer compartment, gently lifted the set of compartments clear as one.

The girl frowned as she tried to identify the two dark shapes nestled in the lower confines of the box and even when the old woman had lifted the official looking papers clear of the items, the girl still couldn't identify what it was she was seeing. Only when the pieces were lifted clear of the box did she identify the objects as teeth. But not just any teeth, these were huge teeth, whale's teeth! The resin coated eye teeth of the whale had dark stains at the chipped ends where the giant sperm whale had driven them against the bones of some equally huge sea monster. Further down from the tips, the teeth became a creamy yellow and as she held the wonderfully smooth whale's teeth in her tiny hands, the girl, Phyllis Amelia, could make out the scrimshaw etched into the surface of each.

She held one of the heavy teeth in each hand and stared intently at the shapes of the women in their fur coats as her grandmother held each of her hands in hers and whispered, 'These teeth were taken from a sperm whale in the Pacific Ocean and presented to me on the back of a whale as a present from the captain and ships company, on my third birthday.'

The girl stared up at her grandmother in disbelief and awe and the old woman felt a surge of pride as the girl exclaimed, 'The stories were true!'

Tears welling in her eyes, the old woman nodded slowly.

'Those stories,' She said, 'And much, much, more.'

The girl clutched the two whale's teeth to her chest, one in each hand and leaned against her grandmother in the failing light, fearing she would have to go to sleep before she learned more.

'Tell me the story, Granna.' She begged, 'Please.'

The old lady wrapped her arms around the little girl and clasped her hands behind her. She was pleased the child was interested. Who knows, if she related the stories carefully, here might be someone to remember enough to tell those who will come later, just what their history was.

'Oh, there is more than just one story,' the old lady replied. 'The stories I have to tell you will take many years to tell and hopefully one day you will be able to relate them to your children and grandchildren.'

The child, fingers dwarfed by the whale's tooth in each hand, looked up at her grandmother.

'Can I take them to bed with me?' she whispered, quietly.

'Of course, you can.' The old lady murmured. 'From this time on, they belong to you.'

The girl clutched the whale's teeth to her chest and using her elbows, clambered onto the old wooden bed and lay her head on one of the old, kapok filled pillows, as the old lady moved into the bed alongside her the girl lifted the ivory teeth towards the woman.

'When will you tell me the stories, Granna?'

The old lady went quiet for a moment, as if in deep thought and the girl felt she might have asked just a little too much of her grandmother for one night. She dropped her head and pretended to be engrossed in the ivory shapes in her hands.

Mary Ann Doherty stared lovingly at her granddaughter. In the days of her father, the elders would sit all the family members down and relate the stories of their ancestors so that all would know their history for all times to come but she was now the only person alive who knew the story of her family and this girl was the only person of her family who was interested in hearing their history. She knew the incidents she would be forced to recall would sometimes be painful and at times, devastating, for her to speak about out loud, but she knew it must be told. First, she would tell of the people involved and each night she would relate a piece of the story and tonight would be the first night she would begin to face the demons of her own past.

She smiled as the girl nervously raised her face towards her own and gently folded her right arm around the girl's shoulder, remembering the words of her father, the Samoan.

To the child's obvious delight, she whispered. 'Come little one, there's something I must tell you.'

The old lady talked softly until the girl fell asleep before gently removing the whale's teeth from her granddaughter's grasp and placing them on the dresser beside the bed.

As she lay in the darkness, she could feel the tears welling in her eyes and slowly trickling down each side of her face as her mind drifted back further, to a time long before her time, where the story began.

Chapter 2

Time: January 10th 1838.

Place: Upolu, Navigators Island. Later Samoa.

Her sails had been furled one by one as she approached the island. Now the only sails aloft were the main and the spanker, from the mizzen to the stern, both beginning to luff and spill air as the sheets at each bottom corner were let go. The barque presented a fine sight as she slowed and dropped anchor a good three hundred yards offshore, her bluff bow and square stern not detracting at all from the majesty her three masts and all one hundred and forty feet of shipbuilding expertise presented. She moved gracefully ahead towards the shore until her heavy kedge anchor found purchase on the coral bottom and the breeze against the mizzen sail at the stern began bringing her head to sea.

As she did her slow, graceful turn, those watching from the safety of the palm forest near the shore could see men sliding down ropes from the tops to the deck below, while others stood among the mass of rigging at the top's platforms or in the shrouds just below, staring shoreward at the seemingly deserted beach. As those who were on the ropes reached the deck, they began moving about with purpose, hauling on rope blocks and rolling out the large tuns, or barrels, towards the whale boats that swung outboard on their davits along each side of the ship behind the main mast.

She was a whaler, a Barque, bluff lines, three masts instead of four and unlike those of the pretty ships that plied their trade in cotton or tea as they raced across the world to secure their masters the best possible price in their respective commodities, she was designed for months, even years, of heavy labour among the huge seas and leaden skies north or south of the forties latitudes.

Five months out of Greenock on behalf of her Scottish masters her pickings had been lean until she had chanced upon large pods of spermaceti heading north from the freezing wastes of the Southern Ocean towards the paradisiacal islands and warm blue waters of the south pacific. Captain Benjamin MacDonald had intended to make his home port at Hobarton, Van Dieman's Land, where he could confer with the ship's owners via transports returning to the motherland, but he was unconcerned, even pleased, as the whale pods skirted far to sea of the rocky cliffs of south eastern Van Dieman's Land and moved north towards the islands of the pacific.

MacDonald knew he would have to resupply and that would mean locating some form of trading post or native population who were unlikely to attack or invade his ship. He knew his crew would have heard the stories of murder and cannibalism and to allay their fears and bolster their courage, he had the ships carpenter bolt the tiny, out dated falconet cannon on the quarter deck where it could be seen quite clearly by any potential foe.

He had no intention of using the gun as anything other than a deterrent and doubted if any man aboard had even had experience in such a weapon but instead of exposing his own ignorance by calling for volunteer gunners, he had instructed his first mate, Rogers, and Smith, the carpenter, to place the small cask of black powder and basket of inch and a half diameter iron balls near the weapon, and pretend both he and the captain knew what they were about when it came to expert gunnery.

He knew from the change in his crew's attitude, their sullen, fearful stares shoreward changing to one of brash confidence and anticipation as they realized their impending excursion would be overseen by a force of such magnitude, his decision, he hoped, was the right one. Although he had to shrug his shoulders and raise his eyes towards the heavens when the first mate began whispering questions on how to operate the weapon. He patted the weapon and grinned disarmingly in the direction of his crew before lifting his telescope to his eye, fully aware that there would be more than one pair of eyes staring right back at him.

Mani's eyes scanned the barque and noted the small falconet mounted on the poop deck. He also noted the two papalagi standing abaft the gun mount at the stern railing, the thin brass tube held to the eye of the captain as he scanned the foreshore where Mani and his men were hiding.

Most of the men among the palms had seen this strange action before and many wondered why a man would deliberately obscure his own vision by sticking a metal tube in his eye at a time when the use of both eyes to view the movement of strangers was paramount. Mani alone knew what the shiny tube was for. He had even looked in the end of one of these when offered by the travelling papalagi missionary when he last visited the round house. He remembered scowling at the missionary to hide his admiration for something so beautiful as he ran his hands along the smooth, brassy surface and remembered also the shock of the scene coming so close to him, almost falling upon him as he held the tube to his eye.

He much preferred not to show himself or his men but if the white man could draw him from the cover of the forest with his shiny stick as he did the people of the village when he held the shiny stick to his own eye, then there wasn't much he could do about it.

Mani knew the men aboard the whaler would be desperate for water and supplies but he also knew it would take little to startle them and have them move off for safer havens. The appearance of himself and his men had to appear subtle and friendly if he was to achieve his aim for his was not the need for guns or revenge against the papalagi. Indeed, he respected the men and the guns of their great ships that plied the waters of his islands in search of Tafola, the great whale. It was this knowledge of engineering and gunsmithing Mani would need if he was to protect his tribe of villagers from being completely overrun by the other families of this island. The islands had enjoyed almost eight years of uneasy peace since the great war but with the age of Malietoa Tavita growing each day, it would not be too long before the tribes were plunged into war once more. Mani needed to learn the expertise of the papalagi in all things warfare and survival and he knew also he could not force the white men to help him. He had to be smart and resourceful if his bold plan was going to succeed.

Little did he know the captain had already noted the footprints along the edge of the wet sand and was aware of the presence of Mani's men, the captain's only concern was whether the natives were friendly or not.

Captain MacDonald traced at least eight lines of footprints, blending and spreading as they led from the water's edge across the thin line of black sand beach to the forest beyond. The area of disturbed sand, together with those singular lines of prints which seemed to track aimlessly from points along the palm forest edge to join the main groups of footprints, could mean more than twice that number of natives were lying in wait among the tangle of exposed roots and palm fronds.

'On the other hand,' he thought aloud, 'If I were to take the optimistic view, there might only be half that number.'

At his mates enquiring stare, he handed the eyeglass over and motioned in the direction of the beach, careful to keep his expression jovial and his voice down to a whisper,

'A trifle disconcerting, I know Mr. Rogers, but we need to meet with these natives if we are to maintain a viable presence in these parts.' He took the eyeglass back from the mate and grinned disarmingly, 'Prepare two boats and a shore party, with myself in the lead boat, Mr. Mate.'

At the mate's order, the deck came alive with seamen. Two whale boats were swung out, one on each side of the ship, four oarsmen to each boat. As the boats settled in the water, plaited rope fenders were put down the side of the mother ship to prevent any chafing of the boats as the men struggled to maneuver the large tuns into place between the thwarts. Once the boats were ready to move off, the captain turned to the mate and ordered firmly that a third boat should be sent down and made to stand off the shore, ready to support the shore party if the need arise. The mate grinned his approval. Most natives were aware that a boat standing off would most likely be armed and could land a fighting force within minutes of any sign of trouble. It was the perfect deterrent and his shore party would be more confident, able to carry out whatever work had to be done without the need to be constantly looking over their shoulder.

Going ashore presented somewhat of a quandary to the crew. After weeks at sea, with only the brackish, oil stained drinking water left in the few tuns aboard that did not contain whale oil, the idea of bathing in one of the many sandy pools of clear fresh water that lay in the lower reaches of the main river and its streams that ran from the heavily timbered mountains near the centre of these islands to the sandy shores of the coast, was always welcome. Against the idyllic thoughts of lazing on the sandy beach, fresh, clean and rested from their labours, they had to reconcile the wilder and more imaginative thoughts of attack from the unpredictable natives and possibly ending up being main course in some cannibalistic feast. Improbable though this scenario was, it was almost incumbent upon these ignorant and mostly superstitious seamen to imagine the worst.

MacDonald passed the eyeglass to the mate and moved forward from the quarterdeck to descend the short step way to the main deck when the mate called, 'Captain!' The captain glanced enquiringly, first at the mates raised palm, then allowed his eyes to follow the direction of the mates pointed finger. MacDonald allowed his right hand to rest on the railing of the stepway and turned back to face the bow of the ship. He had to crane his neck and lean slightly to his right to get a line of sight between the masts and trypot stacks of his own ship before he could make out the dark outline of the second ship rounding the low headland.

He stared for but a few seconds at the shrouds of sail atop the darker shape of the ship, sails of a grimy grey colour merging with the blue grey of the afternoon cloud on the horizon and giving a clue as to her home port before a familiar whiff carried to the

Elizabeth MacGregor and all work upon the deck ceased as the crew turned to seaward as one.

'She's a Yankee, captain!' The mate exclaimed. 'Can smell her from here, probably a Nantucket man!'

MacDonald grinned. All whaling men knew of the lack of cleanliness aboard a lot of the American whaling ships. The much newer ships and stricter regime of the Scottish and English captains and owners resulted in the European whaling ships being kept to an almost naval standard and much mirth and derision was directed towards the much older and long travelled whalers of the American side.

The Yankee whalers out of New England ports such as Boston harbour, Nantucket or New Bedford had carried the economy of the Americas from the seventeenth century, hitching a ride on the gulf stream from their home ports and sailing as far south as the South Shetlands and as far north as the Bering Sea in their efforts to fill their holds with the precious and much needed oil and fittings of the giant creatures of the deep. But a lot of these ships were old, with decades of oil and grime from the smoke of the trypots and boilers on their decks coating not just every inch of the vessel, but the sails and rigging and men that were their engines.

This ship had not long caught a whale and although there was no smoke from her tryworks and no oil filled tuns obvious on her decks, Macdonald could see the pile of bones on her forrard deck and the open drums of whale pieces that had not been boiled in the trypots, putrefying in the hot pacific sun as the last dregs of oil dripped into the bottom of the drums, creating a stench so overpowering that some harbour masters refused permission to tie up and once they had offloaded their precious cargo, these 'stinkers' were obliged to move off and anchor downwind of any inhabited place. It was the stench of these older ships and the very real threat of fire aboard should the ingrained oil ignite that had the penurious Scottish ship owners and captains working their crews for longer hours cleaning and washing down to ensure no such danger could threaten their livelihood.

All eyes, including those on the shore, followed the newcomer as she drifted in a slow arc to rest abaft and downwind of the Elizabeth MacGregor, a move noted by MacDonald as respectful and he halted the work to go ashore and lifted his right hand in acknowledgement of the Captain of the Sag Harbour.

'She's a hen ship as well, captain' the mate raised his eyebrows at MacDonald as he drew the eyeglass from his face. He grinned. 'I'm believin' there'll be a gammin' tonight, Captain.'

'You're forgetting one thing Mister Rogers.' The captain replied, opening both his palms towards the mate and pretending to look about the deck for someone. 'We have no women aboard ship for her captain's wife to chatter with.'

MacGregor could see that some of the crew had overheard the mate's comment referring to the other boat being a 'hen ship', a ship that carried at least one female, usually the captain's wife, aboard. It was not uncommon for captains, and sometimes, a first or second mate, to have their wives and even children aboard for the long voyages to sea. After all, in lean times, the earnings of even the captain could be very poor and would it not be better if he could feed and look after his family at the expense of the owner rather than lay out the cost of living for a family that would not be available to him for many months or even years, at a time.

The Elizabeth MacGregor was different, neither her captain nor any of the three mates had married so it would be slim pickings for any women looking forward to the sharing of women's banter aboard his ship tonight. Still, the captain looked from the mate to the men now beginning to crowd the main deck just forrard of the quarter deck, and gauging the mood that his crew would prefer to engage in a shore gam, a social gathering where crews exchanged stories, and if either ship was heading in the direction of their home, mail, or some other gift or good news for their families, rather than spend all night on a sober deck, as with the exception of the captain and mates, alcohol was forbidden for crew members aboard most whaling ships.

Captain MacGregor pursed his lips and looked again towards the other whaler before turning his head towards the first mate. 'Mister Rogers,' the captain said loud enough that the crew might hear. 'Take a starboard boat and invite the captain and his family to eat with me aboard tonight.' He waited just a moment, deliberately keeping his back to the men on deck before adding, 'Mister Smith,' at his call, the ship's carpenter and cartographer turned from his place near the davits. 'Take some swappings and a small firkin ashore so the men might enjoy some refreshment after they finish watering the ship.'

Smith had engaged in Greenock and with experience in blacksmithing and map drawing was a welcome asset to MacDonald's crew. Men who could read and write were a rarity in this business and with his skills in ships carpentry as well, Smith was a favorite of the captain, but being only a ships carpenter and with little experience before the mast was not entitled to join the ships first, second and third mates at the captain's table. The captain knew this would not bother Smith, for he was well aware the carpenter was more at home exploring the islands and shores than serving aboard.

Mana heard the cheer from aboard the first ship but had no idea what it was for. He was troubled, with the appearance of the second ship his idea to entice one of the crew to help him looked decidedly in jeopardy. He could smell the remains of Tafola, the great whale emanating from the second ship but to him they were simply white man's ships and he did not know whether they travelled in company or this occasion was simply a chance meeting. He decided to make his own presence known before the ships companies could be startled by the appearance of what they might perceive as savage natives.

Gathering up a large palm frond he gestured to a couple of his men to do the same and began ambling down the beach towards the shore, slowly waving the frond in a welcoming manner. Abruptly the murmur of voices from both ships halted and all faces were turned shoreward. Mana stopped at the water's edge and dropping the frond, he opened his hands in a gesture of suppliance before raising his right hand in a friendly wave. Both captains recognized the gesture and waved back. The native had made it clear he was friendly and wanted to trade. They would eat well tonight.

Chapter 3

Greenock, Scotland

Henry Smith had always been fascinated with the stories of faraway places told and retold on the packing crates and barrels outside the bars and taverns of the Greenock docks. As a lad he had watched his father tramp the Crawfordsdyke road, from the ballast quarries to the glass factory and back to the ship building yards of the Clyde, picking up work wherever he could get it. Young Henry had gained some schooling when his father was able to afford it and when the chance to work in the famous Clydeside shipyards alongside his father came, he jumped at it.

The work was hard, dirty and varied for young Henry and the hundreds of men who would one week be canting and turning the huge baulks of rock elm or greenheart timber that had been transported from the Americas, near the dockside at Blacknall Street, to line them ready for the huge block and tackle cranes to snag and haul them into the benches and the next week shoveling and raking the tons of bark shavings and sawdust that piled up around the shore, and were reduced to a stinking black cess that at first poisoned the waters around the shoreline then, after being heaped up and dried, was shoveled again onto the backs of carts and hauled to the nearby glassworks for burning in the furnaces along with the coal, poisoning also the air, around the green hills of Greenock.

Henry disliked immensely the yard work and was most pleased to move into the shipwright shops and cartographer offices of the Scott family. He especially liked his work when the company ordered his father to help with the testing of a new model of ship and after two or three days of back breaking toil of hauling the boat to the lake and then launching the fifteen foot model into Loch Thom, a lake in the hills above the new shipbuilding works and the fast growing town of Greenock, Henry would spend hours standing on the high ground near the lake and stare out over the myriad of sails of all sizes and shapes that plied the Clyde, imagining with each boat or ship that unloaded their cargoes to the wharves and warehouses, that the town seemed to add a new building or street to its already fast growing footprint.

From his vantage point near Loch Thom, his eyes were drawn to following the rivers course and he could easily trace the line of sails as the river turned to the west and opened up to the firth of Clyde and although the river was obscured at this point by the low hills in the distance, he could imagine the fresh water clashing with the briny, green waves of the Irish Sea and wondered just what it would be like to just keep on sailing, farther and farther until he reached the islands the sailors talked about, the pure white sands of Jamaica, or the warm blue waters of the pacific, until a shout from his father or one of the others would have him being disappointingly jolted back to the reality of another week in the yards.

It was these disappointments that had Henry learning as much as he could about the ship building trade in the hope that one day his chance would come to travel to these wonderful faraway places, *'where they make the wind and the sun warms your face on every day of the year'* as one seaman had put it.

Henry's mother had died in childbirth and he considered himself a lucky child to have a father who loved him enough to care for him and school him in a manner very few of his childhood friends had. Those of his friends, and there were many, whom had lost a parent, or sometimes both, to disease or accident at sea, had little recourse other than depend on relatives for succor or apprentice themselves out to the harsh masters of the workhouses and orphanages. Thus, it was with great sadness he recalled the day the news of his father's death by thrombosis was conveyed to him at work in the map room at Scott's. It was one of the Scott family themselves, he was not sure which, who had conveyed the sad tidings and uttered their condolences and offered him continued work should he decide to stay on.

Henry had intended to stay no longer than the time it took to see his father interred alongside his mother, two simple crosses adorned with names and dates in the Laird street burying ground. Following the short wake in the pub afterwards, he walked the track up along the south Burn to the loch, his favorite place of solace, and sensed another feeling besides that of sadness and loss, a feeling of freedom. He no longer had the constraints of family to ensure he followed the strict protestant rules of his upbringing. His Masonic heritage and teachings of his father had been ingrained in him from an early age but it seemed there was something else, perhaps the free spirit of his mother, he wasn't sure but he could feel the sense of longing to be free of the constraints of the increasingly dirty city he was born in and, if he didn't move now, would surely die in.

Almost if in answer to his quandary, he saw her. Far to his left, clearing the low headland and opening up the river proper. The luffing sails of the barque, as she made her way up the Clyde caught his attention and he knew at once this was no trading ketch plying its way between London or Bristol with leather or cloth, no, she was a whaler, and from whence she came he had no idea. The very thought of not knowing what ports she had visited or where she might be bound, excited him. One thing he did know was, when she left this port of Greenock, no matter where she was bound, he would be aboard!

The Elizabeth MacGregor was a Greenock ship, laid down in the very shipyards Henry worked in, some twelve years prior and Henry warmed to her immediately. It took little convincing the captain he would be of good service to her deck, as ship's carpenters, especially those who could read maps and write, as well as being followers of the revered craft, were very hard to come by in these days of factories and daily paid workers.

But life on deck wasn't the enjoyable sun filled life William had imagined. It was true, the blue pacific waters and the isles beneath the wind, were all the old tars had said they were but to get to them one had to endure the hellish winds of the roaring forties and fifties as well as the stink and gore of the whaling chore and the shortages of food and even drinkable water that was the accepted life aboard a whaler.

Captain MacDonald had noticed the new chum's somewhat reticent manner when it came to cleaning the putrid gore of the pickings barrels or bone piles and shook his head and smiled knowingly as Smith grimaced in disgust at the malodorous stench emanating from the bits barrels and try pots as the crew sat around eating their meals from whatever table like structure each man could find.

It wasn't like he was a poor worker, indeed the carpenter was a willing and strong deck hand but the captain could see this man was a landlubber and this was evidenced in the fact that each time the Elizabeth would call at the humblest of ports, Smith would be the first one to volunteer to go ashore. Then, once work was done, instead of taking his ease among the deck fittings, would spend hours walking and exploring the coves and streams of even the remotest island. It wouldn't be too long, the captain mused, before our Smith would find a life much more suited to his calling than whaling.

The captain could see the Sag Harbour's larboard whaleboat had been lowered with the mate in charge and as was the custom, he instructed one of the Elizabeth's starboard boats away with his own mate on board. The rest he sent ashore and the deck came alive at his orders.

The smell of whale oil and bits grew increasingly stronger as the boat approached the Sag Harbour and Rogers, not wishing to be insulting towards the crew or the ship's captain, repeatedly blew air out his nostrils instead of lifting his hand to his face as they neared.

Surprisingly, the malodorous stink seemed to evaporate or pass over them as they closed on the larboard side of the barque and as the boat was made fast to the heavy hemp fenders, the mate grasped the rope ladder and clambered up to the deck. He greeted the captain and the captain's wife as politely as he could, noting the lustrous grey, almost black, appearance of anything wooden, where the oils and fats of decades of whale blubber had permeated not just the decks and sails of the ship, but the faces and forearms of the crew as well.

From the deck to about eight feet up each mast, the timber grain of the trees could be seen beneath the resin like coating, but from there up, the masts and even the sails were almost black from years of foetid, black roils from the try works passing up and around them, enveloping the tops and rigging in the greasy film before being carried away on the wind.

Captain Ulysses Tuck acknowledged the captain's invite and reciprocated the offer to have his crew land and join in the gammin', and at this, half the crew cheered and the other half looked around blandly, not really understanding just what was being said. Rogers noted then the swarthiness of most of the crew was less the result of ingrained whale oil smoke, although it was plain that some of it was, but more the heritage of some of the Sag Harbour's crew, that contributed to the dark complexions of the men before him.

From the deep red of the Rhode Island Indian to the high yellow of the Portuguese influence right through to the creamy brown of the Cabo Verdeans among the crew, the mate noted a more varied nationality of crew than he had ever seen, homogenized only by the grimy film of whale oil black that reddened the eyes and matted the hair of all on board.

The captain and his wife were the only exception to the rule of grime. As he walked the short distance to the poop where the captain, his wife and the first mate were standing, Rogers couldn't help but notice the bright, brass buttons of the captain's uniform and the pretty brown ochre dress of his wife were in stark contrast to the stained and patched slops he had been used to since leaving Scotland and he kept his eyes focused keenly on the captain lest the wrong intent might be taken from his wandering gaze.

His invitation was met with a friendly smile and a firm handshake from both the captain and first mate and a cordial smile and nod from the woman. Rogers was relieved, he was aware of the rivalry that existed between some of the Yankee ships and the European whalers. Most stemming from the revolutionary wars when whaling ships in foreign harbours had been commandeered by both countries and either pressed into service without payment to owners or put to the torch with no recompense. However, with memory of the war and its attendant acts of barbarism fading and in such remote seas such as these, it was prudent of all sensible sea captains to hold fast to whatever friendship they could curry and these two were no exception.

Captain MacDonald received his guests graciously, apologising for not being married and not being able to provide adequate company for captain Tuck's wife. His comments were met with polite acceptance and mirth and the company watched from the poop, the empty barrels being rolled from the cedar whaleboats on to the sandy beach by the crews of both ships.

Smith had met the natives near the water's edge, Mana had sent some men back to the bivouac camp to gather trading supplies and the rest he had walk into the open beach without weapons of any sort. This gesture allayed any fears the ships crews had, and they set to unloading the large barrels or tuns from the whale boats. Surprisingly, the natives ignored the white skin of the Englishmen but were intrigued at the skin colour of the red skinned gay head Indians who took their name from that place in Massachusetts, and who wore no slops or shoes as most whalers do but instead, a jacket buttoned to the neck, a skirt or petticoat pants made from sail cloth and bright cloth headband or intricate head adornment of beads and feathers. These men were the harpooners, renowned for their strength and hard work on board whaling ships.

Whereas most crew members aboard a Yankee whaler were press ganged or suckered into signing on to the long voyages, the gay heads or Wampanoag Indian had been killing whales long before the white man had discovered the benefits that could be gained from the great sea animals. Little wonder then, thought Smith, that the mates from the Sag Harbour stood watchful over the ordinary crew as they worked, yet these red men could wander as they chose, mixing with the crew and natives alike, much to the wonder and amazement of the native islanders who seemed to warm to the Indian as they would a long lost relative.

Mana had already accepted Smith as the leader and with the native having charge of some words of English, they managed to develop a rapport that made the task of water gathering easier than it normally would have been.

After much gesturing and drawing in the sand Mana had led Smith to a waterfall just upstream from the beach. Here, a length of palm trunk had been hollowed out and placed as an aqueduct to gather water at one end and dispense the same at the other. It was pointed out to the carpenter that if the crews would wait for the tide to allow the boats to be walked up stream to the pool, then each tun or barrel could be filled whilst remaining in the boat and would not have to be manhandled as they were now doing. Smith acknowledged the native's advice and ordered the men to wait until the water level was such this could be achieved and the men rested for the short while it would take.

With the crews taking their chance for a much needed carbolic and wash up to await the arrival of fresh food and swapping's from the natives who had ventured back to the bivouac camp, Smith again walked to the pool to await the boats.

Henry sat staring into the clear waters of the river pool, enjoying the solitude of the island. Compared to the cramped quarters and smells aboard ship where there was simply no place for quiet thoughts or contemplation, this idyllic setting was the closest place to heaven he could imagine. He had been ashore at two stopovers, the first at the Cape Verde islands, off the west coast of Africa where he had marveled at the sparkling blue waters and pure white sandy beaches and the warmth, the warmth was something he had never imagined. Even when one walked into the sea from the shore, the temperature of both the sea and the shore never seemed to vary, everything was warm, but this would not last.

The harsh reality of what he had signed on for hit home when the ship crossed the thirtieth latitude, the blue waters off the east coast of Africa slowly turned a cold green as they approached and rounded the Cape of Good Hope, the cold south westerly wind striking his face had Smith's memory returning his thoughts to Scotland again and as the ship drove ever southwards, driving her gunwales deep into the green troughs, he promised himself that if he ever made landfall in such a place as Cape Verde again, he would make all effort to stay and make his life there.

Hobarton was the southernmost port of call but the captain allowed only a couple of days to revictual and the carpenter's shore leave consisted of standing on the wharf overseeing the loading of supplies. The weather here was clear and crisp, similar to that of Greenock, and totally unlike that of the Cape Verde, but not so cold as to be uncomfortable. Henry would have liked to have had the time ashore to pass beyond the sandstone warehouses and daub and bark huts to the foothills and tree covered slopes of the great mountain that stood like some giant overlord above the town. Gangs of convicts carried gear and pushed carts about the streets with only one or two soldiers to guard each contingent and Henry mentally compared his voluntary indenture aboard a whaling ship to that of those poor hard toiling souls dressed in their broad arrow serge and once again the feelings of being in a prison of his own making bubbled to the surface of his imagination.

With the ship victualled and moving slowly back down the channel, Henry's disappointment was evident as the ship drove south along the D'entrecasteaux channel but his demeanor improved greatly when the ship turned and began its north easterly passage towards the Navigator's Islands and the warmth of the south pacific. He went about his tasks with a renewed vigour as the ship moved into the roads and sightings and catching of whales became an almost every day occurrence for, he knew there would be little chance of him ever seeing the cold waters of the Clyde or the cold waters of anywhere, for that matter just as soon as he could make landfall on a suitable shore.

Henry heard the rustling of the thin paper mulberry trees and cocked his head to one side to acknowledge the native's approach. He knew the native had been watching him for some time and although there was no secrecy about each of their movements, Smith noticed the manner in which the native was constantly in his vision, as if trying to convey a message he knew the carpenter could not, or would not, understand.

Mana moved as close as he dared to the carpenter. It would do no good to startle the white man. He knew that most of these savages that sailed in their big wooden ships had carried a morbid fear of his kind simply because the white pork like flesh of these 'long pigs' was almost as tasty as that of the hogs and sows that proliferated the islands, although somewhat saltier, and shared the floor of the round houses, although the papalagis' teaching's and laws now prohibited the feeding from the flesh of his enemy and great efforts were made to inter the bodies as soon as possible, to Mana, it seemed a waste to bury such a tasty resource.

He knew he had little time to carry out his plan and now would have to be the time. He had watched as Smith had set up the loading ramps earlier to offload and reload the barrels, he saw how each of the men deferred to this man when something broke or needed strengthening. He also saw Smith reading the white man's papers, tracing a line across the sheet with his finger and then directing men to lay ropes and blocks to make a seemingly impossible task easy enough for a child to carry out and there was something else, something about this man that said he had less enthusiasm for his tasks than for the enjoyment of the island itself.

He walked confidently around to be in full view of Smith although both of them had been fully aware of each other's presence for some time. The two men had met only a few hours earlier and were far from fluent in their attempts at communicating, but Henry sensed an air of secrecy about this man, with his curled hair tied once at the back of his head allowing the rest of his curly locks to frizz out in a fan that framed his round, almost fat, face. Mana's forehead was in a state of permanent frown, even when he seemed pleased and grinned largely, instead of conveying his pleasure, his features contorted into what could only be described as a fierce grimace, accentuating the blue and black tattoo lines that streamed from his mouth to the extremities of his chin, no doubt creating, or at least adding, to the reputation of 'fierce cannibal natives'.

His only form of clothing was a stiff reed skirt tied in the middle by an even stiffer reed, or frond, with a myriad of what looked to be softer reed or frond branches hanging from the belt, half of which extended above his waist and the other half below, looking as if it would fall off if the wearer should bend or engage in anything other than the most sedentary activity. But this was not the case as Henry had seen the other natives dressed in identical attire lifting baulks and manhandling the boats in the most athletic and strenuous manner with not a frond or bark piece come adrift and the carpenter wondered just what the texture of this awkward looking garment might feel like against his own soft, Scottish skin.

Once Mana had his attention, the native moved across to the boat where the crew and a couple of natives were filling the barrels. Members of the crew of the Elizabeth were soaping themselves up and rolling about in the water as they waited for their tuns to fill, reveling in the luxury of their tropical bath.

Mana kept staring into Henry's eyes as he sidled up to the whaleboat and patted the gunwale before dropping his arm and patting the side of the boat. Henry frowned quizzically as the native repeated the movement before pointing at the carpenter cocking his head to one side and half closing his left eye as he did, his large nose and questioning grimace presenting an almost comical appearance as he tried to convey his question to Henry by means of facial gestures.

Henry hesitated, he knew there was a question here but he could not discern if this native thought he was the captain or maybe the owner of the whaleboat, or even if he was negotiating in some primitive way to purchase or take charge of the whale boat. He shook his head slowly.

Mana cast around before picking up one of the slender fronds of the paper mulberry trees and fashioned the leaf into a rough canoe shape. He then pointed back and forth from the toy to himself until he saw the realization dawn on Henry's face. 'It's yours, you made that!' and again, the grimace of congratulations had Henry laughing out loud.

Mana totally misunderstood what Henry was laughing at and believing the carpenter's jubilation was a result of his guessing the correct answer, nodded enthusiastically. Just then shouts from the beach heralded the arrival of the native contingent Mana had sent to retrieve the fresh food and Henry began to turn away, but the native stopped him, holding his left hand palm facing towards Henry, careful not to make contact and moving his other hand rapidly back and forth between the two men, first between their mouths, then between each other's chests. Henry immediately understood and reciprocated the movement. 'Talk later?' The ludicrous grimace and the half wink told him he'd guessed right.

Following the return of the barrels of water to each ship, the feast had been one of pork, steamed in a hole in the ground and covered with palm leaves. To each layer of leaves, an assortment of different foods was added, resulting in a treasure hunt of delicacies such as the seamen had never seen or tasted before. A chest of assorted foods had been conveyed to those aboard ship and from their vantage point on the deck of the Elizabeth MacDonald, the captain's and mates watched as the quiet, orderly discussions on the beach broke down to peals of laughter and dance and the raucous rasp of shanties rose and fell among the shrill notes of the squeezebox and fiddle as the alcohol extinguished any inhibitions the white sailors might have had. The coloureds, including the natives, were excluded in partaking of the alcohol but with tobacco their drug of choice, were satisfied with the quality, and quantity, of the pungent weed produced from the hold of the Sag Harbor.

In a fit of magnanimity, fostered no less by copious quantities of ingested brandy, the captain had offered Smith to return aboard but the carpenter had politely refused the invitation and patrolled the beach and perimeter of the firelight with Mana at his side. With both leaders displaying an amicable relationship as well as an element of control, the mood among all was relaxed and informal. Language was no barrier to the whites and hand gestures and grimaces formed the basis of communications between the coloureds.

The gamming was held on the very edge of the beach where the palm and mulberry trees became stunted and gnarled by the exposure to the salt air and spray from the sea. Successive storms and high tides had eroded the soil from around the roots of the trees, leaving a thin layer of rocks and shells to spill out onto the sand from under the bushy roots of the mulberry trees, marking the last line of survival for many unfortunate seeds. Those that fell above the line of shells, would quickly be covered by leaves and soil, guaranteeing germination and survival of the island's food chain, those that fell below the line would have a slim, but possible chance of being either picked from the beach by passing sea birds and excreted at some point inland or being drawn away on the seas to land at some faraway place and begin the cycle of life once again. For those unfortunate enough to fall or be blown directly among the gaps in the rocks and become trapped, life would be over before it began, as the ebb and flow of the salty tide would certainly destroy any chance of survival.

Every few years, a fallen tree, or favourable weather conditions would allow seeds to germinate at the very edge of where the tree line meets the sandy beach. This in turn would create a microcosm of life jutting into the sandy beach as if to establish a beach head for an all-out assault on the sea itself. Soil and seeds would then build up around the freshly germinated plants and it would seem as if the jungle was finally going to defeat the sea in its domination of the water's edge. But inevitably, nature would send its battalions of storm waves to undermine and scour the roots of these interlopers, causing them to collapse onto the beach and bury beneath the sand as punishment for their impudence.

The clearing created by these fallen palms and the subsequent view into the forest was the ideal place for a gamming and the fallen tree barrels leading out onto the beach would form the ideal seats for Henry and Mana as they could keep an eye on both the crews and the ships as they shared facial and hand expressions in their less than perfect methods of communication.

Mana feigned amazement at the tools and workmanship of the carpenter but was very careful not to display too much interest in weapons of any sort. Henry, on the other hand, marveled at the descriptions and sand drawings of the native lifestyle and habitat. Mana was a fine artist and created very effective depictions of his island life, intriguing Smith to the point that, when the natives travelled back to the bivouac in the morning to pick up the final supplies, he vowed he would be with them.

Henry Smith waited until the firkin was well finished and the effects of the ale began to wear off the whaler men before he took two of the more sober seamen and rowed out to the Elizabeth MacDonald. Catching the eye of the watch by waving the lantern as the boat pulled away from the beach, he marveled at the clear sky ablaze with stars upon stars which seemed to run in a river across the centre of the sky before joining their own reflection as they dipped into the inky blackness of the tranquil ocean. He could hear the constant sound of the waves carrying to him as they broke against the outer reef but here, in the relative shelter of the bay, there was not a sound on the water save the barely audible shloshing of the oars as the seamen, tipsy though they were, expertly dug the shiny phosphorescence from the water without creating as much as a ripple as they sent the boat forward towards the ship.

Rogers was on watch, and believing the carpenter was there to replenish the ale supplies of the gammers on the shore, met him at the gunwale as Smith reached the top of the rope ladder.

'I would have thought you blokes had had enough by now, Smithy.' Henry could smell the alcohol on the mate's breath and grinned conspiratorially as the amiable mate patted him on the shoulder then added, 'But unfortunately, the captain's gone below and our guests have gone home.' The captain's store was where all the alcohol was kept and this was situated directly beneath the captain's cabin, making it impossible to access the finer stores without waking the master.

'Don't worry, mate,' Henry whispered, sensing the concern in the mate's voice at the prospect of answering to the captain in the morning for giving away another firkin. 'We're not here for more grog,' he pointed aft towards the hatch to the steerage cabin beneath the upturned spare whaleboat. 'I'm just here to grab my gear. I'm going with the natives to help with the swapping's on the morrow.'

The mate turned his head to one side and leant forward, closer to Henry, not sure what he was hearing.

'You're what?' Rogers asked, as if he was listening to words of a lunatic. He knew full well of the ploys and cunning of these island natives. One minute they seem to be your amiable best friend, eager to invite you home to share their meal, the next, you find yourself as the main course at that meal.

'Don't be so bloody silly man, once out of sight of the ship, these bastards will cook and eat you, you mark my words.'

Had it not been for the need to remain quiet, Henry would have laughed out loud. It was entirely possible he was being naïve, but he knew if he was to get any experience of island life, he simply had to trust Mana. He held his finger up to his lips as the two walked past the main mast and ducked through the main channel towards the hatchway.

Rogers stood at the hatchway, holding the lantern on a rope so Henry could see his way around the cramped quarters. There was not much in the way of belongings, but when he finally reached the top of the ladder way, the mate knew instantly what he was about.

'You're jumping!' He exclaimed. 'For Christ's sake, Henry, we're in the middle of nowhere!' He shook his head incredulously at Smith's stupidity. In a time when the only civilized community within thousands of miles was the ship they sailed in, all sailors knew their safety depended on being aboard that ship at all times, the ship was their island of safety that no man, God fearing or otherwise, would leave or stray out of eyesight from, unless it was absolutely necessary or under orders of the captain. He had heard tales of whole ships company's being killed and eaten, not to mention what atrocities the natives committed on each other, stories of children being gutted alive and roasted on stakes with the heads of their parents sat on stands for the women to abuse and jeer at whilst they feasted on the putrid corpses of their bairn.

'I'm only taking my gear in the event I can't get back in time.' Henry whispered. They need to bring the other trade goods from their round hut and I will come back with them when they do.'

The mate shook his head. 'You are making a damn fool mistake, Henry Smith. If you head into that jungle with those savages, it's a moral we will never see you again.'

Henry grinned at the histrionics of a drunken seaman, and had it not been for the shadows cast by the lantern moving in the mates less than sober hand, the skepticism would have been obvious on his features. 'You will see the likes of me again Mister Rogers, of that I can assure you.' The mate was still shaking his head as Henry disappeared over the gunwale and made his way down to the waiting whaleboat.

By the time the hung over seamen had woken the next morning, Mana, Smith and all but two of the natives had disappeared into the jungle. On the beach in the moonlight, it had been quite easy to see one's way, but as they entered the forest with its overhanging canopy of green, the shadows merged into one and Henry had to stay close to the man in front so as not to stumble or lose his way. Mana made sure Henry was guided and treated well on the first part of the journey, as he didn't want his charge to get cold feet within shouting distance of the rest of the whaler men.

For the first fifty yards or so from the line of shells, clear open spaces interspersed with the odd mulberry shrub dominated the bushland between the palms until the thin tendrils of the mulberry trees came together to present an almost impenetrable wall of vines and creeping plants. Into this wall of green leaves and dangling vines there appeared narrow gaps, not much wider than a man's body, some of which were paths that petered out within twenty yards or so but others, and the trick was knowing which ones, continued on with intersection after intersection like an arterial system through which man and animals of all types were forced to travel.

Every now and then, Mana would divert from the beaten path to show Henry some sight of beauty, be it a waterfall, a stream or a forest flower and Henry would stare in wonder at each of these marvelous creations of nature for a few minutes until Mana would remind him of their obligations to the ship and once again, they would set off inland, forever inland. Or so it seemed.

About four hours into the trip, the path veered to the right and the canopy above opened up and the heavy damp air disappeared to reveal a much-welcomed azure blue sky. Mana stopped and directed Henry to go ahead. Henry saw the buildings even before he had moved past the native, a number of domed shaped grass huts open beneath the roofs except for the poles that supported the structure. Henry could see people moving about inside and beyond the cluster of buildings and as he drew closer, he could see the sea beyond and the waves moving towards the shore from the same direction they had been when they were back at the beach. The realization they had not been heading inland at all dawned on him as he recognized the inlet as the one, they had espied from the ship's quarter deck as they approached the island.

He turned to his new friend and opened his hands as if querying this development and the fierce grimace that served as a smile together with much gesticulating and head movements explained to him that the water here was much too shallow and tidal to transport goods to the white man's ship, and besides, Mana tested Henry's loyalty to his ship by explaining that the natives could have transported all the swapping's to the ship in less than one day but this would have meant revealing the whereabouts of their village and should the ship's company be less than friendly, they could simply land a force and take whatever they wanted, including the natives themselves. Besides, he reasoned, if the white man believed the carrying of all the swapping's to the beach was hard work, he would probably not quibble about putting a higher value on the goods.

Henry had wondered at the freshness of the goods on the arrival of the first natives from the so called bivouac and pursed his lips as he digested this somewhat corrupt line of dealing from his new friend. Mana was silent, he waited for a reaction from Henry which could go either way, depending on how strong his loyalty was to the ship. His fears were allayed when he saw the smile begin to grow in Henry's face and the carpenter's head nodded in approval of the business acumen of the natives. Mana clapped his hand on Smith's shoulder and pushed him gently towards the group of natives that were gathering near the open wall of the largest grass roofed hut.

The people assembled outside the hut were some of the most beautiful people Henry had ever seen. Heavy built, brown skinned women with pendulous breasts rested on one somewhat overly large buttock, their legs folded and crocked to one side whilst they peeled and stripped the long palm leaves into fine twine and baskets. Young women with exposed breasts and stiff grass and palm skirts stared almost sternly at him until a command from Mana had them shrieking with laughter and covering their faces with their hands and shyly turning away. The older women had no such modesty and a few of them hauled their heavy bulk to standing and pressed their palms against almost every part of Henry's body, squeezing as they did so and causing Henry to blush with embarrassment. Henry looked to Mana for help and at the native's seemingly stern command, all the camp broke into uproarious laughter, including the men.

Henry was somewhat taken aback and thoughts of last night's conversation with Rogers, the mate, came back to him.

'What are they after?' He enquired of Mana but the native continued to laugh and did not answer, instead he motioned for one of the younger women to come forward. The woman, who, unlike most of the others, had her hair on one side of her head completely shaven off and on the other, left, side of her head near her temple, a long bundle of tresses, about two inches wide curled from her scalp and fell about her shoulder like a bronze ribbon. Henry was unaware that the colouring of her hair, like that of most other women who surrounded him, was the staining of turmeric that was abundant on the island and used for all manner of things from cooking to make up and even hair dye. The woman wore a small poncho like blouse made from finely stripped flax that looked as soft as silk which provided adequate, but scant, covering for her breasts, which forced the poncho to stand out from her chest and form a verandah of flax that hung over her belly. She was naked from there to her lower belly where a tiny silken, lap lap, hung on a strand of flax tied around her waist. Many of the women were totally naked and seemed unabashed by their nakedness. Henry assumed by her dress, scant though it was, as well as her aloofness towards the others in the village, even the men, that she must hold some standing in the village. Ignoring the antics of the others, she stepped forward and before Henry could introduce himself in the white man's somewhat condescending manner that white men do, she placed the ends of her bunched fingers against the centre of her chest and said, 'Me Salamasina,' then pointed directly and unsmilingly at Henry's chest and said simply 'You?'

Henry was amazed. 'You..you speak English?' more a question than an acknowledgement of what he had just heard. The concept of being able to converse with one of these tribespeople was joyous to the carpenter, who for the moment, forgot he was a carpenter, forgot he was a Scotsman, he was now an explorer who had discovered the life, not to mention the breasts, he had always dreamed of. Henry was aware of the laughter and jeers emanating from the villagers at his discomfort and dragged his eyes back to the face of the young woman and forced himself into some semblance of seriousness. To attain this attitude, he considered the still strong possibility of being this woman's lunch instead of her lover and tried to smile disarmingly. The ploy was lost on the woman and she closed three fingers of her right hand before moving her thumb and forefinger together to be almost half an inch apart. 'Small,' she moved her hand rapidly from side to side, still holding her thumb and forefinger in the same position and repeated, 'Small, small.'

Henry picked up the meaning immediately, he realized that the Queen's English was almost nonexistent in this part of the world and he would be relying on one word having ten meanings as well as hand and eye movement if he was to communicate adequately and be of some use to these people. He smiled again and copied the young woman's gesture. 'A little, you speak a little English.'

The girl nodded, if she was pleased at his understanding, she did not show it, instead she went on in a stilted jumble of English words which she expected he would understand as if he were listening to a speech from the king. Henry had to concentrate intently on each pronounced syllable and even some letters the girl spoke to understand the gist of what she was saying. Henry's attentiveness and concentration was taken as respect for her understanding of his language and the villagers fell to silence as the girl explained her attendance at the missionary house in Apia when her father was king. The word Maliatoa was mentioned over and over, referring to more than one person, including herself, and Henry was forced to commit some of the words to memory as he attempted, with some success, to follow her story.

It seemed there had been many wars and her tribe, or people, had been attacked more than once with grave consequences. Henry could not understand exactly who had attacked them but it seemed this Maliatoa character had abandoned them and they were now left to their own devices. He was about to question her and find out more of her story when Mana intervened by placing his hand on Henry's shoulder, indicating there were stores to deliver to Henry's ship and the young woman took Henry's hand in hers and formally shook his hand. Henry was once again surprised at a gesture so prevalent and respected in his country should present itself in this land of savages and cannibals. He reluctantly turned to follow the men back to the ship and did not notice the look that passed between the young woman and Mana as they moved off.

It took but half the time to return to the shore where the boats waited, even though each native was weighed down with almost half his weight in all types of island vegetables and fruit. The seamen of both boats were by now fully aware of Smith's desertion and stood on the shoreline, boats in the water ready to be pushed out to sea at any sign of a native advance. Three natives from Mana's group broke the tree line one after the other and although they were weighed down by much needed supplies for the whaling ships, the fearful and surly mood of the sailors did not change until the carpenter staggered from the bush with the weight of less than half that of the smallest native across his shoulders causing him to stagger as his feet slipped on the sandy beach.

As he tipped his load onto the beach and raised both arms above his head in jovial relief, the mood among those at the boats changed dramatically. He could see Rogers shaking his head in disbelief and admiration of Smith's courage at wandering into the jungle with a tribe of unknown savages and actually surviving.

Rogers then turned away from Smith towards the seamen that lined the gunwales of both ships and signaled the captain's that all was well and immediately three other whaleboats slid gracefully from behind their mother ships and made towards the shore.

Two lines of men were formed between the piles of victuals near the tree line and the shore and hangovers and imagined hostilities forgotten, the swappings began moving in two continuous lines towards the waiting boats whilst Smith, Rogers and their two counterparts from the Sag Harbour swapped beads, axes and other implements for the choice foodstuffs and fruit, deposited on the beach by a seemingly endless line of natives. Smith seemed to be the only one of the whaler men aware that if one looked close enough at the native line, they would be able to make out the repeated appearance of the same native faces in short sequence, belying the story of the long trek to the native's inland camp but although it would be obvious to the more attentive and observant gay heads, the white seamen paid no attention to the comings and goings of the natives in the short distance between the forest and the pile of supplies. They had washed, fed and drunk their fill and with no evidence of female natives in the immediate vicinity who one might form a quick dalliance with, their only concern was in getting the swapping's aboard and all interest in a continued stay on the island was lost.

Smith heard the occasionally comment from the men lamenting the lack of female company as they loaded the whale boats and glanced knowingly in Mana's direction, he was now fully aware of the reasons for the native's subterfuge. Mana acknowledged his glances and it seemed to Smith the native was always ready to make eye contact with him. For Mana's part he was aware the boats had near enough to all the supplies they needed, and they would soon be leaving. His mind was racing as the second last whale boat drew alongside its mother ship and instead of loading the stores up the rope ladder ways, the captain ordered the boat and its cargo be lifted as one into the ship. The Sag Harbor had all boats stowed in their davits and already men were going aloft to ready the ship to catch the offshore breeze and clear the island before nightfall.

The captain of the Elizabeth MacGregor was in the same dilemma as Mana. Rogers had informed him of Smith's actions and Captain MacGregor suspected Smith would abscond into the jungle as soon as he was aware the ship was leaving. Although he was partially sympathetic to Smith's attitude, as a responsible ship's captain, he had no intention of leaving his capable ships carpenter behind to be at the mercy of savages.

The captain let it be known to the crew, that the Elizabeth MacGregor would not be leaving until the offshore breezes of the dawn were favourable.

Rogers relayed the message of the departure delay to Smith and explained to the carpenter the dangers of staying behind after the ship and its company had departed.

'For Jesus sake, man'. He pleaded with Henry. 'These savages are only friendly towards us because we have the strength to hurt them.' Both men looked to where Mana was helping to load the last of the small wooden kegs with either salt Muli, or pork rumps, or Moa, chicken bodies minus the wings and legs. Neither man noticed the fact that the piles of meat set aside on their wrappings of palm leaves didn't contain any of the choicer pieces that had been surreptitiously set aside by the natives for their own consumption.

Those sections of the slaughtered animals that were missing were for the consumption of the orators and chiefs of the village and the rest were for distribution to the common people and for trade with the Papalagi. To the Europeans, pork was pork and chicken was chicken and as long as it was edible and stored so as not to spoil easily, it was of little consequence. Especially when there were more important things to consider. Mana did not look up, even though he was fully aware of the gist of the papalagi conversation.

Rogers lifted his gaze above the natives and nodded towards the open sea.

'Once that ship rounds that headland out there,' He whispered, 'It'll be all over for you, the next pig in the pot will be YOU'.

Smith shrugged. He couldn't disagree with the mate, he had heard the tales of massacres and cannibalisms and didn't doubt the truth in them but the thought of returning to the icy winds and rigours of the voyage home to Van Dieman's Land or even worse, Scotland, kept him silent for a few moments before he spoke. 'Can you leave a boat and perhaps a couple of men ashore with me tonight and I'll decide in the morning?'

The mate was aghast. 'And lose two good men as well as a perfectly good whaleboat?' He shook his head rapidly. 'No bloody way lad.' He stared intently at the carpenter as if trying to bend the carpenter's will to his own and, not sensing any change in Smith's attitude, he shook his head resignedly. 'Tell you what, Henry. I'll keep a lookout for you on the beach in the morning and if you're still here, we'll come for you, if not,' His eyes moved from Mana, who still had not looked up, back to Smith and repeated a tone of finality in his voice, 'If not, you are lost to us.'

Mana was pleased to see Smith grab the prow of the whaleboat and begin to heave the boat out into the waves. He deliberately avoided the mates glare as rogers clambered aboard and high stepped over and around the cargo to settle on the stern thwart where he could give orders to his crewmen.

The whaleboat was pushed out stern first, the surging surf causing the fully laden boat to ground in the troughs between the waves and the natives slipped and stumbled as they grappled the heavy whaleboat into deeper water. A steady surge of water lifted the boat clear of the bottom and without the mate needing to call, the oars dug deep in unison, sending the boat clear of the surf and on its way to the mother ship with the tattooed natives waving and calling excitedly as their fists punched the air in victory. The whalers could only nod their heads in appreciation of their efforts as their hands, arms and lungs were preoccupied with control of the oars and their boat.

As if an umbilical cord had been cut from himself to the world to which he belonged, Smith felt a sense of rising panic. The reality of losing everything known to him and replacing that which he was familiar with all that was foreign had him staring forlornly after the boat. Only a hand on his shoulder steadied him from calling out to the boat to return and rescue him from his own stupidity.

Mana gestured towards the tree line and the two sat on one of the many rotting logs as Mana's men packed the swapping's into the palm leaf satchels each man had swung from their necks down both sides of their bodies. Smith tried to explain to Mana his need to stay the night but the native insisted, through gesticulating and facial contortions that had the carpenter laughing out loud and bringing his sense of adventure to the surface once more, that he needed to travel to the village to eat and meet the elders of the village. Once that was done, the native explained, they would both return to the beach before morning and then he could decide his future.

As the beach emerged from the grey pre-dawn mist, both the mate and the captain stared at the open sandy cove, devoid of life save a few sea birds fossicking the shore for food. During the night, the tide had swept away all trace of the past days of trade and activity, leaving not a single footprint in the sands below the tree line. Both men knew Smith was gone forever. Lost to the barbaric lifestyle of the south sea native or worse. The mate wrinkled his nose at the thought that was going through both men's minds.

'Can almost smell the cooking pots from here, Cap'n.'

The Captain turned from the gunwale and murmured, 'Not of our control any more, mister mate'. He nodded towards the crew standing by the main. 'Make ready for sea, mister mate. We've a job to do.'

Chapter 5

Mouth of Tafitoala river, Upolu,

Navigator's Island, 1838

Even though it had only been a few hours since they had left the village, Smith's recollection of the village was different to that of his first arrival. His first mental picture of a collection of domed huts was somehow distorted from that of reality until he became aware that the direction from whence they arrived the second time was different and the domed huts on this side of the village were huge! To call these buildings, some of them nearly three stories tall, huts, was indeed a misnomer. He could see the smaller huts he had first encountered, further across the clearing, guessing they must be of lesser importance than the giant domes of palm fronds and grass that stood in front of him. Even the timbers that supported the roofs of the buildings were as thick as his thigh, these posts alone were over eight feet high, driven into the ground and supporting full saplings of banana trees, fixed at the lower end to the solid posts and curved upwards across the supporting frames not unlike that of an unfinished ship turned on its back.

One side of the structure seemed completed and about a dozen natives were relaying banana leaves and grasses up and along a scaffolding of saplings as professional and competent he had seen in any Scottish city.

As he walked towards the larger buildings, Henry noted that not all buildings were as imposing as those in the centre of the large clearing. In fact, there were buildings and hovels of all shapes and sizes but each with its domed roof and typical open sides.

Mana stopped in front of the gathering of people and placed his hand on Henry's shoulder, a gesture that drew a sigh of admiration from at least half of the gathering of half-naked tribespeople and had at least six of the bare breasted females coming forward to place their hands against Henry's body. One particularly pretty female, after pressing her hands against his chest and shoulders stared him directly in his eyes before shocking the carpenter by grabbing his penis through his slops pants and squeezing firmly.

Smith jumped back in alarm and the maiden let go, turning back to the crowd and holding her arms outstretched in a show of bravado. The crowd cheered and laughed uproariously at Smith's embarrassment. Others moved forward and made to grab the carpenter, it seemed to Henry that the first mate had been right, it might be his time to join the choice cuts of pork and vegetables that were being loaded into the cooking holes and covered with banana leaves to the right of the largest building, before the woman he had encountered on his last visit called out. Immediately, half a dozen heavily tattooed warriors stepped forward and ordered the maidens and young girls back away from the sailor. The girls ignored them and, in their attempts to grab at Smith, he was pushed to the ground and at least three girls had to be forcibly dragged from him. Smith was scared, scared as he had ever been in his life. He knew Rogers and the Captain had been right, he was going to go the same way as the explorer, De Langle and his ten crewmen who had met their untimely end in the cooking fires of these people less than a decade ago and probably not more than a few yards from here.

The tall woman stepped forward and clubbed two of the young girls across the side of the head with a wooden axe-like tool, almost knocking one girl senseless and drawing blood from the heads of both of them. Smith felt Mana's strong grip under his left arm and let himself be hauled to his feet. He felt nauseous but managed to keep his head up and stare back at the throng of natives. Henry was fully aware these savage's respected bravery, it was only common sense they would have little or no respect for a quivering coward, which was exactly what he felt like at this moment. He fought and won over the urge to run which he reasoned would probably be the fastest way to a painful death if the woman with the razor-sharp club had her way.

He turned to Mana but his one-time friend and now kidnapper seemed to ignore his plight, save for his one handed support of Henry's arm. Instead, his face was twisted in a grimace as each of the warriors came forward, and after displacing the maidens to the throng of onlookers, thrust their tattooed and disfigured faces into Henry's now deathly pale visage with looks that could only be described as horrific, before retreating to the seated crowd near the front of the building. In the confusion of him falling, Henry's pack had been sent flying and he could see three of the young girls and a woman trying to tear the pack open. He was all but resigned to knowing he would never require the contents of his pack anyway, when the tall woman called again. This time all the commotion stopped immediately and the three girls brought the pack before Smith and placed it reverently at his feet.

Mana let his arm go. Smith was now nothing if not confused as the throng of islanders moved into a half circle either side of an old man and a huge woman seated in front of the largest hut. The old man rose to his feet and walked the half dozen steps to be in front of Smith. His face was much wrinkled and the once tattooed lines from his mouth to his chin and ears had long faded to a dull blue. He wore his hair in a bun and a fan of what looked to be flax leaves and brilliantly coloured feathers protruding from the back of his head, framing his face and softening the fierce appearance of his countenance.

The old man stood in front of Henry for a few seconds, seemingly fearful of the carpenter's presence then slowly and feebly he raised his right arm and placed his hand gently on Henry's left shoulder and opened his mouth in a tentative, but toothless smile. Still terrified, Henry grasped desperately at what might turn out to be a lifeline and tried to smile back but his fear had him so shaken he could barely manage a shaky and nervous grin.

Immediately the crowd roared its approval and the old man nodded his pleasure. Smith could feel Mana drawing himself up to his full height with pride at bringing a white god to the village, a god who had not attempted to insult the maidens of the village by striking them away from his being, a god who had not attempted to defile the maidens of the village, even though they presented themselves and laid hands on his manhood, a god who had smiled upon Malieatoa, the chief, even as the chief had laid hands on him. Mana was more versed in the ways of the outside world than the chief and did not believe for an instant that Smith was a god but the chief and at least three quarters of his village did, and more importantly, so would their enemies.

Smith couldn't believe his good fortune, in his belief, he had been literally plucked from the jaws of death by the old chief and although the chief's toothless jaws probably wouldn't have a great deal of effect on choice cuts of his carcass, he had no doubt the razor-sharp tools of the warriors and women would have little trouble rendering his cadaver into pieces manageable by even the youngest of the villagers. Smith believed he would be forever in the old chief's debt. That belief would last until the first evening.

Henry was led into the largest hut and marveled at the sheer size of the interior of the building. In the shadows towards the centre of the dome, a huge centre pole seemed to support the structure, forming an immensely strong and weatherproof ceiling which, when inside the building, created an atmosphere not unlike that of being inside a cathedral.

Henry eyes were continually being drawn to the curved timbers that formed the ceiling high above them as the villagers seated themselves on the floor of the huge building and accepted the calabashes of banana leaves containing all types of meat, fruit and local vegetables. Food that Henry had never seen, or tasted before. He did note however, that certain foods were only accepted or offered to villagers of certain standing and vowed to learn as much as possible from, and about, these wonderful people. He noted the seating positions of the villagers and the fact that the tall woman sat immediately to the right of Maleatoa, with the fat lady who was obviously his wife, or one of them.

Smith sat among the villagers where the chief could see him face to face and he could see Mana and follow his lead as the choice cuts of meat, fish and fruits were brought to him. He smiled at all who lifted their food in salute and grimaced in respect to their new found God, all the while surreptitiously glancing in Mana's direction and noting the slightest movement of the latter's head or hands as his new found friend guided him through the habits and customs of communal eating in the big house.

As a white man in the situation he was in, and having heard the stories about the savagery of these people he was sitting among, he realized he should have been terrified. Strangely, his fear of these wild savages had all but evaporated, replaced with a sense of excitement to be alone and unarmed in the wilderness of the south seas and as well, a strange sense of belonging, as if he was meant to be here. He noted the tall woman had not even acknowledged his existence since they had sat down and apart from a few curt exchanges with the chief and Mana, had remained aloof and indifferent from all around her until a loud burst of laughter from the village girls on his left drew her attention. The girl who had grabbed Smith by the penis was holding her hand up to her friends and was making squeezing motions much to the uproarious laughter of the other girls her age. All in the round house could see what she was intimating, much to Smiths embarrassment. The girl, encouraged by the laughter of her peers, moved her hands slowly apart as if to describe a growing movement and looked toward the chief for his approval only to be met with a cold, stone faced, stare from the tall woman that even had the chiefs toothless grin fading from his face.

The laughter died in the room and Smith felt even more embarrassed as all attention was directed toward him, he hoped he wouldn't be expected to defend himself or even explain his actions, but the girl was already withdrawing her hands and acquiescing to the withering stare from the tall woman.

Smith looked in the direction of the woman, hoping to thank her once again, with a smile, but a cold stare was all that was forthcoming before she returned to her food.

With the meal finished, the villagers made no attempt to leave the room. Instead, they either rested on their haunches or dragged themselves back towards the nearest pole where they lolled and dozed in the shadow of the roundhouse thatched roof.

Smith watched as the old chief and the fat lady were helped to their feet and led away to their private quarters by Mana and his aides. By this time, the round house was resonating to the snores of both men and women alike and Smith felt himself beginning to follow suit until the tall woman and his friend stood before him. Mana then motioned for him to follow them and led him, albeit with some reluctance, from the big hut, into the bright sunlight.

Mana and the woman led him to a clearing near the stream and, it seemed quite obvious to Smith, out of earshot from the village, as the whispers and stealth the two displayed when first leaving the village became a loud and heated discussion, with Smith obviously the subject of that discussion. Only when the argument had finished was Smith to receive another shock as the woman turned from Mana to him and said in plain, albeit somewhat stilted, English,

'What is your name, Smith, what can you do?'

Even though it had only been a couple of days since he had heard his own language, to Smith it was as if hearing his name for the first time.

'You speak English,' He asked. 'Where did you learn English?'

The woman ignored his question and went on. 'My name Salamasina, I am from Maleatoa! Mana is from Maleatoa!' She paused, then added respectfully, 'His name means Son of chief.'

From both her hand gestures and her stilted English, Smith guessed what she meant was, that she was the daughter of Maleatoa and

Mana was her brother, although she sometimes referred to him as Manaia and he would reciprocate when he was angry or demanding, she would be Salamasina! but if he required a favour, or boon, of her, or even at times when they were both feeling affectionate, Mana would refer to her as Sina. Henry quickly guessed he would have to learn to recognize certain hand gestures as well as inflections in her voice in order to maintain a somewhat fluid conversation with the woman, but he was amazed and relieved he would be able to understand what she was saying and he wouldn't have to rely on her brother's weird gesticulations and facial grimaces any more.

He sensed Mana was somewhat crestfallen at the usurping of his power by his sister and surmised this is what all the arguing was about. He resolved then and there not to come between Mana, who although held back by the language barrier between them, was obviously the more patient and diplomatic of the two, and his sister, who seemed to be more demanding and less diplomatic. Yet he was still somewhat taken aback by the woman's next question.

Now he knew their names, Henry pointed to each in turn, saying their names as he did so. *'Salamasina, Sina'*. She nodded. He then turned to his male companion and pointed to his chest, 'Manaia, Mana.' Again, they both nodded. Henry then laid his open palm to his chest to formally introduce himself, saying, 'Henry.' Immediately both his companions began laughing and waving their hands in admonition of Henry's failure to understand island language.

Each of his companions laid their hands upon his chest and repeated over and over. 'Henare, Henare!'

It would take almost half an hour of laughter, admonition and denial by his companions before Henry finally realised, the only word that Mani understood at the beach when they were loading stores were when the other seamen addressed the carpenter as *Henare,* a well known Samoan name for Henry. Thinking he may have been of Samoan blood, it was this term of address that convinced Mani to approach Henry with his plan. When Henry finally relented and acknowledged his name was the proper Samoan version, Henare, and not the silly English version, Sina stopped laughing abruptly and asked him,

'You like it here?' moving her hand across the clearing in such a vague manner that Smith could not determine if she meant the clearing or the island as a whole. Her next question gave him the answer. 'If you like it, you stay.' She stared into his eyes. 'If you not like it here, you must go.'

Smith was embarrassed at his hubris. He had honestly believed he would be allowed to come and go as he pleased, or at least, as transport would permit. He didn't expect he would be under an ultimatum to either stay and contribute to the village or leave and never return. He turned to Mana who grimaced back at him, noncommittally. He turned back to Sina who continued to stare, her face expressionless. 'What would you do if stay?'

'What would I do?' He asked, then, realizing quickly he was being asked to give what amounted to a tribal resume, before either of the two could ask again, he went on. 'I can build.' He motioned with his hands to describe a building of sorts, a description which was totally lost on them and seeing their blank stares he scratched the shape of a boat in the sandy soil and pointed to the rough etching. 'I can build boats,' That's as good a starting point as any, he thought.

Both Sina and Mana screwed their faces up and shrugged. They already knew that he was a capable carpenter and builder. The main question they had for him was asked again. 'You go?' Lani pointed to the ground, 'Or you stay!' she pointed away from them, towards the sea. Smith laughed, even though she had described his potential actions the wrong way around, he could see exactly what she meant. He stared back into the eyes of the couple and knowing he would probably regret his decision, he knew it was always going to be, 'I Stay! I stay all time!'

Both Sina and Mana looked at each other and nodded their understanding. Each seemed relieved at Smith's decision but showed little emotion otherwise, as Smith waited to see what initiation ceremony awaited him if he might be accepted. After a few seconds staring at each other Mani spoke 'aau I lalo o le vai?'

Sina laughed, 'ioe,' she answered, and Smith was none the wiser until they each held a hand to his arms and motioned for him to come with them. They walked only about twenty yards along the stream bank before they stopped and Lani pointed to the deep pool in the stream and answered his questioning look. 'aau I lalo o le vai? Do you want to go for a swim?'

'And ioe?' Queried Smith, as he watched Mana plunge headlong into the cool waters.

Sina shrugged, as if he really didn't need an answer. 'Yes.' And pulling him towards the water, answered again. 'Yes.'

The three swam and laughed as they enjoyed the cool waters of the lagoon and as the other two laughed and splashed water in each other's faces, Smith floated on his back and let the slow current carry him down the length of the pond towards the line of rocks that marked the lower edge of the still water. He felt totally relaxed and at peace. Why, he wondered, would anyone want to live anywhere else other than here in paradise? His thoughts drifted back to the cold drizzle of the Scottish towns from whence he had come, to the hard shipboard life he had experienced in his travels and even to Hobarton, a nice enough town but not comparable to the idyllic life here in these beautiful islands.

He had drifted to the shallow water among the rocks and lay on the smooth rocky bottom with the water just lapping against his ears, distorting his hearing as it splashed against his head. At first, he thought it WAS the slap of the water against his ears until he noticed it was getting closer. He turned to see Mana and Sina waving and gesticulating as they ploughed through the water towards him. He banged his head against one of the stones and jammed his fingers among the rocks as he tried to get to his knees on the slippery bottom, by the time he did, the other two had caught up to him and were pointing towards the high mountain towards the centre of the island.

Smith followed the direction of their outstretched fingers and could see a thin tendril of smoke rising up from behind the outline of the mountain to the east of where they were and drifting away to the south. He was none the wiser and quizzed Lani on just what it meant that they were so upset about?

Mana looked to Sina also and she took charge. He pointed towards the village. 'Go now.' She said, and Smith and Mana followed without question

They arrived back in the village just as the villagers were rousing from their after-lunch nap and went straight to the chief's hut.

The chief too, had heard the booming cannon sounds and although he still had the same slow, lazy, almost condescending smile on his face Smith could see the concern in his dark eyes as he motioned two young girls to his side.

The girls held long, thin, packages wrapped in a soft, almost silken, flax like material, tied at each end with a thin but strong twine which both Mana and Salamasina looped over their heads and motioned for Smith to do the same.

The chief conversed with both Mana and Sina and although he ignored Smith completely, the latter could tell by his hand and eye movements, the conversation was mostly about him. Mana's expression never changed as he listened intently to the old man's words, which to Smith was strange because he had never seen the man engage in conversation without his usual gesticulations and grimaces.

Sina had moved off but she now returned with three western style coats, one which Smith recognized as his own. At this point the chief turned to Smith and embraced him before raising his hands and bidding all three of them farewell, although Smith had no idea just where he was farewelling them to.

They had walked about two miles in silence, Mani leading with Sina bringing up the rear, when the native called a halt. Sina and Smith sat on a fallen log near the western bank of the river they had been following for the last mile and a half, whilst Mana squatted on his haunches in front of them and explained to Smith with Sina doing her best to overcome the differences in the language barrier, the reason for their journey.

The river, he learned was the Tafitoala and they would be following it to its headwaters on Mount Fiamoe, a journey of about fifteen miles to the highest point of the island.

From his ship and from some clearings near the beach, Smith had easily made out the saddleback ridge of the mountain and was keen to attempt a climb and learn more about this island paradise he now called home, but over the next three days and nights of sweating and clambering over slippery, muddy trails. Negotiating fallen trees and steep banks covered with vines and slippery moss, climbing ever upwards towards the summit, his two companions appraised the new comer to the realities of his island and this so-called paradise.

Each evening, the two natives would relate the story of Maleatoa, the great chief, who died and left five sons, each of which claimed the right to rule over the island chain and each of which had staked a claim over part of the territory wherefrom to launch attacks on his siblings in order to become the ruler overall.

Sina, it seems was named after Queen Salamasina, a queen of Samoa many centuries ago and an ancestor of, Maleatoa Taimalelagi, the couples father, and one of his wives, which one though, Smith also couldn't quite understand, given that each King, as well as any prospective leader, was named Malietoa, a title which literally meant 'great warrior' and which Mana stated with great reverence, was given to the original chief by the defeated leader of the Tongans who, is said to have called over his shoulder 'Malie To'a, Malo e tau...' (Great warrior, thank you for the war!) as they retreated to their boats to save them being main course at the victory feast.

With each stop, be it for a night's rest in the pitch dark of the forest at evening, or a patch of cleared forest near the river's edge to gulp down much needed food and drink, the two natives related to their companion the danger they and their fellow islanders were in and the urgency of their cause.

Smith listened, fascinated at the lengths these siblings were going to, simply to gain control of the islands. It seems the islands, far from being the paradise he envisaged, had a history of bloody war and was threatening to become embroiled in even more conflict. He found himself going over and over their stories as they clambered ever higher through the dappled sunlight and steamy jungle.

On finally reaching the saddle of the mountain, Smith could see the land sloping away towards the east, much gentler than the steep western slope they had just traversed. As they stood on the shoulder of the mountain, they could make out more smoke plumes in the valleys before them. Smith thought they must be village fires but after standing for a few moments two new plumes of smoke erupted, followed by the unmistakable boom of cannon in the distance. His companions motioned him to what looked like an old campsite affording them a clear view of the valleys. Dry palm fronds had been strewn about in the storms and a few of the poles had rotted off but at least they afforded some semblance of shelter from the mist. They motioned him to place his pack on the ground and then began to cut and carry fresh palm fronds and poles. Within half an hour they had the shelter as good as new and Smith marveled at the ease of being able to live in this paradise, where all you needed seemed to be at your disposal, but he couldn't help being suspicious of their actions at bringing him here and wondering just what it was his companions had in store for him. He wasn't too long in finding out.

In the days that followed, the three companions trekked down from their shelter, towards the tendrils of smoke that emanated from the treetops along the valley. Each stop for rest or water would have his companions telling Smith of the atrocities committed on their villagers by the opposing chiefs and it wasn't long before he saw for himself just how vicious the atrocities were.

It would be three days before they approached the first clearing where he had seen the first tendril of smoke rising and Smith finally got to see the carnage first hand. Although there were no bodies, as it was obvious the villagers, being further away from their attackers, had been forewarned, and had fled into the jungle leaving the attackers to destroy everything in their path.

The explosions they had heard back in the village, were not cannon fire at all, but barrels of gunpowder being set off to destroy and set fire to the buildings in the outlying villages. Smith estimated the furthest villages were about ten miles west from Apia, the main harbour, the captain had spoken about, and thus the jungle trails and streams would be far too difficult to haul cannon across, but the small barrels of gunpowder would be much easier to carry through the jungle and have far more effect than simply burning the huts that could soon be rebuilt. By blasting the huts, burning the gardens and driving their livestock off, their attackers would ensure those villagers who were dispossessed and who had fled into the jungle could not return, and would have to continue westwards until, with their backs to the sea a virtually unarmed, half starved, populace, when caught up with, would face certain massacre.

Mana had motioned to both Smith and Sina, the presence of villagers hiding in the jungle as they passed and although neither of the two saw any evidence of the terrified natives, they had no reason to disbelieve this jungle trained warrior and by the time they had approached the third village, their worst fears were realized.

As soon as they could smell the sweet, sickly smell of burning flesh, Mana halted, and fearing the enemy might be close, he motioned for the other two to remain hidden while he would go ahead. He was gone but a few minutes before returning and signaling them to follow him.

He cut off the track into the jungle and began angling upslope towards the south, with the other two following. As soon as he reached a clearing where they could look down on the clearing and see enough of the village area to determine whether the enemy had left the scene, he halted, and the three companions scanned the scene below them.

To Henry's surprise, the clearing seemed to have been fortified with shallow trenches and the remains of a redoubt. The earthworks had been created some time ago, with some of the eroded walls being shored up with logs, giving Henry the impression of an older fortification being neglected and run down and then hastily reconstructed as if the villagers had known an attack was imminent. The main community house, or Malae, had been razed, as were most of the smaller dwellings but it was a pile of smoking logs fencing off a corner of the redoubt, that drew their attention. Henry peered into the dappled sunlight trying to make out why someone would light a fire against an earthen wall, until closer inspection revealed they were not logs, but human bodies, piled against the wall where they had tried to escape by climbing over the wall of the redoubt and were either bludgeoned to death or speared and set afire where they lay, most possibly still alive. At least two of the bodies, a man and a woman, had been beheaded, no doubt the chief and one of his wives. The attackers, unable to move fast with the weight of full bodies in tow, had removed the heads for feasting on once they reached the safety of one of their mountain camps.

Henry felt sick, already the vision of his paradise rapidly fading from his imagination, replaced by an uncontrolled hell hole of murder and savagery. Sina broke the silence that had descended on the trio. 'Those are our people.' She said quietly. She turned and looked Henry in the face. 'If you don't help us, they will come for us.' Henry stared back and the penny dropped!

'So that's what this has been about!' He exclaimed. 'But I'm only a carpenter, what can I do against an army?'

'They are not an army,' She answered, matter of fact. 'They are no different from us, except they have guns and we don't.'

'And neither do I.' Henry shot back.

Lani looked to Mana who could sense the mood of hopelessness settling on Henry and shrugged. Henry began to move forward in the hope there may be some survivors, but his companion waved his hand and shook his head sadly. It was his experience that no one in the village would be left alive except the people who escaped before the attackers came.

Mana walked over to where the bodies lay and motioned for Henry to come. Henry gingerly stepped around what may have been body parts and stepped close to the wall where his companion began gesturing with his arms stretching open and closed, pointing at the wall as he tried to explain something that was beyond Henry's comprehension.

Sina began to put her brother's gesticulations into words, explaining to Henry that, being a carpenter and ship wright, he would be able to instruct their people on how to build redoubts and forts as well as adapt their small four-man canoes into larger war canoes. As well he might be able to talk with the missionaries and white sailors that sometimes landed at Apia, in the hope they might be able to acquire some of the types of weapons their enemies were using against their people.

Mana again showed him the heads of some of the dead and Henry could see that most of them, if not all, had been bludgeoned brutally, dying from head injuries inflicted by some type of modern axe, most likely procured from the whalers or trading ships and not musket shot. What they need, Sina explained, was a strong type of defence as well as better weapons that would drive their attackers back towards their own territory and thus deter their enemies from attacking in the first place, thereby negating the use of violence at all.

Henry listened as he studied the wall, or rather the pile of logs and dirt that made up the roughly constructed redoubt and concluded the builders had little knowledge of defensive construction and probably would have been able to escape, or even defend their village had they have had some training in the construction of fortifications as well some knowledge of modern weaponry. What his companions were saying made sense. If these barbaric actions were allowed to continue then a return to the cannibalism and carnage of the not-too-distant past was almost certain and that would spell disaster for these islands, not to mention his own future.

During the weeks and months that followed, the three companions made many trips back and forth to Apia, enlisting the help of their fellow villagers to carry what goods they could inveigle from the whaling ships or traders that sometimes called at Apia or any other sheltered cove. Henry constructed from two single canoes, a double canoe with a light frame between, that could be steered from a rudder between the two hulls and powered by a short lateen sail made from woven flax fronds. This enabled them to reach the ships that moored out in the deeper waters of the bays. For the most part they were driven away from the ships with curses and threats from the frightened mariners but, on seeing a white man at the helm, struggling to control the little boat in the choppy waters, they were eased of their fears and for the most part, allowed the canoe to come alongside.

The promise of freshly picked fruit and vegetables made ready swapping's and the ships captain's saw the ease and time saving of this crazy Englishman's offers to meet the whaleboat at the beach with barrels of fresh water and swapping's. The time saved in conversing with another white man instead of a heathen savage was enough to convince the ships captains to part with their precious axe heads and iron bolts that could, with Henry's talents be wrought and shaped into tools and weapons. Henry never requested any guns and indeed rarely saw any muskets or pistols being carried by the crews that came ashore. No doubt, their captains would be most wary of arming the unpredictable native lest those very weapons be turned against him on some later encounter, but he always made it his duty to amicably question the traders as to what cargo they might be carrying.

He was pleasantly surprised when a crewman from one of the larger traders let on that part of one ship's cargo consisted of casks of saltpetre, for the use of curing meat. The ship was bound for Sydney, Australia, and it took some haggling with the captain to convince him to trade one barrel of a cargo that was part of the ship's manifest and didn't belong to him. In the end it was agreed that Henry would do two days repairs on the ship without pay, and as well, deliver to the captain, a freshly killed pig.

Much was Mana's disgust when Henry ordered one of their pigs slaughtered and brought before the captain in return for a useless barrel of salt, and even more annoyed was he, when Henry took the waterproof tarpaulin, he was using for a shelter and proceeded to wrap the barrel in the waterproof oil cloth to keep it dry. His argument that salt was readily available from the sea was ignored by Henry and stern looks from Sina forced him to hold his tongue, but it did not stop the grimace of disgust and annoyance as he and three other natives lugged the heavy barrel, slipping and sliding over the steep mountain track towards their village.

They heard stories of attacks by men from A'ana and Savaii but, apart from smoke in the distant hills, they saw little evidence of the war. Still, they remained wary and trusted no one on their trips into

Apia. Each night around the fire Sina would teach Henry the customs and skills of the Muasega. Henry was a willing pupil and they found themselves warming to each other, sitting closer together whispering quietly and more intimately to each other than the evening before. Each day Henry would share his skills of woodworking and iron shaping in the tiny blacksmith hovel, complete with forge he had constructed from homemade bricks and bellows Sina had the women of the village create to his patterns. He had fashioned an anvil from the head of a broken anchor Mana had discovered sticking out of the beach at Apia Bay and despite the scarcity of iron to work with, had managed to amass quite a reasonable collection of iron and woodworking tools. Mana was a willing servant and brought him all manner of different shaped wood for the construction of everything from boats knees and wooden pulleys to trade with the whalers that so often put into port with damage or lost gear, and a myriad of handles for every type of carpentering and shipwright tool imaginable. As well, and to both the chief and Mani's delight, Henry created spear heads, pikes and a vicious looking set of war axes, along with fish hooks and gaffs of every size one could think of. As he worked at his forge or sat eating the food Sina brought him, she would watch his every move, as if studying his ways and mannerisms. Often, she would catch him admiring her beauty out of the corner of his eye and at these times she would shed the aloofness of a chief's daughter and lower her head coyly. It was one of these times at the forge she was staring so intently, studying him as he worked. It unnerved him so much, he put down his hammer on the brick work of the forge and stared back at her.

'What is it? What is it you wish to learn from me? He stepped around the forge and laid his hammer down on the anvil, and smiled. 'What do you need to know?'

He was almost struck dumb by her straightforward answer. 'What I need to know is,' She took a deep breath. 'If I'm going to be your wife, I need to know everything there is to know about you.'

Chapter 6
Muasaga Village,
Tafitoala River, Navigator's Island, 1839

The year was Eighteen Thirty-Nine and although Navigator's Island's was still in the grip of war, reverend John Williams made all haste to attend Henry and Sina's wedding. After his initial shock at being proposed to by a woman, and in such blunt terms, it was explained to Henry that, in Samoan society, it was common for a high-born woman to choose the man that would be her husband. Normally, following the proposal, each of the couple's family would meet and discuss the terms of marriage, but given that Henry had no family, he was still a navigator, a shipwright and carpenter and as such was considered high born by the chief of the muasaga and so was approved!

Henry came away from the meeting, a very happy man, although he couldn't help thinking to himself that had he refused Sina's proposal things could have been a whole lot different, with himself being stretched out on the bridal table and being part of the wedding feast. Henry had visited the reverend at his church in

Leulumuega on the eastern side of Opulu and found the reverend to be much loved and respected by the people of Navigators islands. He had first come to Savaii and built his first church at Leulumuega in 1835 and the response he got from Maleatoa Vaiinuupo to embrace Christianity was so encouraging he built a ship from rough sawn Tamanu and bent mahogany spars for masts. She was a seventy tonner, fore and aft rigged schooner of some sixty feet in length. With her ropes made from the fibres from hibiscus trees and her sails made from plaited matting with a white dove emblazoned on her mainsail, the Messenger of Peace took fifteen weeks to build with no proper shipbuilding tools, she was, as they say, 'somewhat hard to handle in a blow,' and had many a close call as she sailed the seas between the islands.

Only last year, the London Missionary Society had purchased a new ship, the Camden, a proper Falmouth built Brig and the reverend John Williams, together with six other missionary families had arrived in the islands to spread the Christian word.

On hearing of a white man, one of the very rare, literate and educated white men, to inhabit Navigators Islands, the missionary was overjoyed to see Henry and learn he was marrying an islander. Best of all, and he made no bones about it, Henry was only one protestant in a world of full of heathens, godless ne'er do wells and Catholics.

Henry and Sina visited Reverend Williams house whenever they were in the vicinity and when he received the opportunity to co preside with their chief over their wedding, which was inevitable, as he was the only white missionary available within about a thousand miles, he was ecstatic.

It was after the nuptials, with all the village and more, engaged in the three days of gorging themselves on the sumptuous feast placed on trellis' in front of the big house, when the reverend approached the wedding couple and invited them to a cruise over to the island of Erromango on the Camden.

An Irishman, Mister James Harris had also attended the wedding and explained that he had recently travelled via Rarotonga and saw the transformation that had taken place since reverend Williams had placed teachers there and begged to be allowed to join them in the hope of becoming a successful missionary teacher.

They had already met the captain of the Camden, Captain Robert Clark Morgan a devout Wesleyan who had gone to sea aboard a British man o'war at the tender age of eleven and served on whalers before finding his calling and accepting the position of master of the Camden. He once confided that during his term on the British man o'war, that those ships were, *'a place where all wickedness is committed with greediness and a place where he saw every vice a man is capable of committing'*.

Morgan left the Royal navy to join the Merchant Marine at the age of sixteen and progressed to whaling. In eighteen thirty-six, he became master of the Duke of York, a whaling ship that was fitted out to bring the first settlers to South Australia. Leaving London on 24 February, they arrived at Kangaroo Island on 27 July. After disembarking his passengers, Morgan sailed away to continue whaling, calling in at Hobart town for supplies and then proceeding to the whaling grounds. In eighteen twenty-eight, whilst whaling near Tahiti and Navigators Island, he became interested in the work of missionaries in the area and following Reverend Williams being ordered to sell the Messenger of Peace, but in acknowledgement of his successful attempts at converting islanders to Christianity, the London Missionary Society purchased the Camden. In eighteen thirty-eight, to combine his love of the sea and his commitment to missionary work, he applied to the Society and was given command of the Camden.

On hearing the tales of adventure aboard a new and comfortable ship from captain Morgan, and at the urging of Reverend Williams both Henry and Sina were eager to accept the gift of what would be a honeymoon trip of a lifetime.

The Camden hauled anchor and left Apia Bay for Erromango on 30th October, Eighteen Thirty-nine, for the thirty-day return voyage. Sina was just as enthralled as Henry at the sight of the islands from the sea. For, although she had lived all her life on and around Upolu, the furthest she had she had ever been away was no more than a couple of miles offshore and to see the shoreline alternating from cliffs to sparkling white sands, then heavily forested bays to black sand beaches, all from the comfort of the wide gunwales of a beautiful ship that simply moved by itself under the power of the wind, was an experience she would never forget. It wasn't long before they lost sight of the islands and ventured into the wide expanse of the south pacific, but far from being boring, the lessons in navigation and sailing given by Henry and almost every crew member from the cabin boy up to the captain, whilst being surrounded by a myriad of sea wildlife meant there wasn't time for Sina, or Henry, to be bored. The couple spent hours riding face down on the whisker nets that stretched from the bowsprit to the bow gunwales of the brig and laughed at the thrill of watching the dolphins and porpoises breaking the water just inches below their faces as the ship plunged into the low troughs of crystal clear water.

From their vantage points around the ship, they could virtually select the views of the sea life they wished to encounter. From the massive span of the wing tips of the southern albatross as the birds hung suspended on the slipstream just aft of the stern, so close you could reach out and touch them, to the guessing game that all on board would partake in as a whale would break the surface in the distance. With a call of *'thar she blows',* all persons who were not otherwise engaged in ship board duties, and some that were, would rush to the gunwale and try to guess the type of whale. Apart from Henry and Captain Morgan, the others on board had rarely seen a whale up close and were stumped as to how the captain, in particular, could guess it right every time. It wasn't until sometime into the trip that he divulged over their evening meal, the secrets to guessing the type of whale and much diverse were the reasons. It seems that humpback whales were much likely to broach, rather than simply 'blow' and have much longer pectoral flippers and Southern right whales had no fins at all on their back and roughened skin that looks like a pile of stones on their heads, and cachalot, or sperm whales are easily recognised by their enormous square heads and narrow jaws. Each evening after the day's most fun filled education, the newlyweds would attend a short service conducted by the Reverend and retire to their cabin for a period of love making, thereafter to be rocked to sleep by the gentle swell of the Pacific Ocean.

In just four days the Camden was approaching the island of Rotuma and the Reverend's decision to call into the island in the hope of picking up an Erromangan native he hoped would advantage his communication with his tribal compatriots, would lengthen their trip considerably but neither Henry nor Sina were bothered. They were having too much fun to care and if the reverend could utilize the sailing time between Rotuma and their destination to learn at least some of the language of the erromangans, then this indeed would speed up their voyage and at the same time, hasten the native heathens embrace of his holy work.

Both Henry and Sina remained on the ship, expecting a same day return of the captain and reverend and their group of ten. Strangely, although the Rotuman population seemed very friendly and accepted their gifts in return for introducing them to the elusive native, there seemed to be always an obstacle or incident that befell them in their efforts to espy their quarry. Indeed, as

Captain Morgan voiced on more than one occasion his suspicions that things 'did not seem right' and 'all effort must be put into ensnaring the recalcitrant heathen' before continuing their journey, but after the noon of the second day passed and the mood of the Rotumans seemed to change from one of welcome acceptance to one of surly and grudging acquiescence, it was decided to forego the capturing of the elusive native and press on regardless.

What they did not know, was the native they were searching for was aware of the murder of two of the chief's sons on erromango by white sandalwood traders just a few weeks before and was loathe to have any association with any white man. It was decreed that white man should face native justice and that any white man who enters past the marked tree on erromango would suffer the fate of being killed and eaten.

The next port of call was the tiny island of Tanna where the ship disembarked three Samoan teachers, and once they were ensconced in their make shift huts, the captain gave orders to make sail. Once within the confines of the wheel house he again voiced his concern that the natives were becoming increasingly unpredictable the further west the ship sailed and although the reverend Williams agreed, his argument was that 'We simply must make our presence known to these heathens.' He drew a deep breath and iterated what everyone knew to be true. 'For too long these natives have been shamefully abused by white traders and seamen, we must show them that we are men of god and they need have no fear of us.'

On the morning of the 20th November, Erromango was in full view and the Camden glided slowly up into Dillon Bay on the west coast of the island. The bay was a wide open expanse that slowly narrowed off into a healthy sized tidal river. The ship made its way towards the river mouth before letting go just one anchor and all her sails, Henry noticed that the ship was still some distance of the shore and the mains had only had the clews let go, allowing the sails to luff and spill wind. None of the sails had been fully furled, and more than half of the leather straps that normally held the sails furled tightly to the yard arms were hanging free. Henry enquired of the captain, as the latter made his way to the lowered whale boat, 'We won't be stopping long then?'

'I don't believe so, Mister Smith,' the captain replied, 'We shall see what transpires during the next few minutes.' Then he added, 'I fear the good reverend is too trusting of the locals, and shall thank you to remain on board and be ready should the need arise and we have to make all haste to return to ship.'

The reverend and mister Harris were already in the first boat and the crewmen began pulling towards the shore. Henry looked towards the shore beyond them and could see a beautiful bay running up to a sharp valley, almost like a gash in the mountain from which a white torrent of water cascaded down the rock wall, disappearing into the trees, before exiting the forest as a crystal-clear stream, running gently across the beach towards the surf.

Three natives appeared from the forest on the northern end of the beach near the stream, Mister Harris hailed them but they withdrew into the trees, except one. A hand full of large beads was then thrown and the natives appeared once again before grabbing up the beads and again retreating. At the captain's call the rowers in the first boat halted their advance in the surf before the beach, and waited until the second boat caught up. They were too far from the ship for anyone aboard to hear, but it was obvious the captain was remonstrating with the men of God and requesting their reticence from advancing any further. The reverend refuted him and threw a bucket towards the young native who had remained on the beach, near the stream. The reverend indicated to the native his need for a drink and to everyone's surprised the native boy picked up the bucket and walked back up the beach to the line of trees before dipping the bucket into the stream and retracing his steps, wading out to the first boat and handing the bucket to the reverend. The Reverend turned back to the captain and laughed. 'You know we like to take possession of land, but if we leave a good impression and leave, we can return and locate teachers to bring here.' He hesitated, grabbing the gunwale of the boat to steady himself, and added confidently, 'Babel was not built in a day, you know'.

Encouraged by his mentors' words, mister Harris leapt from the whaleboat and proceeded up the beach towards the forest. The reverend followed in his footsteps and mister Cunningham made to join him but the captain signaled him to stay. He could see more natives approaching the reverend and wondered why there were no adults among them.

Already the reverend was trying to communicate with the boys and they each appeared to be at a loss to understand each other. By this time, mister Harris was into the tree line and the line of people had strung out the full width of the beach, from the tree line to where the boats were waiting in the surf.

Even from where they were at the ship's railing, both Henry and Sina heard the shout. Not a shout of warning, nor aggression, but a mournful cry of desolation and pain as Harris staggered back from the trees and fell into the stream as the adult males fell on him and began clubbing him to death. The ship's crew watched in horror as the stream turned red with Harris' blood and a horde of natives lunged from the forest and began chasing the reverend and the captain down the beach. In an instant, mister Cunningham was aboard the second boat and helping the captain inboard. The reverend moved very rapidly for the large man he was and was almost to the first boat when the force of the waves caused him to stumble, he was back on his feet in an instant, his hand reaching for the prow of the first boat when a native delivered a blow to the back of his head that would surely strike him unconscious, but again he struggled to his feet and reaching for the outstretched hands of the whaleboats crew before two more blows struck him and a mass of arms dragged him back from the water and safety, up the beach to his doom.

The natives followed the boats as far as they could into the surf, grabbing at the prow of the first boat as the crew tried to turn in the surf and only when the second boat came alongside and they feared a larger force, did they withdraw to the beach. With the terrified crewmen pulling on their oars for dear life and unable to protect themselves, they were forced to face the hail of spears and clubs falling among the two boats, bouncing off the gunwales and thwarts, narrowly missing all except one seaman who took a wound to his thigh

The ship's crew watched from the gunwales in helpless horror as the gentle stream became a ribbon of blood and the young native men all joined in with rocks and clubs, pummeling the reverend's body until it was unrecognizable.

The ship was a good two hundred yards from the beach and to those in the whaleboats it seemed miles, yet to those aboard the ship, still in disbelief at what just happened, it seemed they were far too close to danger and men began running to the rail and calling those in the boats to row faster, although they needed no second bidding. Within minutes, the two boats had come alongside, and were being hauled up into their davits.

Captain Morgan leapt from the still balancing whaleboat as it cleared the bulwarks and ordered the anchor weighed. The ships company, Henry and Sina included, needed no second bidding. The crew, relieved the captain had already ordered the capstan bars inserted, grabbed the bars and began turning and the anchor came free of the bottom and sails were luffing even before the final whaleboat was secure in its davits. The Camden drifted sideways at first as the current took her, instilling a moment of panic lest the ship be thrust upon the beach allowing all of the ships complement to suffer the same fate as that of the two missionaries. Then, as the sails filled, the ship stalled, then began making way, confidence replacing fear as the Camden came under the control of the helmsman, gathering speed as she sailed around the cove and stood off the shore in deep water until Captain Morgan was certain the native population posed no further threat, but he had to admit there was no hope of saving poor Reverend Williams or Mister Harris. The amount of blood that had flowed down the once beautiful stream assured all that any life that once existed was now extinct, and when the smoke from the cooking fires about two hundred yards distant from the tree line, began trailing upwards through the trees into the air, it was obvious to all what the aftermath of these brutal murders would be.

Already the natives would be stripping the flesh and separating the body parts to be divided up between the chiefs for ritual eating. The pits would be prepared and the stones heated up before the body parts, wrapped in purau leaves would be cooked among the hot stones.

The Camden stood off for about two hours before the captain, not wishing his passengers the mental sight of what was happening behind the wall of trees, and not wishing to put his ship and crew in any further danger, ordered the ship about and set sail for Sydney.

Much was Henry and Sina's protestations at learning they could be months before they would return to Navigators Island but the captain was adamant, he would have to report this disaster to the nearest British authorities, without fail.

A stroke of luck then befell the newlyweds as the next morning a sail was seen on the horizon, a ship, sailing directly towards them. Captain Morgan had the Camden hove to in the other ships path and on seeing this, the captain of the Highlander, a whaling brig out of Hobart Town bound for Navigators Island and the whaling grounds, stood off, and a boat was put down to inform the captain of the dreadful incident on Erromango Island.

Much was their relief as Captain Lovitt, Master of the Highlander, on hearing of their ordeal at witnessing such a dreadful sight, agreed to take them on to Navigators Island free of charge, Mister Cunningham had agreed to proceed to Sydney with the Camden and testify at the enquiry, which would no doubt ensue.

Much relieved that, because he wasn't on either of the whaleboats and therefore would not have to testify at the enquiry, Henry and Sina hurriedly packed their belongings and clambered into the whale boat after thanking the crew and Captain Morgan for their efforts to entertain them and happily climbed out of the boat and up the ladder on to the deck of the Highlander. After thanking the captain Lovitt for his kind assistance, the couple were led below.

The crews' quarters were much more spartan than those of the Camden, after all the Highlander was a fully stocked whaler and although clean, as most British whaling ships were, she smelled strongly of the remnants of the giant sea creatures she had come to hunt. At the evening meal, Henry related the story of their voyage in the Camden, deliberately omitting to mention the whales they had seen to the north of their path lest Captain Lovitt set off in chase, causing them more delays in getting home.

The captain, first mate and bosun listened intently as Henry related the story of Reverend and Mister Harris' brutal demise and subsequent consumption, and shook their heads in disbelief and visible relief as, they explained, they were intending to go ashore on Erromango themselves had it not been for Captain Morgan hailing them down.

'I shudder to think of the dreadful fate that might have befallen you had not Captain Morgan acted with alacrity in getting the ship under way.' Captain Lovitt said, still shaking his head at the thought of the beheaded bodies of Henry and Sina being cannibalized by the heathen islanders. 'But don't worry, rest assured, the Highlander won't be stopping off anywhere until we reach Upolu, and there the both of you will be safe.'

'Yes,' Answered Sina, gratefully. 'All three of us are safe now.'

'Three?' All Heads turned towards her, questioningly.

Sina smiled at the questioning looks from the white papalagi, including her husband. She was aware the customs of the whites called for privacy and little mention of pregnancy, but the Samoan custom was to celebrate the gestation and birth of a child and she didn't hold back. 'Yes,' she said gleefully. 'I am with child.' She placed her hand on Henry's and raised her eyebrows. 'And now there are three of us!'

There was a moments silence as consternation at placing a pregnant woman in such danger as they had just been delivered from, saw accusing stares aimed at Henry from the captain and his officers, before Salamasina added, 'Henry didn't know.'

'Oh, I see,' Captain Lovitt grinned at Henry's obvious embarrassment.

Henry stared back at Sina. 'Why, why didn't you tell me? He whispered, the thought of his unborn child being torn from his mother's womb and hurled into the fire, horrifying him. 'We would never have left the village, had I known'.

'You were not to know, and besides,' Sina replied. 'A Samoan woman is strong and knows how to carry a baby in public and not hide away her condition. Life will go on the same until I am ready'.

'And just when will that be?' Henry asked.

'I think I am about half to go.' At this comment, the captain and his two mates deliberately avoided staring at Sina's stomach, and looked to Henry to continue the conversation.

Henry read the questions in their faces and calculated for them, confirming their assumptions.

'Four and a half months!' He exclaimed. The magnitude of the situation finally dawning on him. 'A baby in just four and a half months!'

Salamasina and Henry stared at each other for a moment, before captain Lovitt broke the silence. 'I would consider that, having just been delivered from a most dreadful situation, you folks have just been in receipt of some momentous news that will certainly bring joy to an otherwise disastrous trip, and this would call for a celebration.' He hesitated and motioned to his mate with an outward flapping of his hand. 'Mister Mate if you will, please.'

The mate needed no second bidding and leapt up from his chair and moved to the side board, He removed a bottle of the finest brandy and five china cups from the locker and proceeded to pour a healthy charge into each cup.

Much to the mirth of the captain and his mates, both Sina and Henry gagged and spluttered as they drank their first large sips of the fiery liquid, but managed to consume the nips in time for the second charge of liqueur.

There were no double bunks aboard Highlander and although Henry and Sina attempted to squeeze into the narrow bunk in an attempt to kindle a romantic connection, they were forced to abandon the idea in the interests of comfort and Henry retreated to the second bunk, and they were soon asleep, weary from the day's exertions and no doubt the brandy aiding in a good night's sleep.

Sina assisted the cook in the well appointed galley, whilst Henry assisted the ship's carpenter during the day. During the evening meals, both Sina and Henry acquainted the ships officers with what they might expect to find on and around the islands in the way of hospitality, or lack of, or, in the case of erromango, downright hostility! Thankfully, no whales were sighted during the voyage to Opulu and both were pleased captain Lovitt opted to put them down in their home bay at Tafituala instead of sailing around Opulu to Apia.

In return for this favour, William arranged for the ship to be victualled and watered in friendly territory, a great time saver for the captain who was wont to be away on the hunt as soon as possible. All the villagers, particularly the chief, were very pleased to see the newlyweds and a feast was organized on their behalf as the returning heroes from the cannibals of erromango. Interesting, Henry noted, as he feasted on the assortment of pork and vegetables spread out on the calabashes before him, that just a few short weeks ago, reverend Williams and Mr. Harris most likely would have been the main course at a similar feast.

Celebrations were tinged with sadness as reverend Williams, or Villaimu his native name, was hailed as a great man of God by the chief, stopping short of hailing him as a great leader, as no one could be as great a leader, or Malietoa, as himself.

As they feasted, Mana informed both Sina and Henry of the island's events in their absence. Apparently, the islanders from Savaii and A'ana had withdrawn to their respective territories and apart from the odd skirmish which had resulted in nothing more than a few burnt huts and some stolen pigs, all had seemed quiet. Now that he knew more about this island and its inhabitants, not to mention the vagaries of their language and customs, which could change with the moods of one, or more, chiefs, Henry felt it was time for him to acquaint himself to how such a paradise could be so engrossed in a cruel and seemingly unwinnable, war.

Henry listened intently as both Sina and Mana began explaining the cause of the war and whose fault it was. It seems there was a great chief Maleatoa Savea, so called because, in the war against the Tongans, who had invaded and ruled Samoa so cruelly and unjustly, life for the Samoans became unbearable. At the hands of the Tongan tyrant, the Samoans rebelled and in the great war that followed, Samoans defeated the Tongans and as they ran down the beach towards their canoes and safety, the Tongan chief called over his shoulder 'Male To'a, Malo e Tau! (Great warrior, thank you for the war!).

There followed a succession of Great warriors, Kings and Maleatoas who, it was reported, were the sons, half-brothers, step sons and nephews of the many wives each Maleatoa had. It seems there was a princess Salamasina, the only female Maleatoa, and who Salamasina was a namesake, to whom each and all people in Samoa seemed proud to be descended from, especially his companions and their father, the chief.

Two hours later, Henry was still trying to come to understand who, or what, started the war but in the end, he accepted that convolutions of succession and familial jealousies left Samoa with generations of intermittent bickering, fueled by something as trivial as a family argument about who was related to whom. He learnt that Samoan lineage does not have a written history, all Samoan history is carried by word of mouth, from generation to generation. As well, Henry thought, even though written history can be misconstrued or even deliberately misinterpreted, at least, the British way of recording history has some sort of reliance on fact and can be referred to by all disputing parties however far into the past they need to go.

Henry couldn't even fathom the depth of which the rivalry went, but he did understand that in the past, rivals were capable of killing, but disputes seemed to only last until the day's supplies of rocks, stones and spears were exhausted and then the battle would be over. In these days of musketry and cannon, the group armed with the most powerful weapons could create all manner of death and destruction even to the point of wiping out not just a whole village, but a complete island population. Henry could now understand the villages dilemma, it would not suffice to be a peace loving village in this place where savagery and barbarity lie just beneath the friendliness of these islands.

Henry acknowledged his companions need to protect themselves and over the next few days, he devised a plan of how it could be done.

Chapter 7
Corner of Henry and Andrew streets
Strahan, Tasmania, 1937

Maryanne lay awake in the total darkness. She couldn't hear the child's breathing, instead, the gentle rise and fall of her tiny chest against her right arm was all she needed to know she was sleeping peacefully. Maryanne wouldn't sleep this night. She slowly turned her head and looked towards the window where whatever light there was outside would creep around the faded curtains and let her know what the weather was doing outside. There was no light. No moon, no stars, no light at all, just the distant roaring of ocean beach, some five miles away to the west, just enough sound to carry across the gentle westerly breeze that whispered through the little town of Strahan, through its quiet graveled streets and around the clapboard houses and blackberry covered brick chimneys interspersed with grassy paddocks lined with radiata pine trees that normally stood tall and proud in the moonlight. But tonight, the shapes of the giant trees joined land and sky within the inky blackness and together with the gentle rustling of their needles on the wind, created dangerous conditions for any foolish soul that ventured out without some type of lantern, and there were not many souls that would waste the precious fuel in these straightened times on such a night. These were conditions which would only be perfect for ones who could sense, rather than see, their way about in the blackness.

Mary Ann closed her eyes and strained her ears for the telltale sound she was waiting to hear and it wasn't long in coming.

A tiny sound of chain links touching against each other where the cloth that had been so carefully wrapped around them had frayed in the long ride home, the scrape of a beast's hoof against a loosened cobble and the rattle of the dislodged stone against the road surface. Then silence, as men and horses halted as one, listening for any movement other than their own and their animals.

By the time the mounted men moved forward again, Mary Ann was out of bed and standing in the tiny lounge. She kept her eyes closed as she moved to the window and avoided looking at the fireplace lest the tiny coals that survived the nights fire dull her vision of the scene she imagined, rather than actually saw, in the street outside her window.

Her eyes, now accustomed to the dark, could vaguely make out the shapes of two men on horseback and one, no, two beasts between them as they made their way past her window towards the stable near the bridge. Mary Ann waited until the men had herded the first beast inside the barn and imagined she could hear the steel latch fall across the two wooden lugs that held the door closed.

The barn wasn't big enough to hold all of the animals and men as well and Mary Ann knew at least one animal would have to remain outside whilst Jack Crane, her son in law, and Dan, his brother could dispatch the first beast.

Jack and Dan were experts at this game. They had been taught well by their father to 'come to the crack of the whip' as they leapt over the schoolhouse fence much to the dismay of the school teacher who was too afraid of their whip wielding father, and even more afraid of the feared Ada Sarah, their mother, and joined their father in the dray for a night of rustling cattle. Now, with their father and mother both passed on, the expertise instilled in the boys became the bane of Herbie Watkins life as the well-known farmer and horse breeder who farmed the Henty River, seventeen miles north of Strahan tried in vain to halt the drain on his livestock.

Jack knew the town would be asleep and few would venture out on a night such as this, and anyway, they would be able to see any lantern they would have to hold from a mile away. They only person they had to fear was his mother-in-law, Mary Ann. He liked Mary Ann, but Lydia, his wife and Mary Ann's daughter, were very much estranged from time to time and he really didn't wish to get entangled in women's family arguments.

Mary Ann stepped quietly outside, she knew the men were too careful to let her hear the latch fall but she could smell the sweat and steam from the animals and almost hear the snuff of the second beast as it shuffled uncomfortably against the hitching post outside the barn.

She listened for, and heard, the creak of the barn timbers as they took the weight of the first beast collapsing against the rope block hanging from the rafters. Still, she waited.

She waited until the men were firmly ensconced in their work before she made her move. But it was not towards the barn where the men were busy butchering the first beast, but towards her own shed at the back fence of her own place. Her eyes were well accustomed to the darkness but still she had to feel around for the latches on both the shed, and the gate.

As soon as she had the shed door opened the jersey cow inside moved forward and nuzzled her shoulder.

'There, there, Daisy' she whispered. 'Quiet now.' As if in answer, the cow stopped and only moved forward when her owner did without any pulling of the rope already around her neck.

Quietly Mary Ann lifted the two wires that passed for fencing along her back fence and led the cow through, surreptitiously glancing back towards the shed across the road where the two men were hard at work. She knew she had gotten through the easy part of her task and peered into the darkness beyond John Henry's fenced paddock and under the pine trees about sixty yards away.

She couldn't see Red Eye, but she knew he was there. Red Eye was John Henry's bull, a mad, savage beast that was quite capable of killing a man or horse, let alone a defenceless woman. She was not sure of his breed but with his rusty coloured coat and bloodshot eyes, he was aptly nicknamed by the townspeople. Mary Ann knew what she was doing was illegal and John Henry would not hesitate to call in the constabulary and claim the progeny for his own if he could but she knew also her granddaughter had to have milk and the sale of the poddy calf from this most prolific breeder would certainly give them sorely needed cash money.

She didn't have much time. Red Eye, for all of his five-hundred-pound bulk had a reputation of moving quickly and quietly around in his paddock before attacking an unsuspecting intruder. If she allowed the bull to get even halfway across the paddock before she could get Daisy through the gate and get the gate closed again, she would be in a world of trouble. Each time she looked towards the pines as she fumbled with the gate, she swore she could see the bull charging out of the darkness. Daisy seemed to sense her fear and placing her nose under her elbow, lifted Mary Ann's shoulder, forcing the steel latch up and over the post. Then the cow gently pushed against the gate and quietly ambled through. Of course, she thought, this wasn't the first time they had done this and the cow was probably looking forward to carousing with her amorous, but deadly, beau.

Mary Ann held the gate from opening too far and looked again towards the trees. She was right the first time, a shadow, somewhat lighter than its surroundings had left the cover of the trees and was moving across the paddock towards them.

With her heart pounding with fear and praying the bull would not bellow at this disturbance at least until she was into her own yard, the old woman quickly pulled the gate shut and closed the iron loop over the post. She slipped quietly into the darkness. The night was only young and she still had work to do.

Jack and Dan both looked at each other. They had hung the carcass of the first beast and were just cutting the skin off the second when something alerted them. A shaft of light shining through the crack between the barn door and the jamb had cast upon a movement of something outside the barn. Probably a cat, thought Jack, knowing the dogs were all on their chains and Lydia was well in bed, knowing not to come out on such a night. The two men stared at the sliver of light playing upon something outside. The men's first thought was it may be Herbie Watkins had followed them or even worse, Sly Bacon, the nickname the town had given Bill Cunningham the constable, had been alerted to their antics! Dan threw the canvas sheet over the hanging carcass and Jack moved towards the door and lifted the bar, pulling it open just enough to see what it was that was putting such a fright into two grown men.

Dan had moved the lantern behind the upright beam in the centre of the shed so the shadow cast by the beam would fall on the doorway and anyone standing outside could not make out the shapes hanging from the rafters.

As Jack opened the door the flickering light from the lanterns shadow fell on the dark face of his mother-in-law, Mary Ann.

'For Christ's sake, Mary Ann,' He hissed. 'What the bloody hell are you doing out here at this hour.'

'I'm sorry Jack,' Mary Ann lied. 'I couldn't sleep, and heard a noise. I thought someone might be rustling your cattle.'

Both Jack and Dan were relieved there was no Herbie Watkins or the constable to upset their night, but still they were annoyed to say the least. 'Don't you ever sleep, Mary Ann?' Dan asked, then added, hoping she hadn't seen the carcasses hanging from the rafters. 'We're trying to get some work done here!'

Mary Ann moved into the barn and much to the men's chagrin, eyed the piles of offal and skins lying on the floor, the men had forgotten to cover.

'It's a nice cool night to be killing,' She nodded towards the carcasses, knowingly. Then said matter of fact, 'No flies to annoy you.'

Both the men knew the jig was up. No doubt she had been watching all the time. The woman was a bloody nuisance but she was family after all, even if she was dark.

Jack grinned slowly and pointed to the pile of offal.

'What pieces would you like Mary Ann?' He pulled the hooves and hocks out of the pile and grabbed the axe off the bench to cut the hooves from the ankle bones.

Maryanne smiled gratefully, as if he was doing her a kindness by giving her just the hooves. 'No need to make a noise cutting them off, Jack.' She looked at the heads of the steers lying in the corner. 'Just the hocks, and if you could cut a flap off the cheeks, I would really appreciate it.' Jack was about to argue but she added, 'I could make Wacky a nice brawn with those.'

At the mention of the girl's name, Jack relented. He, like most in the family had a soft spot for the child and had even commented on her being a bit skinny and could do with some nourishment.

'Here,' he said, a harsh tinge to his tone, just to let the woman know there were to be no more favour's here tonight. 'Take these and be gone.'

The men loaded her outstretched arms with two hocks and hooves and two cheek flaps. Which, even Mary Ann had to agree was a substantial burden even though most of it was bone. Bone which would be scrubbed, along with the hooves and placed in a soup which would be relished as their evening meals for days to come. The cheek flaps from the steers would be skinned and pulled, then pressed into a steel pot by hand, heavy weights would then be placed on top of the lid to form the mold which would be boiled with the gelatin which she would obtain by burning the hooves until the outside casings would split, revealing the gelatin inside. The weighted meat cake would then be left in a basin of cold water to set. The delicacy could then be sliced onto sandwiches and eaten with gusto. There was but one more task to accomplish this night.

Her night vision all but destroyed by the light of the shed lantern, Mary Ann had to gently pick her way across the road, unable to avoid the piles of horse and cow dung that assailed her senses as she slipped and slid in them. She ignored these obstacles as she clung to her precious cargo for fear of dropping any in the darkness and never finding it again.

She reached her kitchen and placed her burden on the wooden table and covered the pile with a towel, grabbed up a small hessian bag she had prepared for the occasion, then gently closing the door behind her, she made her way back to the blackberry bushes near John Henry's gate and waited.

Mary Ann strained her eyes and ears to pick up the shadows of the two beasts she knew would be cavorting under the shadows of the pines. She had to be very careful not to call the cow too soon lest

Red Eye had not been satisfied in completing his business of insemination, and follow Daisy back across the paddock to the gate, making it impossible to retrieve the cow without the bull seeing her and attacking. Even though John Henry's fences were quite substantial, an aggressive animal the size of Red Eye would have little trouble tearing the gate apart and trampling Maryanne's body into a muddy pulp if he was aroused. Even his annoyed roaring would be enough to alert John Henry to the theft of his prized bull's fluid and bring the wrath of the constable on her.

She waited in the darkness until her eyes finally began to pick up the faint outline of the trees, and beyond them, to the right, a bulky shadow that must be the animals she was looking for. As she stared, the shadows seemed to separate, the smaller one moving out into the grassy paddock, leaving the large one to retreat further into the warmth of his lair. Sated, Red Eye had done his job, and Mary Ann gave the bull a couple of minutes to get comfortable among the pine needles, before she gave a short, low whistle and waited. Within a few seconds she began to make out the ghost like figure of Daisy, as the cow seemed to float soundlessly towards her in the gloom. She held the gate closed and waited until the cow arrived at the gate, her eyes still fixed on the spot she last saw the bull, then as Daisy arrived within a gate's length of her, she quickly pushed the wooden gate wide and almost smacked the cow's haunches against the timber as she drew it closed behind her. It was a cool night, but Mary Ann realized she was sweating with fear, her old heart pounding, as she looped the lead rope over the cow's head and quietly led her back across the road towards the gap in her own back fence. Once inside her own territory, she reached inside the hessian bag and turned the contents out on to the floor of the cow shed. Daisy seemed to acknowledge the strokes of the old lady's hand across her neck and began to eat the oats from her hand before turning her attention to the feed that had been tipped out of the bag. Maryanne quietly closed the door behind her and made her way back inside her home. They would eat, they would have milk, and within ten months, the sale of a new poddy calf would give them sorely needed income to tide them over until her husband came back from the river once again.

It was almost daylight when the old lady finished cleaning and stripping the meat ready for the brawn she would make later today and as she slipped into the bed beside her granddaughter, she only had a couple of hours until the girl woke. She could still make out the gentle rise and fall of the little girl's chest as she slept, oblivious to the nights nefarious actions. In the darkness, Mary Ann couldn't see the work box on the wardrobe but she knew her granddaughter would be asking for more of the story as soon as enough daylight crept around the faded curtains for her to see.

Chapter 8

Upolu, Navigators Island

1839

Apia Bay was a picturesque, almost a mile wide, north easterly facing, bay, cleft almost in half by a sandy headland that jutted three hundred yards into calm water fringed with sand and palm trees. Here and there, large Banyan trees dominated the breadfruit palms and lesser coconut trees along the shore, providing much needed shade from the noonday sun. The masses of tendrils from the roots of the banyans spread out almost six feet from the base of the tree to climb alongside the trunk, entwining both the trunk and each other in a huge mass of branches and vines that overshadowed all other trees. To the west, a line of steep hills ran along a peninsular that jutted into the ocean, forming a barrier between Apia Bay and the much larger, but reef encircled Vaiusu Bay, providing a back drop that culminated in a conical hill that sloped towards the bay and stopped only a few hundred yards from the shore. The northern shore of the peninsular was also strewn with reefs, but nature had blessed the southern half of Apia Bay with deep clear water running right up to the eastern and southern shores, allowing ships a safe harbour in all weather, with the exception of the rare tropical cyclones that spared no one, whether they be on land or sea.

Even though both he and Mana had visited the shores of Apia Bay a few times he hadn't really approached the huts and hovels of the more permanent, white, inhabitants. Usually, he spoke only to seamen as they pulled alongside and tied up to one of the jetties. Henry had explained to his companions the advantage of reconnoitering and they readily accepted his plan and although it was a hard slog crossing the valley from the spur that was their usual route down from the mountains, to a much lower spur, about a mile inland from the shore above the bay, this point gave them a clear view of the bay as well as the movements of the ships and boats. Between the trees and scrub, with the help of the spyglass, they could, for the most part, make out any movement on the beach as well.

There seemed to be two rivers entering the bay. The larger one, Mana called Vaisigano, had its reaches high up on the mountain range that ran down the centre of the island. A myriad of streams and runnels that coalesced into a series of spectacular waterfalls and crystal clear pools, before reaching the fertile plain about a eight miles from the shore of the bay, becoming a single ribbon of water that entered the bay through a wide, brown, sandy mouth. The smaller river, Mana called the Vailima, ran down from the very spur Henry located their observation point on, was not visible through the forest but Henry could make the line of trees edging the river that meandered across the forested flats until it too, emptied out into the bay less than half mile north from the Vasigano.

A number of small rickety jetties jutted out into the bay, with one or two small open boats tied alongside. Groups of shacks stretched out along the shore, about twenty yards in from the shore line and about forty in all. Interspersed with these, especially along the southern shore were large areas of mosquito infested, swampy ground between the two rivers.

From his vantage point on higher ground, Henry could make out the more substantial buildings to the north of the larger river, that served as churches for the London Missionary Society. Quite imposing buildings in this setting of ramshackle huts but still would not hold their own amongst the trading ports of Van Dieman's Land or New Zealand. There seemed to be always one or two traders or whalers in the bay, all anchored as close as possible to the southern shore where it seemed the water was much deeper, but managing to keep enough water beneath their keel so as to be able to make haste for open sea should the need arise. Through his spyglass Henry could make out the members of the crew walking the decks, back and forth, making sure the islanders who peopled the tiny skiffs that clustered around the larger ships, bartering and selling their wares, did not succeed in reaching the deck of the larger ship, although even from here he could see natives attempting to hook their makeshift wooden grapples into the chain plates that held the shrouds in place on the sides of each ship. Before launching themselves from the canoe and up the frail fibre ropes and on to the bulwarks. There to offer anyone who would listen, their wares, be it coconuts on a string around their neck or a calabash of fruit over their shoulder, they would continue to palaver their wares until the deck sailor would approach and either purchase their wares or send them back over the rail, usually into the water. Every ship's captain knew that the natives would steal anything whatsoever, whether it be of value or not, and even if all the gear was stowed from sight, the natives were the most cunning spies for their chiefs. If they noticed a chink in the ship's security, a lack of weapons, or perhaps even a shortage of crew members, that could be a sign of weakness and the ship could be an easy mark for a dead of night attack. The paranoia that gripped the crews of the ships as they were forced to visit these ports for victuals, was for the most part unfounded, but one could not avoid the stories of attacks and massacres by natives, who last year, had accorded the ships the most friendliest of greetings, would now have little trouble bashing the brains in and devouring the bodies of the whole ships compliment. Little discussion was made of the kidnapping, rape and murder by the white ne'er do wells and sandalwood pirates against the innocent natives who owned these islands.

Henry watched as the crews of the ships that stood close in remained at their stations until the ship had been revictualled, and half of the crew taken off after the last boat of stores had come ashore. These ships would then stand off and anchor in deeper water, as protection from thieving heathens as well as allowing the other ships to move carefully in and have their turn at the fruits from the shore and hovels that served as shops and bars. To the north of the smaller river, a large, flat, sandy spit jutted out into the bay, almost separating it into two bays, from where he was standing, he could hear the laughter and singing as whale boats tied alongside the jetties that poked out from either side of the sandy beach and the crews headed for grog shops and shebeens that were scattered along the shore.

It seemed to Henry the clash of two societies was painted in this scene of beautiful white sandy beaches lined with palms and looking out on a turquoise blue ocean, yet the natives appeared sad and resentful with only the few pennies the crewmen threw them to purchase either their goods or their bodies, or both. In comparison, the dirty ramshackle huts the crews frequented were loud, raucous, and anything but sad, if the laughter emanating from them was anything to go by. Occasionally, especially when it appeared a ship was about to leave, some of the sailors would stagger from the shade of a grog shop and approach the small groups of young islanders standing in the shallows as they cleaned their catch.

Even from this distance Henry could note the body language of the young boys as they gently but purposely pushed their dugout canoes and lightly built skiffs, back into deeper waters, away from the slowly advancing men, until the seamen gave up their advance and turned away towards the jetty where their shipmates were waiting. From this distance, Henry couldn't make out their exact words, but the rise in voices from their shipmates as they jeered and catcalled at the seamen's failure to cajole even one of the young islanders, convinced Henry of the fragility of the island's safety. Everyone on the island was aware kidnaping and indentured labour was common amongst the islands, the practice of taking young islanders, boys and girls, and forcibly indenturing them to an unpaid life at sea, or worse, to be sold into slavery at the next port of call. Each seaman knew the captain would pay a bonus for each extra able-bodied person who could work aboard ship for nothing and later be sold off at the blackbird markets in Australia for a handsome profit. A disgraceful practice, Henry mused, but legal around these islands where the brown skinned people were thought of as less than human.

Henry noted the names of the ships that would be most likely to carry the items that his village would need to sustain a defence against the more powerful tribes of the islands. The larger whaling barques or smaller brigs would only be useful for waste rope or used sail cloth, perhaps a few surplus iron nails could be swapped for clean, dressed timber for planking or knees for a damaged whaleboat, or fresh meat and vegetables. But it was the smaller traders on route from the Americas to Australia that were loaded with the very things that Henry would need.

Guns and powder would be handy, but the likelihood of obtaining decent long barreled muskets capable of accuracy, was very slim. More likely he would be offered trading muskets, commonly traded to islanders or Indians who would be ignorant to the dangers of these weapons. Most were over used and worn out, rejects from some far off war and much more likely to maim or kill the operator than do any harm to his opponent. No, what Henry wanted was cannon! Something small enough to manhandle through the steep mountains and conceal throughout the forest, yet powerful enough to decimate a war party of opposing tribesmen. Three cannon the size of a large falconet could be carried into the attack, sited in a log with grooves already cut at differing angles where two men could lift the barrel out of one groove and change direction of the shot. Once fired, the cannon could then be lifted out of its groove and spirited away to be set up at the next firing site.

Henry put the spyglass down. He had seen enough of life in the village and was convinced he could easily fit in with the ex-seamen and other detritus from society who populated the shanty town, and taking Mana with him as his 'boy' he bade their four helpers return to their mountain huts to await their return.

The trek down off the hill was hot and sweaty under the forest canopy but soon the canopy opened out to a brown sandy beach, the cool sea breeze a godsend after the heavy dank air of the forest. The sandy track along the beach was a pleasant walk, the large banyan trees spread their foliage wide, shielding the ground from the heat of the day and allowing short grasses to spread out from the trunk until the well-trodden path cut through the grass to the clean white sand beneath. The track meandered around tree stumps and palm trees between the beach and the forest and here and there a shack would present itself, tucked away in the scrub on the right, near one of the few small streams that run from the hills beyond and petered out to a thin film of fresh water that cut through the sand across the beach to the sea.

Occasionally the track would divert from the trees down to the beach proper as it skirted a lush swampy area and the men could hear the myriad of mosquitos and other weird and wonderful insects as if, annoyed by these interlopers, their protest was to rise from the swamp in their thousands, as if to attack, then, unexpectedly, settle in silence as they passed.

To Henry it was as if the whole island, even the insects, were on tenterhooks, waiting for a spark that would set off a catastrophe.

Apart from the few natives on the shore and among the waves, there seemed to be little sign of life until they arrived at the first collection of shacks. If this shabby group of thatched roofs on a series of poles was the beginnings of what was to become a thriving and prosperous port, as reverend Williamu had described the future of Apia, then, Henry mused, it had a bloody long way to go.

He peered into the gloom beneath the woven palm frond blinds and was surprised to find the inside of the shack quite clean, albeit sparsely furnished and even though he was fully aware there was people here he was startled when a voice called 'The boy stays outside!'

Mana, anticipating this welcome, had already halted and was standing near a palm, directly in line of sight from the inhabitants of the shack. Henry motioned for him to stay but he needed no second bidding. He didn't trust these men and it took every bit of his courage to stop himself from running. The voice called again. 'English? Deserter? Freeman?' Henry laughed at the inference.

'All of the above!' He called. This time it was the turn of the other man to laugh and his companions guffawed with delight. 'Well then, come in friend'.

Henry stepped into the hut, his eyes quickly adjusting to the gloom as he searched around the hut for the faces to the voices. There were four men sitting against a bench encircling the centre pole of the building, which was much bigger than Henry first envisaged and looking through the building beyond the poles Henry could make out more grass shacks among the long grass and scrub. Men of obviously different nationalities and races and island women lounged and sat around the poles of the buildings. He turned his attention back to the men in the centre of the hut.

'Henry Smith.' He introduced himself, much to the guffaws and laughter of the others. The bearded mad to which he addressed himself, stopped laughing and pointed to each of the men in turn. 'This yers Bill Smith, Bob Smith, Harry Smith, and thet gentillman in the corner,' He paused and drew a deep breath, his pointing finger indication a man of obvious south American descent 'Is Roderigo Juan Carlo Ignacio Smith!!'

The men broke into raucous laughter, causing some of the men sitting outside to stir and approach the hut, but Henry, not to be outdone, nodded to each man in turn before stopping at the south American and smiling, answered quietly, 'Well, we obviously must be related.'

With that the hut erupted in uproarious laughter, which even brought a nervous smile to Mana's otherwise stony face. He had no idea what was being said or if the laughter was a sign of friend or foe but when the men began to shake Henry's hand he did feel somewhat at ease.

A demijon of rum was produced from a large wooden chest and tin cups suddenly appeared as if from nowhere. Henry insisted on paying for the round and this was his immediate initiation into the group.

The bearded man, who introduced himself as Bob, explained, as Henry suspected, that these men were all refugees from white society. Most, if not all, had jumped ship from clippers and whalers from all over the world, some, sick of the hardship and low wages of the many whaling and sealing voyages to the frozen wastes of the southern oceans, found it was much easier to fish and subsist here on a warm south sea island where they were free of the constraints of white society's laws and conditions. Others, like Roderigo, had served their government amid bloody wars and strife, only to be abandoned to their own devices once they were too old to charge down the guns for the benefit of the wealthy classes. On calling into these islands more than once aboard their respective ships, they could see that after living on seal blubber and risking their lives each day for a pittance nothing in their lives could compare with the islanders free and easy lifestyle. Providing, of course you chose your island very carefully. Bob also explained the lack of native population in Apia as a result of the mosquitos that rose from the swamps of an evening and proceed to literally suck the life blood from anyone, whites and islanders alike.

Henry related the tale of the reverend Williams and Mister Harris' demise and the men gathered around the shack eager to hear, first hand, what the circumstances of that terrible voyage were.

Later that afternoon, when he had considered he was well enough trusted, he confided in Bob, his need for cannon and shot. He thought Bob might jib at his request for armaments, but the man never wavered at his questioning. After all, these men, illiterate and intolerant of society as they were, had experienced and taken part in everything from slavery to piracy and the atrocities that went with these crimes. They, of all people, were aware of there being little justice in the world and if one were to survive, then one must take advantage of every situation. Henry let it be known he was in the market for armaments and that he would be prepared to use his people, and cannon, to defend anyone who helped him should they find themselves in trouble.

This offer was accepted by the little community, after all, they were all aware that, given the volatile nature of islanders, the situation could turn nasty overnight and any and all of them could find themselves at the mercy of a thousand murderous islanders. No one mentioned the fact that any dispute between themselves and the locals, would most likely be caused by some immoral interaction by the whites against the natives, but believing in their god given right of white supremacy, they mightn't be right, but they could never be wrong! If Bob was aware of the location of Henry's village, he didn't let on and Henry, in turn, did not offer up any information as to its whereabouts. Instead, he made it known he would return from time to time to see what news they had of his requirements and bought another round of drinks and bid them adieu.

Both Henry and his little group would make at least five trips to Apia Bay over the next couple of months. Each time Henry would have to approach the chief and ensure Sina did not follow them. Only at the chief's insistence, would she relent and consent to stay in the village while the men trekked of to their base camp overlooking the bay and he and Mana together, would head off down the ridge towards the shacks. It was on the fourth trip to Apia Bay that Henry had the pleasure of espying a British warship, HMS Favourite, anchored not far off the shore. The ship had both anchors down and all sails furled tightly, it was obvious she was staying for some time.

Henry went first to the shack where bearded Bob lived only to find it virtually abandoned. Bob was sitting near the shack in the shadow of a large banyan tree. He had sited himself where he could view the ships crews' comings and goings and where they couldn't see him. His companions of the previous trips had faded into the gloom of the forest at the arrival of the warship, for every man on the island was fully aware they could be pressed into service in the name of the crown if the captain of the Favourite had a mind to. Indeed, should they, unbeknown to them, be found guilty on some far off shore, of only a few of the nefarious crimes each of them had committed over the years of their less than committed servitude, each and every one of them could find himself swinging from the end of the gibbet by sundown.

Bearded Bob asked that Henry not give any mention of their presence to the crew of the man o' war and Henry assured him he would hold his confidence.

Henry and Mana approached the jetty where some of the crew from the ship were guarding the whaleboat. The soldiers went instantly on guard as Henry and Mana approached, but relaxed, as Henry introduced himself in his best British accent. Before any of them had time to answer, a shout from further along the shore caught their attention. Henry looked up to see mister Cunningham striding towards him and both men held their hands out as they approached each other, each clasping the other's firmly in welcome.

'Mister Cunningham, so good to see you.' Henry said, warmly.

'And good it is to see you, Henry.' The other man replied, before dropping his voice so the other men might not hear. 'We have just come from Erromango, Henry.' Henry nodded solemnly, as the other man went on, 'The news isn't at all good, I'm afraid.'

Mister Cunningham went on to inform Henry they had been sent to Erromango island to retrieve the remains of Reverend Williams and Mister Harris. On arriving there, Captain Croker, his second lieutenant and Mister Cunningham, together with an armed contingent was dispatched to the shore where a volley of musket fire announced their arrival to the natives. Aware of the soldier's strength and fire power, the men of the village remained hidden and only two young boys stepped warily from the cover of the trees and stood, awaiting the wrath of the papalagi soldiers.

The captain of the Favourite, Captain Croker, demanded they lead his contingent of men to the place where the remains of the reverend and Mr. Harris might be. On hearing this, the boys immediately flung themselves prostrate and began wailing uncontrollably. The captain, unimpressed at this display of apology, ordered they be beaten until they stood on their feet. He then lined the soldiers up in two rows and ordered his men fire their muskets into the trees to deter the natives he knew would be hiding therein.

As the smoke cleared, the soldiers heard the sounds of the conch horn, the battle call of the natives. From three sides of the beach the natives began running around in the open, and in full view of the soldiers. They did not appear to be attacking, seeming to run around in panic, in an attempt to avoid the bullets that must be raining around them. Calmly, the soldiers formed into square formation, muskets pointing outwards. At the sight of this and another ships boat which was being lowered down the side of the Favourite, the chief, who until this time had remained hidden within the trees, became aware his club and spear wielding warriors were no match for these well armed and trained soldiers and a battle of this nature could have only one outcome, the complete decimation of his tribe.

He ordered the now frightened natives to sit and lay down their arms while he heard the white chiefs demands.

At first the chief denied all knowledge of the killings but after being confronted by mister Cunningham, he admitted the killings and begged the captain's forgiveness, citing that, sandalwood traders had killed two of his sons and kidnapped his daughter, just two weeks before Reverend Williams had arrived on the island. He showed the shore party where he had instructed his men to erect warning barriers of saplings so that anyone seeing them could collect water from the beach but would not be allowed to venture further into the forest, towards their village. Both mister Harris and reverend Williams had ignored their warnings and had paid the price for their ignorance.

After disarming the natives, much to their dismay, the party was led to a clearing where it was plain there had been campfires but no remains of any humans, cooked or otherwise, could be found. The captain demanded of the chief to take them to the real scene of the savagery and the chief, having his bluff called, led them to a clearing further up the stream and closer to the native's village where a native waited with a bundle of bones and a skull wrapped in palm fronds. Upon inspection, mister Cunningham declared that these were probably not the bones of the reverend or mister Harris, due to the fact the skull had not been shattered in the way the two missionaries must have been. Resigned to the fact the two men must have been consumed in the normal way by opening up the skull and bones to access the marrow and brains and then the bones would have been crushed and powdered, to be placed in the food of the warriors and chief. It was possible, mister Cunningham pointed out, that some of these bones were of his friends, and in taking them they at least, would be ensuring that at least some parts of the reverend and mister Harris would at least be given a decent burial.

The captain ordered the bones to be taken to the ship and after admonishing the chief and declaring the white man's god would wreak vengeance upon the tribes of Erromango if they should continue this barbaric practice, he ordered the natives to erect a cairn of stones at the place where it was most likely the two men were consumed and decreed no native should ever disturb the pile of stones upon pain of death. After conferring with Mister Cunningham, it was decided it would serve no purpose holding a service for the two lost men, or punishing these heathens for avenging their own loss. Rather they should remove the remains to a place of reverence and safety.

With the chief begging for forgiveness and promising never to follow false gods again, the party packed up what little remained of reverend Williams and mister Harris, or some other poor souls, and made haste for the boat.

'So, what now?' Henry asked.

'Well,' Cunningham said, 'The captain and I have decided, rather than take the remains to Sydney, where reverend Williams was less well known, we should have them interred here, at the church where he is very well known and loved.' He paused, looking out to the warship where he knew captain Croker would be watching, and added, 'In the event there being a dearth of civilized people in the vicinity, I was hoping to catch up with you in the hope you and your wife might attend the service.'

'Of course.' Henry answered, deliberately omitting his wife's condition, so as not to overshadow the occasion.

'The captain has invited both you and your wife to stay aboard ship until this spot of bad weather passes, and once it clears, we can convey the remains to the reverend's church, what do you say?'

'I'm afraid I will have to arrange for my wife to come over from our village.' Henry answered, looking towards the leaden skies in the east. 'If we head off now, we can be back here day after tomorrow, will that suit?'

'Fine,' answered, Cunningham, 'I'll let the captain know your circumstances, and we'll await your return.'

Henry and Mana opted not to return to bearded Bob's hut, but set off towards the camp up on the spur. A half day travelling saw them stow their gear and food at the at the spur camp and head off towards the summit camp at the top of the mountain range that divided the island. They could see the storm on the horizon and each man could feel the warm sea breeze as it came off the forest below, quickly changing to a cold, moisture laden, fog. In the distance, out over the sea, they could plainly see the towers of rain, like solid buttresses of water, reaching from sea to sky, obliterating all around from sight. Both Henry and Mana knew both the wind and the rain would increase once the cooler air reach the higher ground of the mountain and they made haste towards the camp. By the time they approached the summit camp, even Apia Bay had been obliterated by the rainstorm and the fog at their backs had turned to sheets of icy rain. Henry's confidence that it would only be a passing rain storm dissipated, as the warm air, being pushed from the valleys below, collided with the icy, moisture laden clouds higher up the mountain, causing a vicious finger of forked lightening to spiral across the only part of the mountain that was still visible. *So much for a passing rainstorm,* Thought Henry as the summit camp came into sight. He knew they would have to stop the night in the summit camp and hopefully they could carry on to the village tomorrow. He could see a couple of natives peering out from under large palm leaves they were holding over their heads and already the streams of water were running off them with such a force, they were landing a yard or two away from the holder. He was thankful they had managed to cut plenty of palm fronds and the many layers had made the camp totally waterproof but that didn't ease his shock of staring straight into the face of his wife as he entered the humpy. Sina was lying on her back, her knees pulled up and splayed wide as she rocked her head back and forth, trying to ease the pain of labour.

Henry was mortified! Stuck here on a god forsaken mountain top in the middle of what may turn out to be a cyclone. 'What the hell do you think you're doing here?' He asked, the look in Sina's eyes told him not to be too forceful in admonishing her.

'Came to walk home with you!' She grunted as the pain from her labour began to ease. The rain began to beat heavily on the roof of the little humpy and the natives, not wishing to be uncomfortable, had all moved inside, the steam from their bodies creating a sauna like atmosphere as they stared in wonder at Sina and her pain. Henry began to shoo them away, but both Mana and Sina stopped him. Sina explained between spasms, that a pregnant woman should never be alone, lest evil spirits enter her body and destroy her child.

'Well, Said Henry, looking around at the throng of villagers jammed into the little humpy, all kneeling in the cramped space, waiting for something to happen. 'There's not much chance of that!' Sina motioned for him to come forward and remove her earrings, but Mana stepped forward and obliged her. She explained that it was custom to remove the earrings so that they could not choke her child and deform its body while in the womb.

Henry shook his head. He had no idea what to do. There was no way they could make it back down off the mountain and the only light outside was the flashes of lightning that seemed almost continuous now the storm was reaching its peak. A disturbance outside caused him to turn as two of the natives began an agitated conversation, pointing towards the way they had come and threatening to run off and leave them.

Henry stared back along the track through the pouring rain. He thought it was the lightning causing his mind to play tricks on him, he imagining he could see a dim light dipping in and out of the bushes, going first this way, then that. All manner of imaginings came into his head. Was it the lightning simply reflecting off the wide palm fronds that bent low across the track under the weight of the rain, shining even slicker now that the rain had washed them.

Both he and Mana stared into the down pour, straining their eyes in an effort to make out some shape or form and as the voice called to them from the storm, it was the last straw for the natives who were in no doubt the Aitu from the forest had come to invade the woman's body and it was time for them to leave. Only Mana held them back from flying off into the scrub in all directions. Threatening all sorts of repercussions on them for abandoning a chief's daughter, he managed to halt their headlong charge towards home just as the hail from along the track came again, this time Henry recognized the voice. It was Cunningham!

He ran a short distance along the track and called out as loud as he could and was answered immediately, as Cunningham burst from the trees, a hurricane lamp held high in front of him.

'By all that's wonderful! Henry exclaimed. 'Are you a sight for sore eyes, what are you doing here?'

Cunningham explained that, just after Henry and Mana had left, a native had approached them and, in stilted English, indicated someone was in some difficulty. At first, they didn't believe the native and surmised it was some trick to lure them away from the ship, but the native was insistent and seeing as they had known Henry's party was travelling the same track, and had departed less than half an hour before them, they surmised they couldn't be far. Given the circumstances of the reverend Williams and mister Harris, the Captain was taking no chances with the safety of a British citizen and ordered a search party after them.

Henry led mister Cunningham around to the humpy and indicated towards his wife. 'I sincerely thank Captain Croker for his concern, but it's not me that is in pain.' He added despondently, 'But we ARE still in a world of trouble.'

Cunningham took one look at Sina and summed up the situation, he put his hand on Henry's shoulder and laughed. 'Not to worry, old chap, in a past life I used to be a doctor.'

At the mention of the word doctor, the one word the villagers seemed to understand, at least half of the villagers cheered, more in relief they were not being invaded by Aitu, than respect for the learned physician, before a woman, who seemed to be guiding mister Cunningham's party and who Henry had seen in Apia, near Bearded Bob's shack, came forward and offered her services, it seems she was the local midwife and was recognized by all the villagers, including Sina. She was actually on her way to visit Sina's village and decided to tag along with Cunningham's party for safety.

In between moans of pain, Sina, now rejuvenated by the presence of the midwife and the doctor, began ordering the majority of the natives out of the humpy. She explained to Henry that Samoan custom is that an expectant mother should have her friends and relatives around her to ward of Aitu and prevent them from deforming the baby,

Still, you can have too much of a good thing, and Sina ordered the majority of the villagers outside and even though it was still pouring with rain. Henry and Mana began cutting palm fronds and creating a small skillion against the wall of the humpy.

This done, the party settled in for a long night awaiting the birth of Salamasina and Henry's child.

The wind had turned decidedly chilly and all the natives had huddled together for warmth in the skillion, the steam from the jumbled bodies seeping out into the cold night air, to be whipped away on the cold wind. Henry, Mister Cunningham, the midwife and two others, Mana and the bosun off the Favourite, attended to Salamasina's needs. Salamasina's low, periodic grunts, intensified to a low moaning, rising sometimes to a shriek, as she battled against the pain of childbirth. The sounds of the woman's pain, intermingled with the uncaring snores from the bodies in the skillion, emanated from the main humpy as the moonlight finally won its battle with the storm clouds and flooded the clearing with its pale, almost blue, ethereal, wisps of steam as the jungle began warming again.

Around three o'clock in the morning, as the wind outside faded to stillness and the clouds began to dissipate completely, allowing the moonlight to permeate the gaps between the still dripping leaves of the palms and Aoa, or Banyan, trees, even the deepest sleeper in the skillion, was jerked awake by the final shriek of pain as Salamasina finally pushed her son into the world.

At first, both Henry and Mana stared in wonder at this bundle of joy the midwife had lifted into Salamasina's exhausted arms. Then, as their eyes become accustomed in the dim light, to the features of their son and chief, their looks of admiration and awe, turned to stares of horror and revilement. The baby's head was horribly deformed. It had no facial features whatsoever, no eyes, nose or mouth and, except for a large fold of skin where its chin would normally join its neck, its head consisted only of a large bulbous lump, totally devoid of the features one would expect from a new born,

'AITU'. Mana screamed, jumping to his feet and racing outside the humpy, picking up his spear as he did so and railing at the evil forest devil that had invaded his sister's body and created this monstrosity. At his screams, the jumble of sleeping bodies within the skillion came alive and tumbled over each other in an attempt to evade the forest spirit that must be honing in on them as they slept.

Henry simply stared at his newly born son, devastated at the prospect of having to drown his baby, yet knowing, without even a mouth to breath, it would surely die within moments. The baby was indeed struggling to breathe, its head wobbling back and forth, until, the midwife, together with Salamasina, quite calmly, but gently slid their fingers under the caul of skin that covered the baby's head and slid it up and over its face to sit on top of the baby's head like a rubber turban, revealing an alert and healthy baby boy underneath.

Mana had reentered the humpy and watched in amazement as the skin of the caul was folded back on to the baby's head. He had never seen this before, but he was aware of what it meant. He raised his spear high and called out as loud as he could. 'Afio mai lau afioga' then, turning to Salasamina, he shrugged, questioningly.

Salamasina looked to Henry, who nodded his assent, before whispering 'Villiamu'.

Both Henry and Salamasina had agreed on his name being the Samoan name meaning 'across the ocean', or, 'wide ocean'.

Mana then ran outside and addressed the rest of the natives who were still shivering in the cool night air, but were unable to go back to bed lest they miss part of the event that was unfolding around them. Mana called again, 'Afio mai lau afioga, Villiamu'.

Mister Cunningham had stood up from where he had been simply observing the midwife and Salamasina conduct the birthing and concluded he was not really needed and although he had heard of babies being born with a caul covering part of the head, this is the first time he had witnessed it so dramatically, first hand. He explained to the still shell shocked Henry that the covering of skin over the head was considered by many races, including the islanders and some white societies, to bring good luck for the wearer.

He was called away from the conversation by Salamasina, who explained that to be considered a wearer of good fortune, a coin, or something of value, would have to be wrapped in the skin of the caul before the caul dries out and loses its shape. Then the caul must be placed around the neck of the owner and be kept there for life.

Only the three white men held pockets in their britches, the natives, having no need for pockets or items to keep therein could not deliver any items of value to place in the outstretched hand of the midwife. Her urgency was not lost on the two men as with every moment of air exposure, the caul began to shrink, making it unsuitable for this purpose. Henry could see the disappointment in his wife's eyes as he desperately sought through his pockets for something of more value than the few shillings and pennies he brought forth and poured into the palm of his left hand.

A shout from mister Cunningham saw all eyes turn to him. He had produced a number of coins that were somewhat grimy and faded and as he laid them out in his palm the men and women strained their eyes to make out the denomination of each individual coin. Cunningham knelt down close to the lantern and held his outstretched palm beneath the pale, yellow light. He could see that three of the coins were but pennies, brown and stained and useless for this purpose, two were farthings and one was a bright sixpence, but it was the largest coin that captured his attention, he strained his eyes to see the inscription around the inside of the outer rim of the somewhat grubby coin and as he turned his palm towards the lamp a shimmer of light fell upon the coin and he could make out the unmistakable crowned and mantled coat of arms on one side of the coin and as he turned it over in his palm, the head of George the fourth stood out prominently, with the words Guliemus 1111 D.G. Brittania Rex FD. It was unmistakably, an English half crown, an ENGLISH, SILVER, half crown!

Without a word he handed the coin to the midwife who blessed it before handing it to both Henry and Salamasina to be kissed and placed in the now shrinking skin of the caul and neatly folded and pressed into rough square shape. Salamasina explained the skin of the caul would then harden and compress, locking the coin into the caul forever. It would then be placed around the baby's neck on a leather thong, never to be removed. Thus, ensuring good luck and health for all the wearers life.

It was Mana who provided the thin strip of leather that would serve as the thong and although Salamasina placed the caul around the babies neck as a gesture for all there to see, once the throng of well wishers had moved back outside to the fire that had been stoked and piled up with forest litter that had been stored in the humpy, she carefully lifted the thong from around his neck for safe keeping, placed the now mewling baby on her right breast and promptly fell asleep.

It was daylight by the time the three white men had warmed and dried their clothes by the fire that was now a large cheery blaze that warmed up the whole clearing but in light of the night's events, they opted to catch a couple of hours sleep before heading back down into Apia Bay.

Chapter 9

Corner of Andrew and Henry streets

Strahan, Tasmania,

August, 1938

Mary Anne sat in silence in the living room of the four roomed house on the corner of Henry and Andrew Street. If Harry was home the radio would be scratching out the sound of the national broadcaster into the room in his usual seat in front of the fireplace, occasionally taking time to tap, tap, his pipe on the whitewashed brick hearth as he listened intently to the national radio broadcast, but Harry was away in the river and it would be months before he was home.

But there would be no news tonight. Instead, the old woman stared into the flames, fighting back the tears of fear and sadness that threatened to erupt from her dark sad eyes.

Wacky had come in from the paddock two days ago, a slight cough and runny nose. By evening that day, there would be no easing of her symptoms and Mary Ann felt the goosebumps of chills on the littles girls' upper arm as she undressed her for bed. Not being a big eater, it was little surprise to her seeing the girl push her food disinterestedly around her plate. The old lady admonished herself for being overly concerned at something that for a child was a rite of passage, all children get the sniffles from time to time. Still, she couldn't help begin to feel the fear that sat in that dark place, that secure compartment in the back of her mind where all bad memories were kept safely locked away from everyday life.

When it was time for bed, the little girl went unquestioning to her own room and without complaint of the old lady's refusal to relate any more of the story, a sure warning sign that something was definitely amiss with her beloved granddaughter and as she tied the piece of flannel soaked in camphorated oil over the girl's shoulders and around her waist, she kissed her normally pale forehead. She could feel a warmth emanating from under the girl's skin that might herald a much more serious dilemma and knew she must prepare for the worst.

Mary Ann went to the wood shed and grabbed an armload of logs. On her way back through the kitchen she stacked the wood stove full and turned it down low. Another two loads for the fire in the lounge and a large boiler of water on the stove would prepare her for the night lest her fears were realised.

It was only two years since typhoid had raged through Strahan, many families, both wealthy and poor, losing children, and even some adults, to this dreaded disease. No one was aware that the shallow burying of night soil allowed the typhoid bacteria to survive and permeate the beds of the towns market gardens and milk sheds, transferring from cow pats and milk to humans. Manifesting in a sniffle similar to a simple common cold, before the chills and fevers began to rack the bodies of those infected, causing dehydration and diarrhoea and more often than not, death in the young.

As she sat before the fire, Mary Ann begged her god to spare this little one's life, she just couldn't go through the agony of losing another little one through a moment's indecision. At this thought, the gates of her memories burst open and she lifted her eyes from the brightly burning coals and stared at the door of the middle bedroom. After all these years of pushing the sad memories into the far recesses of her mind, it took just a few seconds of pain to begin to relive them once again. She walked slowly into the passage and poked her head into the little girl's room. In the dim light she could make out the rise and fall of her chest and the beginnings of a sheen of moisture on her brow, not a good sign.

Mary Ann screwed her eyes shut and clenched her fists as if trying to mentally drive the demons out of her granddaughter's body. She tried to convince herself it would only be a cold, and Wacky would jump out of bed, her usual inquisitive and talkative self in the morning, leaving her to scold herself for being such a worrier. Still, the thoughts persisted, and as she wandered back to her seat at the fireplace, her thoughts turned once again to that day, twenty seven, no, twenty eight, years ago, when a heavily pregnant Mary Ann, who had been playing with her three year old daughter in a rare moment of sunshine for August, felt the winter breeze turn chilly and left her daughter Valvina, to grab an armload of firewood from the wood shed to take back inside the house to stoke the fires for when the weather would turn cold later in the day. Her daughter was playing with a wooden peg toy Harry had carved from an odd shaped scrap of Huon pine and she could hear her three other children playing outside the fence in the cart road. Ten year old Lydia, her first born, or Liddy, as she was known among the family, Harry, or 'boy', as he would be known throughout the Doherty clan for the rest of his life, had a special place in her heart as he reminded her so much of her father, the Samoan. Forever barefoot and dark, uncaring of his appearance or comfortability, would see him would remain a much loved and admired among his siblings. She could hear the delighted squeals from Violet, her third child, as 'Boy' played some sort of vulgar trick on her by chasing both girls with a sloppy cow pat, threatening to smear it all over them. She called over her shoulder for them to keep clean and keep an eye out for Valvina as she carried the wood into the house and restocked the stove, placing the extra logs on the hearth next to the fireplace and glancing back out of the door where it appeared Valvina was annoying the cat by running over its tail with her toy. She took time to rummaged through the medicine cupboard and stirred the bicarbonate of soda solution into the water in an effort to relieve the heartburn that had plagued her each time she bent down or exerted herself. The price of pregnancy, she declared to herself. Never mind, just two months at most, to go and another mouth to feed. God knows, she loved her children, but at the rate she was going these kids were going to keep her in poverty.

The old lady winced as if in pain. A moment of assumption, just a couple of moments inattention! Her memory now had control of her and would not let her free of her demons. She could hear the kids playing and they seemed further away than the tank stand where she and the baby had been playing. They hadn't heard her, and she hadn't checked to see if they heard her! She hurriedly stepped out into the back yard onto the old convict brick pavers where she and the child were just a moment before. She cast around, taking all in before calling to the children

'Liddy!' she called, but already she could see the kids were too far away to have heard her the first time. They stood in the road near the bridge at the creek. Staring back at her. They had been told not to go near the creek when it was in flood and believed they were now being admonished for their disobedience. They stood unmoving whilst Mary Ann ran towards the creek edge outside the back fence line.

Mary Ann could see her neighbour, John Henry, in his paddock, looking in her direction and wondering what the woman was fussing over this time. Mary Ann had almost reached the creeks edge as John Henry realized what was happening and was galvanized into action as he heard the woman's scream of panic at the sight of the wooden toy floating against a pine branch. John Henry ignored the danger of sunken logs amid bramble tangles and launched himself into the mat of reeds that covered the surface of the stream.

Not seeing the baby in the water, Mary Anne was casting about in the hope of seeing her playing somewhere on the wet, grassy banks, but of her daughter there was no sign. Not believing she could travel fast enough to be anywhere near the slowly moving waist deep creek, all were put to task seeking out the toddler. It was a shout from one of her other children that had them running to a spot near a sunken pine log before John Henry, still wading about in the freezing water reached down and dragged the baby's body from under a log and struggled up the bank, shaking the little body in a desperate, but futile attempt to revive her. Mercifully, Mary Ann's memory seems to fail her at that point and she found it hard to recall anything from that moment on until she remembered waking next morning to the muffled voices of Doctor Whitehead and the constable speaking with Harry in this very room. Word had been sent to locate him and thankfully, he had been on the harbour boat, Glen Turk, pulling a raft of logs from Kelly Basin to Strahan, halfway along Macquarie Harbour, when told the dreadful news. Her beloved daughter had been removed to the morgue in the cottage hospital, a couple of miles away.

Mary Ann stared again at the coals in the fireplace, losing herself for a few moments in the dancing flames that licked at the freshly placed logs. She turned towards the door of what had been the Valvina's bedroom and slowly got to her feet.

The door to this room had always been hard to open and she had to place her upper arm against it in order to get it to swing. She knelt down beside the bed and reached under it. Her right hand found the handle of the small suitcase and drew it towards her. She struggled to her feet and placed the suitcase on the bed, before placing each thumb on the brass latches either side of the handle. She pushed outwards with each thumb and the latches flicked open as freely as if they had only just been closed.

She lifted the lid of the suit case and stared at the silken christening jacket that was to be her daughter's keepsake of happy times, instead of a sad reminder of memories she just couldn't let go of. A strained croup cough had her slamming the case sharply and grabbing up the lamp before hobbling to the bedroom where her granddaughter was.

The girl was trying to sit up in bed, but she seemed too weak to achieve this and Mary Anne settled her back in the bed, before placing an extra pillow behind her. The old lady could see the child was struggling for breath and tears filled her eyes and ran down her dark cheeks.

Boiled water was all she could give the child and even then, she would vomit the main portion of that into the china bowl Mary Anne held under her chin, whilst she waited for daylight.

As daylight came the child seemed to rest, although her breath was raspy and her temperature was very high, the sheets and pillow case were soaked with the sweat from her frail body.

The old lady opened the front door and hobbled as fast as she could to Mrs. Baxter, the midwife's, just three doors down.

Tux Baxter was a very experienced midwife who could lay claim to the delivery of many of the children on Strahan and was a close confidante of Doctor Oxley, who lived at the Cottage hospital, on the way to Regatta Point, a couple of miles away.

Used to being called at any ungodly hour of the night, Mrs. Baxter was out of bed in an instant and after running to Mary Ann's house, she took one look at the sick girl and concurred she was indeed very ill and immediately dispatched her son to Doctor Oxley's residence for help whilst she and Mary Ann changed the child's bed clothes and rubbed camphorated oil into a fresh flannel.

It was just over an hour when the doctor's pony and trap pulled up outside Mary Ann's door. Mrs. Baxter led him inside to where Mary Ann was placing cool compresses on the little girl's face and forehead.

Both women stood at the end of the bed in quiet acquiescence to the doctor's ability. Mrs. Baxter, a look of concerned professionalism on her face and Mary Ann, eyes closed in prayer for anyone who could deliver her granddaughter to health and the safety of her own arms.

The doctor felt the throat and neck of the girl, took her temperature and gently pressed open her mouth to reveal her tongue. As he did, he motioned both women to come close. Careful not to come in contact with the saliva and plegm from the girl's lips, he pointed to the white coating on the girl's tongue. the entire surface of Phyllis' tongue was coated with a white, almost paint like substance dotted with red and pink points, not unlike that of the white strawberries that grew wild in the back garden. Mary Ann looked from the girl's face to the doctor's and almost fainted with relief, when the doctor announced, 'Strawberry tongue, not typhoid.' Then, not wishing to get Mary Ann's hopes up too high, clarified his statement with, 'Still a sick little girl, Mrs. Doherty.'

Doctor Oxley went on to explain that the symptoms of scarlet fever were almost identical to that of typhoid, but the chances of recovery were much higher, especially with good care and bed rest.

After making a cup of tea and scones for the good doctor and the midwife, Mary Ann saw them off with as many thanks as she could muster in her state, then made a bee line for the girl's bedroom.

After checking on Wacky, she moved out into what was once Valvina's bedroom, opening the case once again, she gently and lovingly ran her hands over the shiny cream coloured ensemble and gently lifted it to her lips and kissed the christening jacket, before placing it back in the suitcase. She felt a relief as if a great weight was lifted from her shoulders and she knew she would never forget, nor stop loving, that little girl she lost all those years ago, but her priority now was to make certain she was never going to lose another.

Wacky would spend the next month in bed and a further six weeks recuperating. Mary Ann took the doctor's advice and boiled everything the girl came in contact with, including her clothes, and when her husband came home from the Gordon River, she would often catch him standing at the little girl's doorway, 'Just looking to see she was alright.' And the old tube radio was turned down so low, the nightly national news cast was barely audible, lest it should disturb the girl. It was on the fourth week of recuperating and grandfather away in the bush once again. To the old woman's delight the girl clasped her hand and asked, 'Can we start the stories again, Granna'

Chapter 10

Apia Bay,
Navigator's Island, June, 1840-1852

The ceremony to bury Reverend Williams and Mister Harris' bones took place at the little church on the northern shore of Apia Bay. It was not mentioned that these may not have been the actual bones of the two missionaries but they were still interred with all the reverence as if they had been.

Salamasina was there to display her newly delivered baby boy and the name Villiamu struck a chord with everyone present at reverend William's funeral, given that Villiamu was also the Samoan name for William.

Once the ceremony was over and the bones of the two men had been interred under the porch of the little church, Henry and Salamasina bid Mister Cunningham and Captain Croker adieu and watched, as the Favourite sailed out of Apia Harbour towards Tongataboo. None of them knew it then, but just a week later Captain Croker would be killed by a musket ball from a Tongan native's gun and trouble would once again threaten these otherwise idyllic island nations.

The little group made their way out of Apia and over the crest of the mountain, stopping to gather a few stores at the summit camp and reflect on all that had happened in the last forty eight hours.

Salamasina sat beneath a sandalwood tree and put Villiamu on the breast. 'Hungry little critter' mused Henry, and his wife smiled.

'He will need all of his food and more if he is to grow big and strong'. She answered. Henry couldn't help thinking of the trials his baby would have to bear growing up in the islands. He knew life should be better here than England or even Australia, where racism was rife and Villiamu would always be known as 'Afakasi' or half breed whether he was in British territory or enjoying the freedom of the islands.

Salamasina sensed what Henry was thinking as they stared at the baby and was more circumspect and practical. 'He will be strong, he has royal blood and the caul to protect him.' She laughed.

Henry nodded in agreement but couldn't help thinking of the troubles that threatened to erupt across the islands almost every month. Even as they readied themselves to leave for their village, they could see smoke in the distance along to the north of Apia, a sure sign the natives were fighting again. As they packed up, he felt a fear for the life of his baby, something he had never felt before and to console himself he promised himself he would teach this young man all he was capable of to put his son above the next man and hopefully, he would one day become a leader of men.

On May 3, 1841, with Villiamu just fourteen months old, Malietoa Tavita Vaiinuupo died. Immediately, each family leader declared himself to be Malietoa and the seeds of war were once again sown in Apia.

The fighting first broke out at Mulinu'u peninsular, on the north shore of Apia Bay and resulted in many being killed and a fort being constructed to protect the citizens of Upolu. Henry had his tribesmen erect several log and earthen barriers on each of the tracks leading to their village in the hope they would provide a fall back positions should they come under attack. The old chief was continuously complaining that he should be the new Maleiatoa and both Henry and Salamasina had to convince him that he already had much more property and wives than any other Chief. Henry and Mana had managed to salvage two old falconet cannon from a wrecked ketch that had fallen foul of the reef on the northern shore of Apia Bay after the skipper had steered his boat among the rocks during a drunken rampage and promptly left the island during the following days on the next boat that would take him.

It took some weeks of blacksmithing to get them working again, but they were serviceable and Henry found sleeping easier at night once the cannon was installed within the logs of the barricades.

The fighting continued until 1848 when an uneasy truce between the warring parties seemed to settle the factions, although families very much kept to their own villages and children were not allowed to stray far from their parents.

In eighteen forty-nine, the American consul, Prichard, constructed the first store in Apia and life again returned to some sort of normality. Once peace was established, Henry began to once again travel regularly to Apia on trading trips. Ships would begin calling and trading in earnest, using the store as a go between for everything from building supplies for the island to vegetables for the whalers to tinned food for the villagers, a luxury Villiamu had never seen before!

Young Villiamu loved these trips to Apia. Rickety timber structures made from bare poles still served as wharves and jetties and all boats larger than a canoe still had to moor out in the bay. But it was easy to hitch a ride aboard a canoe and clamber over the side to offer his services to load bales of flax, rope for caulking, or even to clamber into the rigging to help replace torn sails and broken yardarms on the beautiful ships that passed through Apia.

Back home in his village, it was the job of the young boys to look after the goats, chickens and any other animals that were forever trying to invade the village gardens. The boys set traps, built fences and tried beating the goats that became the bane of their lives by managing to outwit them and find their way into the maize and vegetable patches. Villiamu began to notice the goats were attracted to the coloured cloth dresses of the village women and decided to use a flag made from brightly coloured flax on a stick. For some reason, the goats couldn't resist these flags and the boys would tie a flag around the lead goat's neck and the rest would follow to a place where they could be tied up, away from the gardens of the chief and the moaning women. This left the boys to the much more important task of watching the ships enter in and out of the many bays around Upolu.

Villiamu loved the sea and these beautiful ships that sailed on it. He would listen to the tales of the sailors and whalers and when he replied to the seamen in English, they would readily fill his imagination with tales of giant whales and sea monsters.

Notwithstanding the troubles that erupted from time to time within the many tribes and islands of the Navigators, or Sa'moa, as the natives called it, growing up on Upolu was idyllic. Young Villiamu grew strong and athletic, conquering both sea and land with his prowess at canoeing, climbing and his willingness to learn from his father all the arts of navigation, sailing, and the tertiary skills of writing and reading.

He was the only one of his tribe or indeed, of his island, who could both read and write. By the age of ten, his printing scrawl had been replaced by a beautiful flowing copperplate, unseen in the islands, except for his father and the very rare, white, missionaries that visited his part of Upolu. Occasionally, his father would take him to Apia, where he would watch the whaling ships and occasional trader drop anchor in the bay and observe the beach come alive with natives and white men alike as they competed with each other for the wares and favour's that could be traded. Vegetables, coconuts and fresh fruit for bits of iron, candles and lamps as well as brandy and rum for those white men who could afford it. His father had remarked that Apia was growing into a real trading port, with a substantial wharf being constructed and increasing number of ships visiting, as the reverend who had died, had said it would. Still clinging to the past, Bearded Bob and his cronies, still inhabited the shacks on 'The Spit' that sandy headland in the middle of the bay.

His father recalled the hatred of reverend Williams for these godless beachcombers, ex-convicts and deserters and shook his head in amazement at the change from indolent ne'er do wells to productive gardeners and wood and scrimshaw carvers who had begun to make a half decent living from gainful, albeit intermittent, employment.

But Villiamu's real excellence was in swimming. As young as he was, Villiamu could swim the mile or so to the outer reefs of the many bays around Upolu, then dive from the rocks into the white surf that sometimes pounded the outer reefs, disappearing from the view of the canoes of his friends, only to surface a hundred yards away, a large Bonito, Mackerel or even the dreaded Barracuda on the end of his spear.

Much to the dread of his father and the joy of his mother, Villaimu's favourite trick was to hunt the reef sharks that inhabit the sandy bottoms of the bays. At first, he and his friends would tie six or seven coconut shells as a rattle to attract the sharks, then a bait of either pig or dog flesh would be held over the side and a noose would be guided over the shark's head and Villiamu would slip over the side and gut the shark with his knife, all the while avoiding the other marauding sharks that were intent on feeding off both him and the caught shark. The first cut would be behind the gills of the shark, instantly filling the water with blood and almost blinding him. A second cut on the other side and a slash from anus to throat, revealing that prized piece of flesh, the liver. Villiamu would quickly cut the liver free and throw it into the boat, closely followed by the body of the shark, and while the remaining sharks fed on the offal of the first, Villiamu would take a lungful of air and quickly slice open two more even whilst they were feeding on the entrails of the first, and repeat the process, before climbing back into the boat and consuming a large slice of raw shark's liver, his prized delicacy, while his friends had the task of hauling the other two sharks on board.

During his juvenile years, Salamasina gave birth to two more children. Two brothers, Louis and James and even though they were two and four years younger than him, Villiamu lost no time in herding them down to the sea for their education in fishing. It was on one of these trips that their lives would be changed forever.

Chapter 11

Apia Bay, Navigator's Island

January, 1852

On the twelfth of March, 1850, the sixty ton schooner Velocity left Sydney for a voyage to San Francisco and return. She was under the command of Captain Kirsopp, who had captained her on two previous occasions, under charter to that feared entrepreneur Benjamin Boyd, of Boyd Town, just south of Sydney.

Officially, she was a trader, shipping between the east coast ports of Australia and the west coast of the Americas. Unofficially, she was one of the first indentured labour ships to prowl the south seas, and to all who knew her and the infamous Benjamin Boyd, she was a slaver! A blackbirder! Sailing throughout the islands of Melanesia and Polynesia, luring unwary islanders into a life of slavery and torture with the promise of good work aboard the whalers and traders of the islands, only to find themselves traded to the drudgery and abuse in the farmlands and cane fields of eastern Australia.

In 1847, the Velocity in an initiative by the cruel entrepreneur, Ben Boyd, had managed to 'blackbird' sixty five islanders to Boyd town from various parts of the pacific and land them at Sydney. From there, the bewildered and half starved natives were herded and forced marched the thirty or forty miles towards the farmland between Sydney and Yass, there to be put to work as slaves for any landowner who was prepared to pay good money for them. Not surprising, the majority of the slaves absconded and were discovered, hiding terrified in the surrounding bush, and on the streets and slums of Sydney, seeking out a return to their home islands and the infamous schooner that had brought them to this hell hole. But the Velocity had sailed, she had had the first taste of this lucrative and legal trade sanctioned by the white governments of the Australian colonies, making her owners and skipper uncaring to the fate her of former cargo, and she wanted more!

In 1852, after two successful voyages trading in human cargo, the Velocity was once again on the hunt! She had left port and sailed deep into the pacific, seeking out another boat load of human cargo from the unlimited supply these islands offered.

She had called at Navigator's Islands on her way to San Francisco with cargo for the Americas and Kirsopp and his first mate, together with the all black crew, had eyed off the groups of young men and women as they fished the bays and harbours around the islands. Each canoe load of islanders that pulled alongside the schooner to trade their goods and favour's, convinced the skipper of rich pickings and many dollars in profit for the owner, Benjamin Boyd. She was carrying a load of cargo from San Francisco to Hobart town in Van Dieman's land, but the captain had made sure there was plenty of room in the hold for enough indentured slaves to be further transported to Sydney. He had already sought out the prospects of a supply of slave labour from the Melanesian islands, but a short stopover at the Navigators islands on the way back to Hobart Town would save a lot of time and effort seeing as how the islands closer to Australia would be, by now, forewarned and quite possibly forearmed, against a violent incursion into their peaceful lives by the heartless crew of the Velocity.

The schooner only carried a crew of six, so Kirsopp had to be very careful not to go ashore with the natives, lest they be outnumbered, rather let two, or maybe three, of the younger, less experienced natives come aboard on the promise of the much sought after blue beads the heathens were so enamored with. Once aboard, the natives would be taken below, plied with grog and regaled with tales of riches and the chance to own the fine jackets and trousers the crew were wearing.

Papers would be produced assuring them of good food and pay beyond their wildest dreams, they had only to make their mark and within a short time, they could return to their home islands, rich people. The concept of time and contracts was totally lost on these people who had spent their lives rising with the sun, eating when they were hungry and moving freely about as they pleased, whether on sea or land. To travel the vast distances to the colonies of Australia and beyond, there to be enslaved and flogged if they disobeyed the indecipherable scribble that was on the white man's paper, was incomprehensible to them.

As they laughed and joked with those members of the crew who could understand the language, at least, in part, whilst eyeing off the pile of blue beads that served as currency, unbeknownst them, their canoes would be let go and the Velocity would be far from their home islands before they realised they had been victims of this unholy deceit. Very few natives had ventured to other islands from their home island thus the threat of being killed and cannibalised by natives from a different island was very real. Escape from the boat, once it had sailed from sight of their home island was extremely risky. Once clear of their home island, the women would then become the property of the crew and would be repeatedly raped and forced to cook and clean for all on board. The males would be locked below, before the next load of human cargo came aboard and terrorised into acceptance of their fate under pain of being thrown to the sharks that were encouraged to approach the boat whenever the slaves were allowed on deck.

Mistakenly, the white ship's captains believed that one islander is as all islander's and this could not be further from the truth. Even the islands of the Navigator's would, at some stage or another, be in conflict with any and every other island of the same group. This hatred, though usually short lived, was obvious to the crew members once the heathens were stored below deck. As they came out on deck to eat drink, defecate and clean themselves, the crew would notice the bruises and black eyes of the fighting parties. This was another advantage of taking younger men. Although, occasionally, especially if he had an abundance of cargo, and as an example to others who may get ideas of escape or fighting into their heads, and usually, but not always, a woman, as they were of less value that the males, the skipper would decide that one of more recalcitrant and disruptive captives should be beaten bloody and tied to the stern of the schooner and left hanging over and the remaining natives forced to watch as their fellow captive was torn limb from limb by the feeding sharks.

It was a somewhat expensive way of keeping the majority of their cargo in line, but with an abundance of populated islands available to the blackbirder's, what matter if the price of an uneventful voyage was one native per trip, most skippers of these hell ships would consider that a fair price for doing business.

Another means of securing cargo was to have contact with the sandal wood traders who would have a ready supply of natives standing by after they finished their quota of sandal wood they were allowed to take, as agreed by the chief. Once loaded on one ship, the cutters would then turn on the workers and herd them on board another ship as bonus cargo for the slavers.

The Velocity had already taken on twenty heathens from the surrounding islands as cargo and gracefully slid across the waters of Apia Bay to drop anchor about one hundred yards offshore.

There were two other ships in the harbour, both whalers, and captain Kirsopp studied them through the glass. The first was an American whale ship, the Lalla Rookh. Strange name, thought Kirsopp, as he moved the glass onto the other ship.

She was the Aladdin, and Kirsopp knew her! She was a Hobarton whaler and would most likely be returning to her home port. It would be best if the Velocity stayed well out of her way, given that both boats could arrive in Hobart Town around the same time and with the cargo he was carrying, it wouldn't do to have someone witness the Velocity in her capacity as a slaver, especially as the troubles caused by the taking by force of the natives also had repercussions for the crews of the whale ships.

Although a new source of workers to overcome the shortages of labour in the colonies of Queensland and New South Wales, indentured labour was sanctioned by governments across the colonies, these same governments who proclaimed to be encouraging the heathens of the islands to a 'voluntary apprenticeship' in a more civilized society, conveniently turned a blind eye to the abominable practices of kidnapping, rape and murder as long as the problems of labour shortages were solved. Nevertheless, black birding and the people who committed these atrocities were despised by missionaries and whalers alike. Not surprising, as most of the sailors and missionaries were, in fact, native themselves.

Sandalwood cutters had raped, kidnapped, killed and pillaged islands right across the whole of the south seas, decimating tribes of natives who resisted their demands of first, the most sought after trees of sandalwood, and when the chief refused to allow them further incursions into their islands, they had not hesitated to inflict atrocities against the innocent for their own ends. A lone trader would not raise any suspicion at all if she was simply going about her business of trading goods, but if it were to be found out she was carrying a hold half full of their relatives, right here, in enemy territory, there was no doubt in Kirsopp's mid what his fate would be.

He made sure the velocity was anchored well away from the other two ships and he ordered the crew to row ashore and fill two barrels of water, revictualling would have to wait until Hobart. He also ordered the 'cargo' kept quiet by giving them extra rations and decided as soon as night fell the Velocity would be away before the Aladdin realized she was a slaver.

Chapter 12

Mouth of the Tafituala River,

Navigators Island,

1852

Villiamu had taken his younger brother Louis, from their village and together with three other boys set off to fish the white surf breakers, about a mile out from the mouth of the Tafituala river. The mouth of the river was surrounded by shallow mud flats, except for a deep water channel that ran all the way in to the shore, okay for fishing the small tiddlers with the hand thrown grab net, but when the sea was right, the only place to ensure a large feast of tailor, Barracuda or reef shark was off the headland of the next bay north.

Taking the canoes, the boys could leave the sling nets behind on shore and row out to the edge of the channel where the white water marked the deeper open ocean, and around the headland about a mile into the bay to the north of the river mouth. Here the boys knew, was a patch of open, yet calm water where sharks would abound.

About half an hour rowing had the canoes at the edge of the reef and the rowers stood off the choppy back wash whilst Villiamu slid over the side into the warm waters of the gulch.

He had only been in the water a minute or so and could see a number of decent sized fish moving in and around a large fissure in the rock, the bits of kelp and shellfish broken off the reef by the pounding of the breakers, creating a fall of feed down the fissure and forming a feed column. Villiamu swam into the gulch and began poking and prodding the seaweed fronds that covered the face of the rocky walls in places up to two foot deep. The clear water was full of waves of seaweed and tiny shell fish that cascaded down the gulch with every wave that struck and tumbled over the reef. He placed his feet against the wall and kicked his body back into the clear water. He could plainly see the shimmering, almost mercurial silver hue, of the surface, where the canoes were, but instead of being steady in the water directly above him, to make it easier to land a heavy fish, he could plainly see the paddles of both canoes hitting the water, hard and fast. The canoes were heading away from him, towards inshore. Puzzled, and more than slightly annoyed, he kicked towards the surface just in time to see a dark shadow pass overhead. He stopped swimming and blew a large bubble of air from his lungs to halt his ascent as the shadow of the whale boat passed over head.

In the volatile atmosphere of the islands, it was entirely possible that war canoes of some marauding party would launch a surprise attack on his small group, but a whale boat? Villiamu was confused and looked around to see what was happening as his head broke the water about twenty yards behind the whale boat. This was no native canoe on the warpath, *at least we can be thankful for that!* he thought. But he instantly recognized the threat for what it was. This was no group of whalers out for a day's fishing to supplement their otherwise bland diet of whale meat and biscuit, as he looked towards the headland, he could see the tall, single main mast and shorter mizzen mast of the Schooner, as she inched her way around the headland, following the whale boat and being careful to hold the breeze, lest she be driven on to the rocks that were now perilously close. There was no way a whaler, or even a trader would risk moving this close to shore, unless she was up to no good.

He could see the canoes moving fast towards the shallow water of the reef, his friends driving their paddles frantically into the water, but the whale boat had spotted them and with added momentum and four oars, was beginning to gain on them. He called to his friends in the canoes, urging them on. He knew that if the men in the whale boat caught them before they reached the comparative safety of the shallow water on the shore reefs, his brother and his friends would be spirited away to an early death by their captors.

He began swimming after the boats but he had no idea what he could do when he caught up. He could see and thought he could hear, his little brother calling to him for help but his arms were beginning to tire and he felt himself falling behind the whale boat. It seemed all was lost as the whale boat gained on the two canoes, but his friend, Tamu, knew what he was doing. He shot his canoe in front of the other and they each rowed line astern through a narrow gap between two submerged rocks. Villiamu heard the men in the whale boat curse as the boat lurched on to its side, almost unseating the rowers and causing the boat to grind to a halt. This loss of momentum and speed allowed the canoes to gain the shallow water and he could make out the boys leaping from the canoes and running up the beach, one of the larger lads holding his brothers hand as he dragged him to the safety of the tree line. Villiamu turned away and began to swim towards the beach as the crew of the whale boat, realising they had lost their quarry quickly regained control of their boat and headed in his direction.

He was almost halfway to the beach when the boat caught him. His arms and legs were tired and felt too heavy to pull him through the water. He could feel his head dipping lower and lower each time he swam a stroke. He dove under the water in an effort to elude the men in the boat, but the crystal clear waters of the lagoon made it easy for the slavers to track his movements and all they had to do was to cut his escape to the beach by rowing across his path and let him exhaust himself as he tried to avoid them.

Kirsopp stood in the stern of the schooner and held on to the mizzen stay. He knew the southern side of Upolu would be devoid of whalers, with the Aladdin and the American ship laying over in Apia harbour, on the other side of the island. Thus, he had the Velocity move slowly into each bay as they ran along the southern coast, pretending to be fishing the unusually calm waters. As they moved slowly along the coast, he had his crew scan the shores of each bay, searching for groups of fishing natives. The mate had first alerted him to the islanders near the reef and convinced him it would be easy pickings to simply come alongside, drag the heathens out of their canoes and be away, without the boat even losing way. Far better than risking their lives chasing black heathens through the jungle! A good plan, on the face of it, but this plan was beginning to turn into a fiasco! His eyes darted from the whaleboat to the shore and back to the water beneath the Velocity's keel. The skipper was used to the best laid plans of mice and men going awry and had lowered the whaleboat alongside the schooner in the event the natives attempted to run into the shallows and put the Velocity in danger. Unfortunately for him, the natives chose the wrong bay to fish, and not knowing how deep the water was in this bay, the Blackbirders were forced to chase them in the whaleboat.

Kirsopp could see they had lost the whole group of fishers, bar one, and even that one was leading his men a merry chase! Had they been within earshot, he would have called them back to the schooner and been on his way. He knew the native village would not be far away and very soon the place could be swarming with cannibals' hell bent on revenge. He could feel the rage building inside, and felt a good deal of satisfaction as the mate picked up the oar and brought it down on the swimmer's head. Two more times he lifted the oar and brought it down. The second time missing altogether as he heard the slap of wood on water, but the third, although he didn't hear it, he saw the wooden pole stop just beneath the surface and hands reaching towards something in the water, giving him the satisfaction of victory.

Again, he searched around and, seeing no one, edged the schooner towards the whale boat.

The mate had laid a warp around the native's neck, keeping its head above water as they towed the unfortunate black back to the Velocity.

Once aboard, Kirsopp inspected the islander and judged him to be a fine specimen. Young, but well built and capable of commanding a good price in sale rooms of Sydney or Brisbane.

Apart from a lump on his forehead, and bruised ribs where the second blow had struck him, Villiamu seemed unharmed. After retching a stomach full of sea water onto the deck, he was taken below and tied to the same railing as the other unfortunate prisoners. His arms were chained to a railing that ran along the sides of the schooner's hold and he could feel the heat from the bodies of his fellow prisoner's either side of him but he did not lift his head.

The training of his father had taught him to keep still and quiet, 'Listen and learn everything about your surroundings until you can devise a plan to escape from your predicament.' His father had said.

Each native asked him, in turn, which island he came from and what island this was, but he pretended not to understand. He shifted in his seat and groaned, feigning pain as he moved his thigh to rub against one of the exposed ribs of the Velocity's hold. Once again, he had his *Tama* to thank for ignoring the island flax loin cloth and creating his heavy cotton drill slops, hidden pockets and all.

He felt the hard lump of his knife in his pocket against the side of the boat, it was only small knife, short, knobkerrie carved wooden handle but with just an inch and a half long, razor sharp blade seated in a leather pouch. Another thing he had his father to thank for. As he sat, feeling his strength returning, he began to devise a plan. He knew he had no hope of overpowering anyone aboard ship. Even if he overpowered the crew, his fellow prisoners would most certainly turn on him as soon as they were freed and he would find himself swimming in the open ocean, or boiling in a pot!

Night passed, and then another. The heat inside the hold was bearable, given the fact that Kirsopp had left Samoa as fast as the breeze would allow and the vents that served to maintain a supply of clean air to the hold were kept open to allow the prisoners at least one small comfort. Kirsopp had taken advantage of the wind and made a direct line towards Van Dieman's' Land, all the while keeping a fast eye out for the Aladdin, or any interloper who might interfere with their lucrative cargo.

Unfortunately, the incident at the navigator's all but forgotten and thinking they were free, greed got the better of the skipper and by the third day, as they turned west, towards the Fijian islands, another source of slave supply, the schooner was forced to slow against the wind. The natives below were finding it hard to keep control of their bowels and already the ammoniac smell of urine began to mix with the sweat and vomit from the prisoners. Just before dawn on the third day, Kirsopp had the prisoners come on deck, each man shackled to the railing to allow him to defecate and urinate over the side without messing up the deck. Welcome buckets of water were thrown over each prisoner and it seemed the men were actually enjoying the escape from the confines of the hold, at least for a short time. The mate inspected the hold and noticed that at least two of the men had vomited and urinated in the hold. He ordered that Villiamu and another native, grab buckets and begin scrubbing in order for the prisoners to go below. Disease was something he had to keep at bay. Typhus, or even worse typhoid, was something that had to be avoided at all costs. It would be a disaster for the velocity to lose some, or even all of its cargo for the sake of a few buckets of water. The first man took hold of the leather bucket and willingly tossed it over the side and hauled the filled bucket in, but Villiamu, after catching the bucket thrown at him by the mate, simply dropped his bucket to the deck just as Captain Kirsopp came out of his cabin. At first, he thought the savage too ignorant to understand what was being ordered of him and nodded for the mate to strike him across the shoulders with his club. Villiamu winced in pain as the blow awakened his earlier injuries.

Once again, the mate ordered him to take up the bucket, and once again Williamu shook his head, this time defiantly.

Kirsopp felt the anger rise again at the actions of this upstart. He stepped forward and grabbed the waddy out of the mate's hand. As he brought the wooden club back, Villiamu spoke. 'I am the son of a chief, and I wash for no man!'

Kirsopp stopped in his tracks, but not for the reason Villiamu thought. The mate also looked frantically at the rest of the prisoners who didn't seem to have any idea what the ramifications of speaking English were and were just enjoying as much as they could of the pre dawn light as it began to glow in the east.

'Who are you?' Kirsopp demanded.

'I am Villiamu, son of Salamasina and Henry. I am a chief and friend of the consul, you will take me back to my village!' He knew his idea wasn't quite going to plan so he decided to play all his cards at once. 'If you can't take me then you will take me to a place where I may write to the consul and he will come and get me!'

Kirsopp stared at the boy for few long seconds. His first mate hung his head and avoided his gaze. He knew he would be blamed for this. A native, any native, was fair game in labour conscription but an English speaking native, especially one who knew the American consul in Apia, was dangerous, very dangerous. With opposition to black birding awakening on all continents, an incident of this nature could very well destroy any chance of developing the colonies, and it would be his fault! Boyd would kill him! There was only one thing to do. No evidence should remain of the accident that befell this unfortunate soul. He motioned to the mate who expertly slipped a leather thong around one of Villiamu's legs and pushed the lad over the side.

Villaimu didn't even have time to take a breath as his body slammed against the transom and flipped over the stern. The thong wasn't around his ankle where it was intended to be, but had tightened around his thigh, just above the knee. Villiamu pulled his body up to an almost sitting position as the waves washed over him and he scratched for the right pocket of his slops for his knife. The sudden weight of his body in the water against the transom of the schooner caused it to act as a sea anchor and with little wind, the boat slowed dramatically, unfortunately, the thong had tightened around his pocket and was prevent him from accessing it. He began to panic but needn't have bothered, a shout from the second mate had the whole of the crew cursing as they looked towards the east. In the light of the rising sun each man could see the shadow of the whaling barque's sails and masts racing across the water towards the Velocity, the hull of the following ship beginning to loom out of the dawn and that meant that in another few short minutes she would also see them!

Kirsopp raised his flensing knife and cut the leather thong with one blow. The prisoners were ignored as the crew hauled on all sail and the schooner turned towards the south, away from the path of the looming ship.

Villiamu's head broke the water in just a few seconds and already the Velocity was picking up speed. He wasn't aware of the other ship's presence and cast around, searching for any sign of land or something that might save his life. The sun's rays had by now brightened up the sky, already he could feel the warmth of the sun's rays as they shimmered across the top of the water. A single bobbing head in a thousand miles of ocean, no way could he even hope for salvation as the Velocity began to fade from view, her sails the only thing visible until a shadow fell across him. He looked to the east and saw the whaling barque, Lalla Rookh, bearing down on him.

The Lalla Rookh was first laid down in 1835 at Dartmouth, England, for the New Bedford whaling fleet and as such she was a relatively new Barque Of some 323 tons displacement, she was yet to adopt the 'stinker' nickname of most of the older whaling ships of New Bedford and despite her long voyages and the taking of thousands of barrels of oil and other whale products she remained a clean ship. She had surprised her master, Captain Gardner, with the taking aboard of nine hundred barrels of sperm oil from the New Zealand whaling grounds and with more pods being seen every day, she was in a hurry to make Hobart Town to off load and return to the grounds, there to once more fill her hold, before heading back to her home port of New Bedford via the Marquesas.

With a prize of more than twenty four thousand American dollars in her hold and the voyage only half over, it was a happy crew that called into the Navigators Islands for fresh food and water for the voyage to Hobart Town. She had spoken to the Aladdin in Apia Harbour and was aware of the schooner, Velocity, anchoring closer in, just before evening. Captain Gardner had taken little notice of the smaller boat and when the dawn watch mentioned she had cleared out, the only concern of the Lalla Rookh was to avoid the Aladdin as the two barques cleared for sea. The Aladdin, to continue her quest for sperm oil and Lalla Rookh to have a clear run to Van Dieman's Land.

Just four days later, the lookout saw the schooner ahead of them in the early dawn and was about to signal to the helmsman to come away to port when the schooner, who also must have seen the Lalla Rookh, turned abruptly to the south. Nevertheless, captain Gardner ordered a slow turn into the schooners former wake, a move which saved Villiamu's life.

Villiamu began swimming as he had never swum before, directly into the path of the near three hundred and sixty ton barque. With each turn of his head, as he stroked the water, he could see the barque looming larger as both he and the ship drew together. The ship looked like a mountain standing above him, threatening to plough him under her monstrous bows and the boy was certain he would be run down and tried to turn away, down the side of the ship in the hope someone, anyone, would see him.

The lookout, Chepi, saw the coconut bobbing about on the glassy surface, and determined it was some jetsam off the schooner, until he noticed the coconut swimming on a collision course with the Lalla Rookh. He signaled the captain that something was wrong and the first mate ran down the steps of the poop deck and along the starboard side gunwale. He reached the forrard mast stays and saw an arm raise out of the water, before it slowly began swimming again, towards the bow of the ship. The Lalla Rookh was heavy in the water, able to make seven knots under full sail, but with the ever so slight breeze coming out of the north, her tops'l and mizzen were the only ones alive. Still, the mate was loathe to stop, or even slow, a fully rigged ship just for one islander who was probably tossed over the side of the schooner for some criminal act anyway, until he heard Villiamu call out in English.

Both the captain and Chepi heard the call and whilst Chepi wasted no time organising one of the rope ladders used for climbing down onto the backs of the sea monsters they hunted, Captain Gardner gave the order to heave to. But it was too late to stop the ship and by this time, Villiamu had almost disappeared under the tumblehome of the starboard side. Chepi untied one of the hauling warps and leapt over the gunwale. Holding the rope in one hand, he swung down the ladder, four steps at a time until he reached the water. Balancing on one foot, he leaned out as far as he could and grabbed the hand of the boy, plucking him from the water as if he were a palm frond and heaving him up to the other members of the crew who had climbed down to help.

Villiamu was exhausted. *'Thank you, thank you.'* He whispered, clinging to each seaman as he was passed up and over the gunwale, onto the deck.

Captain Gardner and the first mate were there to help steady him on his feet, amazed at his survival. By this time the whole crew were beginning to gather around and as Villiamu kept repeating his thanks in breathless English, Captain Gardner, noticing his mode of dress, correctly assumed him to be no ordinary islander and bade him come down to his stateroom.

During a hearty breakfast Williamu related his tale to the captain and the first and second mates, who in turn, related it to the crew.

'And here's me thinking you had fallen over the side of your boat.' The captain shook his head in amazement. 'And we would have gladly returned you to your ship, had that been the case.' He sighed. 'But unfortunately, it's not.'

The captain then went on to explain that the Lalla Rookh was on her way to Hobart town and the best he could do to get Villiamu back to his people was to drop him off somewhere safe in Van Dieman's Land in the hope he might catch a ship heading back to Navigator's Island.

The act of black birding, although abhorrent he explained, was not illegal, and since Villiamu was a half caste, the captain of the Velocity had broken no laws, with the exception of throwing him overboard, and that would be hard to prove. He guessed Villiamu's age correctly, and opined that an eleven year old boy, of Villiamu's experience could sign on as ships boy on any whaling ship out of Hobart, especially since he could read and write, but Lalla Rookh's passage home would be from New Zealand, through the Marqueses, and thence to New Bedford, Massachusetts, North America, and God knows where from there. It certainly would take them nowhere near the boy's home island, certainly for years to come. He offered a berth on board to Hobart and a share of the lay for working his passage. 'Beyond that,' He sighed, 'I can do no more.'

Villiamu once again thanked the captain for saving his life and voiced his intention to join a crew of a whaling ship as soon as he was able to, but not at the decision of slavers. Captain Gardner laughed and congratulated him on his choice of employment and his stamina and bravery in helping to save his own life. The captain indicated his first officer before moving to the chart table and becoming engrossed in his papers.

'The first mate, here, will get you signed aboard for the trip to Hobart Town.' Handing a sheaf of papers to the mate, without looking up.

'Name?' The first mate enquired, laying the papers on the table.

'Villiamu.' The lad replied. He had often watched the local natives lining up for work on the ships and boats and stood to one side, listening to the questions from the midshipmen, memorizing all of the questions and answers. He knew just what to say and the answer to the questions the mate from the would throw at him.

'Age?'

'11 years, sir'.

'Experience?' The mate eyed him warily. The lad before him was as fine an example of a well fed, strong native he had seen for some time. The seaman squinted his eyes and stared the lad down. Let's test your honesty, he thought to himself as he ran his rough palm across his grizzled, tobacco-stained chin whiskers.

Villiamu told him of his work among the ships in Apia, explaining the parts and pieces of the ships and the difference between a Barque and a Brig. He showed he was just as capable of tying a bowline as he was throwing a lead. And when he described his experiences of the wars in Samoa, the mate couldn't help but admire and feel sorry for the lad. It was a disgrace how the powers that be had let the once proud society of these islands degenerate into gangs of murderous thugs, killing each other and stripping each of their property and rights whilst both Britain and the Americas ignored their plight in their haste to exploit these islands. He felt genuinely sorry for these people. He placed the pen on the desk and wished he could sign him on as a crewman but it was obvious he could work his way, for the remainder of the trip to Hobart town anyway.

'Well, son,' The mate sighed, 'it's one hundred and thirtieth of the lay and found, less slops and boots.'

At Williams questioning, raised eyebrows, the mate explained, 'About five American cents per day, and any clothes and boots you need will be deducted from that sum.'

'I have my own slops and I don't use boots.'

The mate held the quill towards Villiamu and watched as the boy took the pen and, instead of scribbling an x to make his mark as almost all other seamen do, wrote his name in perfect copperplate English. The captain looked up and caught the mate's eye. They both knew it would be no problem to take a native to sea under indentured labour, but it could be a problem they didn't need, if this lad happened to be a runaway and both they, and the ship's American owners, could be implicated in the abduction of an Englishman, if this obviously educated, English, boy was being sought in all ports.

The two men directed Villiamu to the deck, ostensibly to familiarise himself with the ship and leave them time to discuss what to do or say in the event customs at Hobart Town discovered an English speaking boy was not part of the ship's crew manifest.

Both the captain and the mate were aware that before leaving the port of New Bedford, the ship would be issued a bill of health certificate. Thereafter at each port of call as she entered in to the port, the Lallah Rookh would be checked for any symptoms of disease among the crew. A clean bill of health meant the ship was free to enter into any other port safely, but if the port authorities even suspected a crew member might be a risk, especially one that wasn't even on the manifest, the ship could be given a suspect bill, which meant they could be laid up in quarantine for weeks, until any suspicions were allayed. If the Lallah Rookh chose to leave the port without clearance, then that ship would not receive clearance to any other port and would not be able to resupply or even enter in to any port until she reached her home port, years later. As well, each American whaleman is issued a Seamen's Protection Certificate which describes in detail the man's appearance, birth place, age and colour and any identifying marks. Captain Gardner was a fair man, but even he knew that for the Lallah Rookh to be held up in Hobart Town indefinitely simply because he chose to help a native out, would be a disaster which he would be responsible to both the owners, and the crew. He had to think of a way to offload the boy before the wharves of Hobart Town hove into view.

'Captain,' The mate began to voice his concerns, but the captain broke in.

'I know, I know, mister mate,' he said, staring at the chart table and shaking his head. 'I'm aware of the problems this could cause us but I think I might have an idea.'

Oblivious to their concerns, Villiamu made his way along the deck, past men who were busy repairing rigging and replacing worn ropes. First, connecting the old and frayed rope hanging from high up in the trees of the mainmast to a new sisal rope from the hatchway leading from the bits store below the bow of the ship, through a series of wooden sheave blocks hanging from the yard on the mainmast. With two men in the cross trees on the mast, the new rope going up was counterbalanced by the old rope coming down thereby allowing two other crewmen to easily drag the old and frayed rope down out of the rigging in a line across the deck to a hatchway between the fore and main mast where half a dozen older seamen sat picking the rope to pieces and bundling it into tied piles to be used as caulking.

With new rigging set, he stared up into the rigging as the mainsail was being set. With the breeze now picking up, all sail was being clapped on for a fast trip to Hobart Town and the yardarms of both the fore and main masts were lined with sailors unfurling the sheets of canvas. As the breeze caught the mainsail, it filled with an almost deafening thud and the ship lurched forward, timbers and ropes creaking as they took the strain.

He was still looking over his shoulder, marveling at this familiar practice he had witnessed from the shores of Apia but never so close up as to be directly below them, when he tripped and stumbled on a pile of old flax, almost sending him flying over the largest pair of feet he had ever seen.

Expecting an admonishment from the owner of the feet, he steadied himself and prepared to apologise but the owner of the feet, and the flax, began first.

'Oakum,' The owner of the feet said quietly, before getting to his feet.

Villiamu stared up into the face of the tallest man he had ever seen and as he scanned the gaudily decorated seaman from his overly large head to his huge feet, which seemed to splay across the deck planks as he stepped, almost as if they had a life of their own. He had seen this man before! This was the man, or should he say, giant, who had lifted him from the water.

'Oakum'. The seaman repeated. 'Old rope used to caulk the planks of boats.' He nodded towards the eighteen feet long whale boats hanging outboard on their davits from each side of the ship. The flax leaves protruding from his colourful headdress rustling back and forth as he did so, making his head seem even larger than it was.

Villiamu knew what oakum was, but not wanting to appear like an impudent upstart and pretending to be more knowledgeable than the most experienced whalers in the world, the boy chose his words very carefully. He had already recognised this man for who he was. He was a gay head Indian, the most talented of all the whaling men and much sought after for their skills, especially with the harpoon! They were more common on the Nantucket men than British ships and although Villiamu had heard much about them from his father, he had only caught a glimpse of one from his vantage point on the beach as the harpooner strolled along the deck of another ship moored at Apia. A rare sight, as these temperate 'warrior whalers' rarely ventured ashore to the flesh pots and taverns of the more populated ports.

'You are Whampanoag (Wampanog).' Villiamu said and bowed his head slightly. The gay head was slightly taken aback at the extent of this young man's knowledge and respect of his tribal name and proudly drew himself up to his full height. He acknowledged Villiamu's use of correct English and stretched out his hand. 'Yes, I am Wampanoag, my name is Chepi. Aboard ship they call me Red Billy.'

He pointed to William's chest. 'You?'

'Villiamu, and I wish to thank you for saving my life.' Villiamu replied.

The Indian began to stammer and struggle with his pronunciation of Villiamu's name. His face became contorted and the boy laughed at the Indians struggle to pronounce such a simple name. Two other crewmen were looking on and they also began to laugh. Seeing the gay head beginning to get embarrassed at their jibes, Villiamu broke in. Holding up his hand to cease the Indians embarrassment, he pointed first to the gay head's chest and then to his own, laughing, 'You Red Billy, me Black Billy!'

Hearing the crew members laugh at the boy's suggestion, the Indian's huge face split with a relieved grin, he had saved face and to a proud Woahpanoag that meant a lot, his tobacco stained teeth growing ever larger as his mouth widened with glee. 'Where you are from?' The gay head asked, warming to this young lad, but his cheeriness turned to concern as Villiamu, reminded sadly of family and homeland, looked back along the starboard quarter of the ship and out to sea, along the ships wake. The boy lifted his arm to point and Chepi could see the tears welling in his eyes as the events of the past few days finally overcame him.

The lads mouth dropped and his lips quivered as he struggled to contain his emotions. It was now his turn to be embarrassed and the seamen on deck that were within earshot averted their eyes to the boy's sadness and went about their business. To a man, they could each remember their first voyage and even as experienced as they were at long voyages away from home, there were times when each of them regretted leaving their loved ones standing on the wharf at new Bedford, seeing them waving goodbye until the harbour disappeared from view. Most of them had been very young when they first left to take up the life of whaling, now their own thoughts turned to home and loved ones they would not see for many months to come. Still, God willing, they would be going home! He wasn't aware of it, but it was entirely possible this young lad would never see his home or his parents again!

Chepi placed his hand on Villiamu's shoulder. 'Come,' he said, guiding the lad around the cauldrons and brick ovens of the tryworks, just forrard the mainmast. He led the boy around the fore mast to a nest of pens, just aft of the foc'sle. The tears dried on the boy's cheeks and he seemed cheered by what he saw. The pens contained two goats with two kids, two pigs and about a half dozen chickens, although he had to bend down and crane his neck to one side, to count them.

One of the goats had climbed up onto the foc'sle roof and refused any of Chepi's coaxing to come down.

'This will be part of your job,' Chepi grunted as he wrestled in vain with the horns of the nanny goat. 'Keeping this old bitch under control and away from the captain's eye, as well as making sure she doesn't eat any of our washing.' He nodded to the lines of washed clothes hanging over the tryworks furnaces as he struggled to stop the goat from butting him.

He let go of the goat's horns, his large hands deflecting the butting head as he tried to coax the animal down and noticed Villiamu pull a small piece of flax cloth from his pocket and began waving it at the goat. Immediately, the animal climbed down from the roof and began to investigate the waving rag. The men standing and sitting under the eaves of the foc'sle were between shifts and desperate for entertainment to stave off the boredom of being between whales. They laughed and cheered at Villiamu's simple solution, but Chepi wasn't embarrassed this time, he knew everyone on board ship had tried, and failed, to keep the cantankerous nanny goat under control, even the captain.

'Lucky you don't have a cow to control on this rolling deck.' Villiamu laughed, his homesickness pushed to the back of his mind as the barque began to list under the thrust of the wind and one of the sailors pointed to the large bundles of cloth covered meat smoking above the chimneys of the tryworks. 'We did,' He laughed. And a fine supply of milk she was too.'

The men laughed again as the boy seemed somewhat shocked at a cow being aboard a whaling ship on the high seas. Chepi explained that it was common for animals to be carried on board New Bedford whalers to ensure a supply of fresh eggs and milk on the long voyages, sometimes more than four years, with little chance of resupply for months on end. It seems Buttercup the cow was a favorite of all the crew and had survived five months at sea since she came on board on Maui, but slippery, rolling decks were not conducive to the safety of such a large animal as a cow and buttercup had slipped and broken her leg in a storm. To save her the agony of being washed back and forth across the heaving deck, Chepi had grabbed one of the flensing knives and with one deft swipe had put her out of her misery. In the spirit of thriftiness, the harpooner had commenced to flense up the carcass of the unfortunate buttercup as he would a whale thus ensuring nothing was wasted and those pieces of beef that were not pickled in brine, were quickly wrapped in muslin cloth and hung to smoke above the chimneys, destined to be a welcome alternative to the almost inedible 'horsemeat' that served as whalers fare once seven days from the last port of call.

Villiamu was given the option of sleeping on the floor of the steerage cabin where the carpenter, blacksmith and about six other hands lived, or a bunk in the foc'sle, with the rest of the hands. But after witnessing the dark confines of the foc'sle after two years of being liberally impregnated with whale oil, blubber, and God only knows what other artifacts of this gritty profession at sea, he opted for a bunk among the straw near the animal pens. This way, he would not be taking a bunk away from any of the hands, who were on four hour shifts and struggling to get enough sleep as it was.

Chepi introduced him to the steward, the somewhat grandiose name of a crewman who was seated on the lower step of the ladder leading to the captain's position on the poop deck, a large basin between his knees and a wooden bucket of potatoes next to him. Chepi advised Villiamu, no crew member was allowed to come aft of the tryworks unless given permission by the mate, except when he was assisting the steward and he would be responsible for assisting the steward at mealtimes serving the captain and the mates. Other times he would be stationed at the animal pens and at the call of the carpenter and the blacksmith, especially since they became aware he was equally as good at either of these occupations.

Villiamu was allowed a couple of hours to familiarize himself as a greenhorn before his work began in earnest, and it did not take him long to recognize the pecking order on board ship.

The captain was, obviously, in total command, followed by first second and third mates. The captains whale boat was on the starboard side quarter in its davits, behind that, the mate's boat and opposite to those, on the port side was the second and third mate's boats. These boats had to be kept spotless and dry, ready for work at a moment's notice.

The carpenter, blacksmith and cooper were next on the pecking order, these men were responsible for keeping the gear, and the boat, in good order and never left the ship unless the vessel was in port. When a whale was sighted most of the crew would man the boats and the tradesmen would stay behind and operate the ship until the boats came home.

Then came the harpooners, of which there four aboard the Lallah Rookh. Usually these were Islanders, Cabo Verdeans or Woahpanoag, who because of their strength, agility and sobriety in a whale boat, expected, and received, special treatment aboard ship. They did not have to clean the decks or gear and spent most of their time sharpening their harpoons and flensing knives.

They were not begrudged these favours by the rest of the crew as it was these men that stood in the prow of the whale boat and held the lives and livelihood of every man aboard in their accuracy and strength with the lance.

Villiamu's days were busy, even though there no whales caught, each whale boat had to be bailed out at dawn. Then, it was to the galley and serving breakfast to the captain and mates, without forgetting the eggs from the chickens of course. Milk the goats, feed the crew, clean the scraps and feed the animals and then himself and the steward.

The best part of the day was the banter between himself and the crew as he went about his chores on deck. Both the carpenter and the cooper played tricks on him as they sent him for imaginary errands to the bad tempered blacksmith. The blacksmith would be on the verge of an angry outburst at his ridiculous requests, but Black Billy's demeanor and well spoken English would allay his ire and even he would smile at the prank. The only chore he disliked immensely, was that of the toe rag operator. The ship had two heads, or toilets, one for the captain, sited at the stern and one deep in the bowels of the foc'sle, which was only used by sick crewmen who were too ill to climb out onto the rope nets that were strung from the bowsprit to the bows. Each day, the members of the crew would climb out into the nets and, balancing above the holes in the nets, taking great care to steady themselves by holding on to the stays, defecated through the holes in the nets.

Occasionally, especially in rough seas, the nets would get smeared with excreta and Villiamu's job was to take a wooden pole with a rag attached to one end, and clean the netting of any of the offensive material, by dipping the long pole into the sea and wiping the nets clean. This practice was known as toe ragging and the piece of rag, the toe rag.

The worst part of his day were the evenings. Even though the sea was, for the most part, calm, and the sky above the south seas was filled with millions of beautiful stars twinkling down at the little ship, he knew that with every mile the ship travelled, it was a mile away from home. Billy's heart ached for his home island and his family. As he lay on the straw filled palliasse, a young goat nestled alongside, he felt so homesick he couldn't bear to walk to the bulwarks at the side of the ship to even appreciate the view of the flying fish and sea animals that seemed to be guiding the ship on its way. It was an eleven year old boy who cried himself to sleep on those lonely nights across that wide, wide ocean, but when the sky began to glow in the east, the promise of a new day gave the boy renewed hope of returning to his family once again. That is, until the captain sent the first mate for him.

Chapter 13

March 17th 1852

Recherche Bay, Van Diemen's Land

It had been a long trip from Navigators Island. Normally, Captain Gardner would have stopped over at two or even more ports for revictualling, but in his haste to get back to the solander's grounds, just north of New Zealand, he had gambled on good weather and it had paid off.

They had eaten the last of Buttercup a week ago and the chickens had stopped laying a week earlier, making it the decision of Villiamu to decide which ones would grace the cooks pots for their evening meal. At least the goats were still giving milk and the young half caste had accorded himself well and showed promise as a sailor. Try as he might, he could not find a way to have him admitted to the port of Hobart Town without certain delay, and delay was something the crew would not countenance at this stage.

Already the salt meat was beginning to go rancid and any vegetables left were all but rotten. He was aware, when it came to the food he had the best fare, but even as he tapped the hard crust that served as bread aboard ship, he could see the weevils dropping onto the table, already he had counted more than six and he knew the crew would be faring worse. He had to solve the problem of the young lad and make Hobart Town as soon as possible, to this end, he had decided to sail south of Bruni Island and north into D'entrecasteaux Channel. It would mean an extra day travelling, but the sight of land would make the crew a lot happier, and since they were in friendly waters, he would have the mate go ashore and secure some supplies to tide the crew over just one more night. This done, he set a double watch to avoid dragging anchor and settled for the night.

He had decided to set the boy off at a settlement of his own kind. They were not Navigator's Island people, but they were black and with no cannibalism on Van Dieman's Land, it was a good chance they would look after him until he could manage to find his way back home.

He had called the boy to his cabin and both he and the mate explained he had earned his way but he was never to speak of his being on the Lallah Rookh. Instead, he was to tell anyone who asked that he had come here on a ship, or boat, called Venus. Both captain Gardner and the mate were aware there was no vessel of that name in these latitudes and therefore it could not be traced back to them. Hopefully he would find his way back to his island or forget the English language and revert back to his native tongue. That way, he wouldn't be believed anyway.

As ships boy, he was entitled to one two hundred and fiftieth of the lay, but as he had not been aboard when the Lallah Rookh had taken the whales, the captain gave him three Spanish silver dollars and a full set of slops, including shoes, for the work he had carried out so admirably. Billy had dressed that night and stood alongside Chepi at the gunwale of the Lallah Rookh as the ship quietly drifted into Recherche bay, Van Dieman's Land, her anchors slapping the waters of the pigsties bay.

It was still daylight as the men wandered about the deck of the Barque, their belly's full of the victuals the mate had secured from the local fishermen. Billy had thought he was going ashore in this place of white, sandy beaches, blue sea and green forested hills.

Much like home, he thought to himself, only a fair bit cooler. Still, he was on the ocean and as the captain had said, it shouldn't take him long to find a ship willing to take him home. He couldn't have been further from the truth!

Chapter 14

Oyster Cove, Van Dieman's Land

March 18th, 1852

Six days before William's twelfth birthday

They could hear her moving before they even saw her. The soft creaking of her timbers and the gentle sloshing of her wake as it came together aft of the transom. She was barely moving and almost invisible through the light fog that settled between the shore and the channel, then they could see her, the outline of her hull merging with the shadows of the water and mist, a ghostly mirage, noticeable only by the swirling of the channel fog her sails pushed aside as she moved silently northwards, along the channel.

Two of the three people moved silently into the white trunks of the gum trees that stood only a few yards from the water's edge, the other, a young man, ducked down into the sags of button grass that ran to the shoreline. It didn't pay to make yourself visible at this hour. They watched as one anchor was let down, the sails turned to work against each other and halt the barque mid stream and the boat was lowered. The people on the shore would have left immediately, the five flounder they had speared in the shallows of oyster cove a few minutes ago, still hanging on fern leaves in two of the women's hands, but only two people, a man and a boy had climbed into the whale boat, with one of them rowing and the smaller one sitting on the thwart at the stern.

The boy seemed to be searching the shoreline, but they never moved. No good ever came here by boat at this hour, so why should this encounter be any different. They stayed quiet until the boat bumped the sandy bottom about thirty yards out from shore and the boy climbed out and began slowly walking ashore. Still the three people remained quiet. Coming up the channel, the pre-dawn light had been sufficient for visibility, but as they neared the tree line the shore seemed to disappear into the mist, becoming dark and foreboding. Billy turned and looked behind him towards the ship. He could see both the ship and the whaleboat, the boat already bumping against her side and although he couldn't see the crew, he saw what looked like the boat floating in the air to disappear into the ethereal shape of the Lallah Rookh as her anchor came clear of the bottom and she began moving north along the channel. He felt fear in his chest. He could handle landing on foreign shores if he could see something, anything. But this shore was dark, foreboding, he stopped and looked again towards the channel. His arms cradling his meagre possessions. Perhaps he should just wait until the sun came up, at least he would be able to see the shoreline and what, or who, was there by then. Did the captain just dump him here? He doubted it. Recherche bay wasn't too far south and the mate didn't seem to have any trouble with cannibals there when he collected provisions last night.

He looked back towards the land and a shadow seemed to break away from it and move towards him, he braced himself for an attack but it never came, instead he could hear the water moving aside as it tried to resist the passage of the person moving through it and saw the light begin to reflect off the ripples that emanated from the shadow as it moved across the water.

The voice was shrill but quiet and calm and he doubted anyone around could hear it except him. 'What you want boy?'

They had seen his colour long before he had seen them and became relaxed as the ship began to move on. Just another black native to be dumped off for them to feed and look after.

The shape was close now, about three arms lengths away, he could see it was a woman and she could see he was no more than a boy, probably five or six years her junior. She repeated her question. 'What you want, boy?' And was somewhat taken aback when Billy answered quietly, in clear English, 'My name is Villiamu and I have been told you can help me.'

As she came up to him in the clearing mist, Billy could now make out the bright, intelligent eyes shining from beneath the dark eyebrows, chubby cheeks set in an almost permanent smile and a full set of clean white teeth. she took him by the elbow, paying no mind to her dress flowing behind her in the knee deep water. When they reached the shore, he could see two others, also natives, coming along the shoreline to meet them. They introduced themselves as Billy Lanne who seemed to be the same age as Villiamu or perhaps a few years older, but not as tall. The other lady was somewhat older and introduced herself as Lallah Rookh which surprised Villiamu it being the name of the ship he had just came off, but he never let on. He explained he had just come off a boat called the Venus and they took him to mean the whaleboat he had just came ashore in and didn't question his explanation at all.

The light was fast approaching from behind and as the mist on the shore cleared, he could to make out a line of drab buildings almost shielded from him by the smoke of the camp fires outside. As soon as he set foot on shore, the dogs began barking, they were aware of a stranger in their midst and had Villiamu not seen the rope leads the dogs were straining against that led to the hollow stumps and logs that served as their kennels, he would certainly have run back to the relative safety of the water. The woman that had his arm calmed him and spoke in a clear voice again. 'My name is Fanny, Fanny Cochrane, welcome Villiamu, to Putalina!'

The mist had cleared by now and the welcome sun was beginning to warm the ground. People were moving about, seemingly unconcerned with this stranger's arrival and the smell of cooking food was in the air. It was obvious that the station was run down, almost derelict, but strangely, for the first time since he left home, he felt safe and comfortable.

The trio led him to a bench against one of the walls of the longest building. They sat down with their backs to the cracked slab timber wall and looked out across the water from whence Villiamu had just been dropped into their midst. The Lallah Rookh had disappeared from view and was all but forgotten as a cracked mug of tea with only half a handle was passed to him and Villiamu accepted it gratefully. He had no idea just how, of even if, he was going to be accepted by these strangers. On any one of a dozen islands in the pacific, he would already be dead and his choice pieces wrapped in palm leaves and buried with hot stones but for some reason, he felt he was among friends.

All three of the trio, Fanny Cochrane, Lallah Rookh and Billy Lanne had prior native names, Fanny and Billy's been lost to history by the forced naming of them by their English masters and Lallah Rookh wasn't her tribal name at all, her name it seems, was Truccanini, or Trugganana and she was by far, the oldest of the trio, a good twenty eight years older than Villiamu. Villiamu explained his predicament and how he hoped he could find his way back home, and with much tut, tutting and sighing the others all declared the only way he could find his way back home would be to sign on as part of a whaler crew. Billy explained that he had just come back from being indentured to a farmer at coal river and he certainly wasn't going back there again. All three had experienced the horrors of the orphanages of Hobart Town as well as imprisonment by bushmen and farmers and the beatings and tortures that went along with those occupations and each swore off ever working for the white man again if they could help it.

'Some white man, good man.' Billy explained, 'But some very bad.' He thought for a moment, then added, 'Have good things, have lots good things, but not smart, not smart very at all. Can't live in the bush, can't hunt, take all fish, not some, take all, then all gone.' He shook his head, as if he felt sorry for the white man being as stupid as he was. 'Black man light little fire and stand close to keep warm. White man light bloody big fire then stand right back!' He nodded, as if in agreement with himself. 'He not very good, he not human, not human' He paused then added, decisively. 'Not like us.'

Each native nodded his assent. Even Villiamu, who thought this was a pretty good assessment of the white man and the conversation dwindled until a bowl of kangaroo tail stew was ladled out of the round cauldron that had obviously served as a trypot in better days and placed in his lap.

Villiamu commented on the tasty stew and the others laughed. 'Make the most of it.' Billy laughed. 'It has to last for week or more before better tucker comes.'

Fanny went on to explain that the settlement was once a convict camp and had been condemned by the 'big guvnna'. They had been here for two years and in that time, there had been no improvements in the conditions of the natives from when it was a convict station. There was very little food and what there was usually rotten by the time it arrived, through the government overseer's office. The only food they had was what they caught themselves and that was getting scarcer as the white man was pushing the black hunting parties further away from where the good game or fishing was.

'The only reason we still alive,' remarked Billy 'Is that Fanny such a good cook and we all like anything she cooks, even grass!'

In the weeks and months that followed, Billy and Villiamu became firm friends sharing their knowledge of the bush and the sea.

Villiamu had evaded cannibals and slavers and Billy had evaded sealers and teachers, all hell bent on their exploitation, simply because they were black. Unlike Villiamu, Billy was cruelly treated from the moment he was born. His first memory was being taken from the west of the island and placed in Wybalenna, on another island, at the age of seven. His parents had both died in that place and he was sent to Oyster cove and then to an orphanage in Hobart where he learnt to read and write in between beatings and abuse. Escaping from a farm at Coal River, he had made his way back to Oyster Cove, the only place he felt safe.

There were at least two dozen natives living at the settlement, with some coming and going on a daily basis. Some would go out to work diving on wrecks in the channel and bringing artifacts back to sell to the white man. Others, would go up into the bush to tend gardens and some would be gone for a week or two, hunting in the hills surrounding the settlement. But most, especially the women, just sat around in small groups, whiling away the days. As Lallah Rookh put it, 'white men take us from our country away, then put us here in strange country with nothin' to do. Why we do anything? Just waitin' to die.'

One day whilst Villiamu was carting seaweed up to the garden in an effort to coax life back into the sour, sandy soil, he was surprised to hear voices of white men by the river that flowed into the cove.

He stepped close to one of the tall white gums and pressed himself against the trunk, a trick taught him by Billy, to merge his shape into the shadow of the tree, and strained his ears to hear what they were saying. He couldn't make out the words, but by their gesticulations and directions they were passing to each other, they were obviously digging for something. Billy kept the trees between him and the men and headed back to the camp.

'Crowther.' Fanny said aloud, as they sat outside the main hut of the settlement. 'Come to take our bones.'

Doctor William Lodewick Crowther was a Hobart Town surgeon and whaling ship owner. It was well known the good doctor was an avid collector of aboriginal bones and artifacts and Crowther also owned timber concessions and a sawmill in the area of the aboriginal settlement. He was also a prominent member of the Van Dieman's Land parliament and as such, wielded a considerable amount of power throughout the island and employed many people, black and white, in many types of occupations. Crowther prided himself on being a fair and honest employer who any person, black or white, could approach and expect a fair deal. By his own admittance, and like many learned people of the Victorian era, he was a more than avid amateur scientist, his favorite pastime being collecting all types of specimens of animals and birds for the observation of museums and colleges in England. A staunch follower of Darwin, and his theory of evolution, he was convinced the Tasmanian aboriginal was Darwin's missing link in the human evolutionary chain.

Billy Lanne liked Doctor Crowther and had done some work for him in the past, but Fanny and Lalla Rookh did not like, nor did they trust, the good doctor. 'You be stayin' away from them, Billy Lanne, them cheat you if you don't watch,' the two women warned, but

Billy motioned to Villiamu to follow, hoping to find work with the good doctor.

As they got up from the bench, a hail from a man coming up from the beach had the two women clapping hands and laughing. As the man approached, he beamed a smile at the two women, especially Fanny, and took off his bowler hat with a flourish and bowed. Fanny hugged the man who would introduce himself as William Henry Smith, her fiancé.

Smith was an English ex convict who had secured his ticket of leave and was looking to stay on the island to settle down and raise a family. He explained that he was only waiting for Governor Arthur's approval and both he and Fanny would be wed.

On hearing Villiamu's name and understanding that he had no surname, William knew instantly this boy was an illegal. Even though the practice of giving the natives an official English name such as William, and then bastardising it by changing it to Black Billy or some similar dehumanising nickname, a subtle, but deliberate method of stripping away their aboriginality in a ridiculous attempt at assimilation, each native on the island under British rule must have a first name, preferably a middle name and a surname. Without these he would find it hard to find a job, would be recognised only as a non human, and would never be able to work on a whaling ship as a Vandemonian without at least a first name and surname.

'What was your father's name?' He asked Villiamu.

'I heard someone call him Henry Smith sometimes,' Villiamu answered still unsure just what his father's name was. 'I just called him Father.'

'Well then,' The ex-convict laughed, 'I would suggest you anglicise your name and call yourself William Henry Smith, the same as me, it's a common English name so people, especially the law, find it hard to dispute, I expect most people will just call you Black Billy anyway.'

'Can you write?' He asked. And in answer William picked a stick up from the ground and scrawled the name in copperplate in the grey dust. The convict nodded his approval and with that, Villiamu, the native boy was gone, and William Henry Smith was born.

Both William and Billy Lanne caught up with Doctor Crowther's working party, clearing scrub, digging trenches and even helping gather some artifacts and bones for the good doctor. The latter was a practice neither one of the boys liked. Interfering with his ancestors remains was abhorrent to Billy, but Doctor Crowther had explained he was studying Billy's history and his work would help Billy's people survive and be healthy, nevertheless, both he and William had to keep their very important work from the women of the settlement. The better days working for the doctor was when the two would be asked to dive on the wrecks in the channel and as far down as Recherche Bay. Crowther's men would pick them up at Oyster Cove and sail down the channel in a small Sloop or Ketch. Anchoring off islands such as the Actaeons or Partridge Island, the boys would free dive on the wrecks of fishing boats and ocean going ships alike, tying ropes to pieces of brass fittings or loading dinner plates and China cups into netting bags to be hauled to the surface by the crew. The boys loved this work and once, when Doctor Crowther accompanied them to the wreck of the Actaeon, he was so impressed with their work he commended them and called them the two Billy's. King Billy, for William Lanne, a true aboriginal, and Black Billy for his friend, the half caste.

Following the offloading of a load of artifacts one day, the doctor invited the two Billy's to his home in Hobart Town, with the promise of work on one of his whaling ships, not surprisingly, the boys accepted.

The Hobart Town of 1853 was a town in transition. From a far flung convict settlement it had morphed into a thriving and bustling town of merchants and chandlery's, all dependent on the success of the whaling trade. And a success it was! The southern whale fishery was booming! After the bay whaling had fallen off, the demand for whale oil increased and deep sea whaling had boomed, with the result that the demand for larger ships capable of navigating the wild Southern Ocean required much more in the way of crews, supplies and chandlery.

Across the ever growing waterfront of Sullivans cove, the convict quarter masters stores and soldier's quarters had given way to coopers, chandlers, victualers and slipways. Dozens of convicts were receiving their ticket of leave passes daily, the overflow of humanity being quickly absorbed into this new industry and large residences of the wealthy whaleship owners had sprung up on the hills around the cove.

Unfortunately, transition is rarely easy for all, and Hobart town was no exception. In its haste to keep pace with the growth of the town, the city fathers had failed to anticipate the human needs. The rapid growth of the inner city and waterfront area still utilized the system of cesspool and night cart disposal of its sewage, as a result, the narrow alleys of Wapping and the waterfront had begun to degenerate into a cesspool of unhealthy alleyways and drains, populated by prostitutes and pickpockets, transmitting all manner of pestilence. Ever mindful of the agitation of townsfolk to clean up the city, the town council organized purges of the town's waterfront, with gangs of special constables roaming the areas where most decent people were afraid to venture, seeking out young, homeless, and for the most part starving, orphans.

It was common to come across a near death, starving child, hiding in a drain or disused brick kiln, whose ex convict parent had died and left them destitute. In 1853, their fate was the cruelty of the orphanage or equally cruel, indentured labour in the more remote parts of the island. It wouldn't be until later that year that ragged schools, that is, schools for the poor, began to appear in the town. The first in Watchorn Street and another two, one in Wapping, at the end of Collins Street and another towards Goulburn Street.

As the convict class were emancipated, another class appeared, that of the unemployable swagman, ex convicts who were aged, diseased, or for other reasons, unemployable. These men and women would wander the roads of Van Dieman's land from Hobart Town to Port Dalrymple and beyond, accosting pub patrons at the door of the local hostelry, begging for a piece of bread or pennies. In a year where twenty five pounds was a yearly salary for a whaleman, these destitute wretches would terrify the servants and staff of the wealthier homes by appearing at the back door, cancerous or syphilitic growths plainly visible in the hope of a sympathetic hand out before moving on.

It was this life of destitution that the two Billy's hoped to avoid, and Doctor Crowther being one of the most influential and kindly employers, the boys vowed to gain positions on one of his ships. Thus, it was, after a couple of successful artifact expeditions, the talents of the boys were brought to the attentions of the good doctor and Billy Lanne, or King Billy, as he was now referred to, was given first a berth on the Aladdin, and then a berth on the Jane, both Crowther whaling barque's out of Hobart Town and just one day after his thirteenth birthday, William, now known as Black Billy, was given a berth on the Offley, as ships boy.

The Jane sailed west to roam the western Australian coast in search of the great leviathans and given that each voyage could easily be over twenty months in length, the boys didn't see each other for a couple of years when, in 1854, after twenty one months at sea, the Offley, with Captain Robinson as her master and 'Black Billy' William Smith as her cabin boy, entered back into Hobart Town.

Billy knew the minute he boarded the Offley, he was born for this life! The rushing of sailors about the deck as they prepared to come away from the new wharf near Castray esplanade. Most of them hungover from the revelries of last night when they had signed on for the voyage in a moment of drunken bravado. The amazing manner in which the great ship was maneuvered from the dock by a half dozen boats, six men apiece, pulling vainly against the suction of the shore, until the mighty ship began imperceptibly at first, then noticeably as the gap between the wharf and her port side widened. As she moved clear of the wharf, the lines from her tows were let go and her sails fell from her yards as giant canvas curtains, halyards on each corner gripped by a dozen seamen and brought taught against the breeze. For a moment, she stalled in the water, her forward motion dissipating as her tows darted back to the safety of the boatman's wharf, before gathering way under her own sail power, and the surge of that power as the mains billowed before the wind and strained the stays. He swore he could almost hear the ship grunt, her brute strength forcing aside the water as she gathered way down the Derwent towards open sea. He stood on deck as long as the mate would allow, staring up into the rigging, the crew stepping back and forth along the yards, some of them swinging down to the deck on ropes, all the way from the tops, to the cheers of their shipmates and the curses of the first mate, an injured man was a liability who could cost thousands of pounds in lost time and manpower.

Only eight days out and Billy saw his first action. Just after breakfast, he was washing the captain's dinnerplates in a tub near the tryworks ovens when a call from the tops came down, 'THAR SHE BLOWS!' the call startled him and had all of the crew, including those off shift, grabbing their oilskins and boots. The boats had been made ready, ropes coiled in their tubs and blocks oiled and harpoons covered with their sheaths and placed aboard.

The mate, under the captain's direction, ordered the ship to chase the whale until it got as close as possible. Twice the animal seemed to slip beneath the rolling waves and they thought they'd lost him, but a steely eyed lookout in the tops noticed him swimming just beneath the green water of the Tasman Sea. It was a Sperm whale, a bull, and each person at the rail held his breath as the boat approached the monster. Sperm whales or Spermaceti, as the captains called them, were the most productive whales in the Southern Ocean, containing at least twice as much oil as their cousins, the southern right, and a much clearer, thinner oil, therefore much more sought after and worth at least twice as much.

When captain Williamson presumed the ship was not going to get any closer, lest the whale sound, he ordered the ship hove to and ordered just the one boat away. With the first mate as boat steerer, six oarsmen, and one harpooner climbed down the rope ladder into the whaleboat. Already, the rest of the crew were lowering the three wooden boards that would form the platform for the flensers to work from, down to just above the water's level as the boat headed away towards the whale.

Normally Billy would be below decks consumed in his chores, but the second mate had approved his entreaties to witness, hopefully, the taking of the first whale. As the whaleboat turned towards the spout of spray the harpooner, an islander, who was as black as Billy, stood tall in the bow of the boat and Billy imagined himself as the brave harpooner who would capture this giant sea monster and haul it back to the ship.

Few whales were taken so close to the ships, but this time the Offley was lucky. The whale had at first not seen the ship, or the whale boat, until the boat was almost upon it. As the boat came abreast of the whale, the harpooner stood high in the bow, and leaning against the clumsy cleat, a cerf cut for the purpose in the thigh board, drove the harpoon deep into the back of the whale, next to its blowhole. Not finished yet, and before the whale could sound, he quickly yanked the shaft from the head of the harpoon and inserted a second harpoon head, driving it home also, before retreating back along the boat and swapping places with the headsman. Already the whale was running and each man aboard ship had his neck craned to see the battle going on just a half mile away from the ships rail. Captain Williamson could have ordered the crew to pay more attention to their duties, instead of lollygagging at the fight on the water, but in the spirit of good spirits, he allowed his men, and his family, to witness the spectacle playing out before them.

Already the first tub of whale line was empty and the line of rope was beginning to sing in the notch cut in the prow, a small sliver of bone holding the rope from slipping out of its notch and preventing it from sweeping across the gunwale as the whale turned, decapitating the men and throwing all crew into the cold green waters of the Tasman Sea. The harpooner, now the head steerer, was bailing water over the loggerhead to cool it down and stop the friction of the inch thick manilla rope catching fire. The harpooner had made one turn of the whale line around the loggerhead bollard in the stern, adding weight to the whale's burden, slowing the running whale line and forcing the men to lurch towards the stern as the boat surged forward. Each man had his oar in the water, backing them as much as the oar shafts would allow, then, as the whale surfaced and slowed, both the headsman and the harpooner hauled in the rope as the oarsmen rowed hell for leather toward the whale, in an effort to get closer before the harpooner, who was now the headsman, locked the whale line around the loggerhead and the chase began again.

For two hours the whale led them a merry chase, until it began to tire. Then, still in plain sight of the ship and all who lined her rails, the whale boat crept quickly up to the side of the whale, the oarsmen deftly avoiding the whale's giant pectoral fins and tail, maneuvering the boat, bow on to the whale's side, the harpooner then picked up the lance and drove it twice into the whale's blowhole, piercing its vital organs. At once a great spout of blood erupted from the whale and a mighty cheer went up from the people on the deck of the Offley.

The whale killed, it was down to business once again. The fires in the hearths were already alight and water was being ladled into the trough below to prevent any fires spreading to the deck timbers. The ladders and scaffold were in place and the specktioneers and skeemen were standing by to begin the work of flensing up the whale. Billy noticed one man standing by the rail of the ship, leather bucket in his hand and looking to the second mate for permission to go over the side.

Captain Williamson had the fore sail and main topsl's turned back with the wind to give the ship way and within half an hour, the Offley had moved up to the whale boat and hove to again. Billy watched as a bucket brigade was formed and the seaman with the bucket climbed down onto the whale's back, walked along the back of the whale and promptly disappeared head first down into a cut in the whale's head. At first, he began baling the clear spermaceti out of the hole and passing each full bucket to another member of the crew who traded the full bucket for an empty one. From there the spermaceti was bucket brigaded up to the trypots to be simmered and cooled before ladled to a funnel in the deck and poured through pipes, into Tuns, that sat beneath the tryworks on the lower deck. Men below would signal a Tun to be full and the crew would cheer as each of the two hundred and fifty two gallon Tuns were filled.

By the time he was finished, the baling man would be completely inside the claustrophobic innards of the whale, covered in blood and oils so much so that he had little hope of ever climbing back out again without help from his crewmates.

Then it was the turn of the spectioneer and his team of flensers. Large wide bladed flensing knives with handles five feet long, would be used to strip the blubber from the carcass and a rope would be passed through a hole cut in one end of the strip and passed through a block on the yard arm. When hauled on, the flensers would cut the blubber free of the whale and it would be hauled up and over the rail, where the Skeeman and *HIS* men were waiting to cut the blubber into blocks and strips called book, or bible, leaves, these to be tipped into the now boiling trypots of oil. Billy's first job as a whaler was stirring these pots to make sure the highly volatile oil didn't burn to the bottom of the pots, turning it black and ruining the oil quality. Billy knew the eyes of every man on deck was on him as he stirred the only means of income they had to their name and they knew the job of stirrer wasn't as easy as it looked. First Billy had to make sure the oil on the bottom wasn't getting too hot, not an easy task with the fires in the hearths fluctuating with the breezes that blew from each and every direction. As well, he had to scrape the oily scum from the top of the boiling blubber and ladle it to the fires to be used as fuel. Then, when the boiling oil was at its best and clearest, it had to be ladled out into the large copper cooling tanks, either side of the trypots, and all this without spilling a drop or burning the oil as the level in the pots went down.

By the time the whale was completely treated, the blubber rendered down, the spermaceti loaded, the lower jaw of the whale removed so the teeth could be removed for sale, the stomach checked for that rare, prized, perfume creating concoction known as ambergris, only found in the stomach of a sperm whale, and then only rarely, Billy was spent. Young and fit though he was, his arms ached from the stirring and ladling, his back ached from lifting and lowering the heavy chunks of blubber into the trypots, his legs ached from running back and forth to the horse cutters at the rail and his chest ached from the stench and smoke from the fires. He was most grateful when the captain's wife brought him a mug of tea and a sourdough bun. She had taken over his job as cooks offsider as everyone on the ship became a fully fledged member of the crew when it came to processing their catch. Billy was much appreciative of her efforts in relieving him of his more mundane chores and allowing him to really become a whaleman, and as he sat near the warmth of the hearth, one by one the crew finished their jobs and sat around the hearths, drinking their mugs of hot char or chickory coffee and smoking their clay pipes with the stems broken off to facilitate easier working, congratulating each other on a good day's work. He thought he was made! Black, dirty and greasy though he was, he had never had a better day in all his life, and getting paid for it!

Once eaten, the crews set about cleaning the decks and timbers of the ship from their coating of oil and grease that roiled off the smoke from the fires, until the sun slipped beneath the horizon and it became too dark to see properly. With the fires in the hearths beginning to burn down, the captain ordered the ship hove to and a double watch put on in the event of another whale showing itself by daylight. Billy watched the last of the day crew go off shift and wandered the foredeck and tryworks area, still reveling in the excitement of the hunt. There were a couple of lanterns still lighted at the focs'le awning, the two harpooners still honing their lances to a razor sharp point. One had struck bone on entry to the whale's body and needed heating and hammering to get it back into the shape and sharpness required by these most fastidious of seamen. That one whale yielded eight Tuns at eighty pounds per Tun, a total of six hundred and forty English pounds, and just nine days into the voyage. Billy sat down on the bench and was still feeling the excitement of the whale hunt when one of the harpooners nudged him awake and told him to go to his bunk.

The Offley would find many more whales as she sailed across the Tasman Sea in that summer of Eighteen Fifty Three, almost to the Solanders at the southernmost tip of New Zealand, and back out north, into the middle ground and although she would do no gammin, she would speak to at least six whaling ships through the captain's brass tube speaker as they passed each other on their long lonely voyages in the hunt for the spermaceti.

On Christmas eve, 1854, the sails of the Offley were sighted in the Derwent River, approaching Hobart Town. The new wharf was abustle with traders, tinkers, prostitutes and purveyors of anything a whaleman just returned from two years at sea might need, and many he didn't.

After passing through customs the cargo was sold and the men lined up at the company's agents, for their wages. The Offley had taken a goodly forty seven tuns of sperm oil, worth eleven thousand seven hundred and sixty English pounds. Billy's share would have been $1/250^{th}$ of the lay, less slops and stores. Billy lived frugally, he had no chance to visit shore and so received the full amount, less two pair of shirts and breeches. He collected the astonishing amount of Forty Six Pounds, Seven shillings and Sixpence! He placed the bulk of the money in the Commercial Bank and kept some for room and board at the nearest lodging house, but not before he signed on for another voyage on the Offley!

Billy's heart sang as he wandered along the wharves to the waterfront lodging houses of Wapping. As he approached the drab, narrow alleys, he turned left along Argyle Street. He didn't need to bed down in some flea ridden slum, he was rich! Billy found good lodgings in the Dog and Partridge Hotel in Burnett Street and set out for the waterfront once again. Normally, the ships agents would found a seaman who was too poor to stock personal belongings but, being a greenhorn, he had no idea he would be at sea for so long without even seeing a store, let alone shopping for necessities. During the voyage he was embarrassed by the same quandary that most greenhorns suffer. That of not taking enough provisions of the basics needs with him. He had but a small duffel bag in which his spare clothing and the barest of toiletries were kept and was forced to approach the slops chest after his meagre number of personal supplies ran out. Not wishing to run up a bill with the ship's agents, which could prove very costly on a 'clean' trip, he had lived very frugally during the voyage having to borrow items from the cook, or the carpenter, everyday items like scissors for his toenails and hair, needles and thread, chalk and slate, for writing tomorrows instructions and even liniment and bandages for the numerous nicks and scrapes that would quickly get infected by the dirty salt water and whale detritus if left untreated at the end of the day. He was very glad of his frugality at the end of the voyage, because it meant he could afford just the thing he needed, a Ditty Box!

He walked past the chandlery stores and Coopers workshops on Davey Street until he found what it was looking for, and in plain sight of the masts of the Offley, he went in.

At first the carpenter ignored him, until he spoke in clear English and gained the businessman's attention. Once he was made aware of the fortunes of this young half caste by Billy's producing of his Commercial Bank savings book, the carpenter was only too pleased to follow the young man's instruction and quickly gather his note book and wrote down his order.

During the voyage, Billy had been so enthralled with life aboard ship, he knew this was the life for him. But not as a lowly ship's boy, he learned aboard ship, there was no discrimination in this trade. As long as you could do your job and hold your own with the rest of the crew and respect other members of the ships company, they, from the captain down to the cook, would respect you, regardless of your colour. Not for him, the class and colour system of the towns and cities, there was a future in whaling, even for a half caste, and he meant to carve that future out for himself. He knew he would have to present himself as an aboriginal half caste as, being a half cast islander, with no papers to prove he belonged in Van Dieman's Land, he could be put on a boat back to Sa'moa or indentured into slavery tomorrow. His homesickness had faded with the excitement of his first voyage, and though he found himself wondering how his family was faring, he felt sure he would see them one day. With money in his pocket, and the respect of those around him, he felt it was a turning point in his life as he handed his instructions to the carpenter and left the joinery store. He headed back to his lodgings, the young man had a plan, and this was the first step in that plan.

On 24th March, 1855, the Offley sailed for the whaling grounds once again. This voyage would last just nine months and once again, a successful forty five tuns of sperm oil in the hold.

Once the offload was completed, and all papers submitted, Billy hurried off the joinery store on Davey Street. From his counter behind the eight paned windows, the joiner had watched the masts of the Offley as she drifted slowly towards the New Wharf, her sails were backed off, one by one, spilling air from one sail to another to slow her way. At the last moment, her anchor was let go and although he couldn't see them, he knew she would have at least two boats with lines attached, ready to slow the ship to a stop before she hit the wharf. As usual, and with precision, the Offley stopped about fifteen feet short of the wharf timbers and ropes were thrown from the ship to be wrapped in figure eight fashion around the curved iron bollards that stood at intervals along the new wharf. He could hear the calls to the crew on the deck as they turned the capstans and wound the ship to rest against the fenders of the wharf.

The joiner looked with satisfaction at the box and took a sheet of cloth from the counter and dusted the Ditty Box for his client. The box was slightly over twelve inches long, nine and a half inches deep and six and a half inches high, constructed of three quarter inch Huon Pine. The joiner had placed inch wide strips of polished Tasmanian Blackwood on each of the borders of both the lid and the main body of the box, leaving the centres just three sixteenths of an inch deep and empty as per his customers instructions. Both the bottom and the insides of the body of the box were lined with a green felt baize, with the lift out compartment, polished Huon Pine. As Billy inspected the box and nodded his approval at the workmanship, the joiner asked why he required the work box in an unfinished condition. Billy explained his occupation required he visit many different ports and spend long days, even months, at sea doing nothing. The Ditty box would give him all of the tools required to keep the few clothes he had room to possess aboard ship, in reasonable condition, as well as a hobby to while away the quiet times, in between whale sightings. He explained he would collect different pieces of timber from each port of call and fix them to the sides and top of the work box until it was considered complete. That way, he would have a constant reminder of his travels and his adventures without having to write them down. Impressed with his theory, the joiner went out the back of the shop and returned with ten thin slivers of bird's eye Huon Pine and passed them to Billy. 'Here,' he said. 'This'll get you off to a good start'. As he wrapped his arm around the small, wooden trunk and walked along Davey Street, Billy had no idea just how important his ditty box would be in telling the story of his life in years to come.

Chapter 15

Hobart Town,

Van Dieman's Land, 1857

The Offley was beginning to look the worse for wear, she had been four years at sea without a decent refit and was booked to make a short run to Newcastle and bring a load of coal back to Hobart, then she would go to Melbourne for a complete refit and return in time to make her crowning voyage, a voyage to the Kergulens or, more aptly named Desolation Island, and Heard's Island to hunt elephant seal.

Doctor Crowther had heard of the Americans capturing huge amounts of elephant seal oil as well as ivory from the seals tusks. Ever the opportunist, he fortuitously overheard the well kept secret from an American whaleman who had been injured at Heards Island and subsequently taken to Melbourne for hospital treatment. Crowther had hurriedly arranged for the Offley's refit during 1857, and as there was some degree of shelter at Kergulen Island, but only an open roadstead at Heards Island, to overcome this problem, he did what the Yankees do. He arranged for a tender ship, the Elizabeth Jane, a smaller schooner, capable of getting in closer to shore when the furious fifties abated enough to allow whale boats to ferry the barrels of elephant seal oil out to the waiting Offley.

This would be a fully fitted out voyage, sparing no expense for the safety and comfort of both crew and ship. To this end, Crowther sent the Barque to Melbourne where unemployment was rife and there were many more hands available to refit the ship. As well, he had the Elizabeth Jane loaded with a mobile house and all the tryworks and flensing equipment needed should the Offley be unable to service the men on shore.

The first signs of trouble began when the refit was finished, the unemployed whalemen of Melbourne, still smarting from many failed gold prospecting trips, demanded they be allowed to crew the ship and that the Tasmanian crew be left behind. This was not acceptable to Crowther, who favoured the usually uncomplaining Tasmanian whalemen over men who were used to the more salubrious comforts of the cities and towns of the northern colonies, but the men were resolute and refused to let the Offley sail and a deal had to be made whereby the Offley would take on twenty two Victorians and have the remaining crew be made up of

Tasmanian whalemen and, much to their glee, both Black Billy and King Billy were among them.

Captain James William Robinson was master of a well fitted out three masted Barque, having more than sixty tonnes of food and gear aboard to service the crew for the expected eight month voyage and was so confidant he had no qualms in taking his wife, son and daughter. She didn't know it, but Mrs. Robinson would be only the second female to ever set foot on both Heard and Desolation Island and in the most trying of circumstances.

As soon as Billy Lanne heard the Offley was to sail to Heards and Desolation Islands, he had approached Doctor Crowther for a transfer from the Jane. This done, he sailed from Melbourne on the Offley and the two Billy's met once again, on the deck of the Offley, both excited at the prospect of seeing the icy seas of the south, and share in the fortune to be made. Among the many people who was on the new wharf the day the two Billy's were about to go aboard ship, was an older seaman seated comfortably on top of a pile of old rope destined for the oakum factory. He could hear the lads chatting about the adventures they might have, once the ship got under way. He stood up and hobbled along the wharf near the boys and sidled up to the lads just before they went on board. 'If I wern you lads,' he said removing his pipe and licking his tobacco stained lips. 'I would be runnin' a mile from dat ship.' He took his pipe out of his mouth and gestured towards the Offley with his fist closed around the clay smokepiece.

The two Billy's were aghast. 'Why?' They asked, in unison. 'This is the chance of a lifetime mate,' Billy Lanne went on. 'If this trip a winner, and it will be, den we'll have trip every two year and we'll have plenty money every year, dey say there's thousands of seals on Herds Island, jus' there for the taking!'

The old man leaned forward on the soles of his feet and nodded down river towards the south. 'Youse never bin dere.' He turned his head towards the lads and looked them in the eyes. 'I have, and dey don't call dat place Desolation Island for nuttin.' He stared away towards the south and shook his head slowly, as if remembering a part of his past that was deeply unpleasant. 'I tell you boy's, dat place be hell on earth, sleet, hail, snow, ice and fockin' elephant seals, dat's all der is, nuttin' else.' He hesitated and looked the boys in the faces. 'And if the first four don't get youse den the seals will! Tho' faces won't look nice an' smooth lak dey do now, when you come back, dey all shribbled up and burnt from de wind and de ice, lak mine.' The boys stared into his scarred and shriveled face, realising he was not as old as he first looked, he had obviously suffered some sort of trauma, his nose seemed deformed at the tip and as he tapped his pipe on his cheek, they both noticed at least three of his fingers were missing.

'De wind , she caus dis.' He shook his head again. 'Don't be makin' de mistake I make, Lak a banshee she is, never stops screaming. You tink you seen wind in storms at sea. You never seen nuttin' till you get's to desolation island.' He stopped and a serious frown came over his face. 'Don't go dere, boys, it be no good for you. You never seen wind until you get to desolation island, believe me, Dat's where they make da wind!'

He could see it was no use and turned away and slowly made his way through the bustling crowd that were filing along the wharf. Some working, as they loaded the final stores aboard the Offley, some hawking their wares to the seamen and sightseers alike and others simply whiling away the days as they waited for an opportunity to make some spare cash to pass over the bars that were spaced out along the waterfront.

Both Billy's were just a little taken aback at the old seaman's reality jolt, but nowhere near enough to consider abandoning the voyage of a lifetime. They could see the crew beginning to position themselves at their post and a hail from both the cook and the second mate had them climbing up the gang plank with the last of the recalcitrant members of the expedition who, if they could have, would most certainly have followed the old seaman into the bars.

And so it was, the Offley set sail from Hobart Town on July 4th 1858, with the Crowther schooner, Elizabeth Jane and her master, captain Abbot, having left port a month previously, to set up camp and rendezvous with the Offley on her arrival.

Billy Lanne was already an able seaman, having shipped on the Jane as well as the Aladdin, so he headed towards the foc'sle and the second mate, for orders. Billy Smith began stacking the last of the stores for the galley below, at the cook's direction.

Captain Robinson, with his wife and two children, a boy of seven years and a girl of just three, standing beside him, had addressed the crew on the way down the river Derwent. Whilst passing the calm waters of Storm Bay, he informed the men that it would be cold, with freezing winds and most probably heavy seas, and with only an exposed open road at Heard Island, the work party and all their stores, including their hut and timber to construct a raft, would have to be put ashore with the Elizabeth Jane while the Offley went whale hunting, or laid up at Desolation Island until the weather eased.

The captain assured the men, that while it would be stormy and cold, the expedition was well founded, with plenty of warm woolens and an abundance of food.

The plan was for the Elizabeth Jane to anchor in the shallower waters of the exposed Bay while the seal blubber and ivory teeth were ferried out on the raft and when loaded, the men would change shifts and the Elizabeth Jane would sail to Desolation Island and calmer waters, there to transfer her cargo to the Offley. Sadly, this well laid plan was not to come to fruition.

The Elizabeth Jane had left Hobart town on 4th June, 1858 and had made good way until the fifties latitude when a persistent westerly forced her to push deep into the furious fifties. She was within sight of the nine thousand feet high Big Ben, that huge monolith that towers over the centre of Heard Island, when a south westerly gale had her plunging her bows deep under thirty foot waves, threatening to punch her decks open. Captain Abbott, believing she would not make Desolation island, another four hundred and fifty miles west of Heard island and her rendezvous with the Offley in Christmas harbour, without causing severe damage, decided to abandon the voyage and as the wind turned a freezing southerly, he decided warmer climes were safer and headed the little schooner towards Mauritius, more than two thousand miles north west, leaving the Offley and her crew without a tender or any shelter to protect the work crews on shore. It would be months and the Elizabeth Jane would have sailed the two thousand miles to Mauritius, there to be sold at auction, before captain Robinson even became aware his tender was not coming.

Chapter 16

Heard, or Heard's Island
29th October, 1858

The men stared silently at the huge volcanic monolith that was Big Ben, the highest pinnacle of Heard Island, as the ship approached from the north. Unlike the verdant islands of the south seas and northern latitudes, this island was grey, forbidding and as the old seaman had said, covered in ice and sleet.

The Offley sailed past two inlets that could pass for harbours in fine weather. One, Corinthian Harbour was the larger but surrounded by sheer cliffs of ice that only got higher and steeper as the Offley passed down the coast. It wasn't until they reached a wide open bay where the ice cliffs finally petered out to a long strip of black volcanic sand interspersed with boulders, about eight miles long, that finally disappeared into the freezing waters of the Southern Ocean. There, much to the consternation of the crew, the Offley began to slow and move to the centre of the bay. The ship dropped both her anchors and backed her sails so there would be less pressure on her cables lest the wind change.

The wind was off the shore and the captain had the ship anchor in about twenty fathoms, approximately a mile off a rocky shore between cliffs of ice and a black sandy beach, strewn with boulders. To a man, they lined the rail and cast about, hoping to catch sight of the Elizabeth Jane or some semblance of her. There was nothing. Nothing on the water, or the land, that even resembled a ship or suggested someone had been here but, even a mile from the shore, they could smell what it was that moved men to come to this god forsaken place. A thick, cloying, musky smell that made even the hardiest whalemen gag and the greenhorn's retch.

To the north of a rocky beach directly in front of the ship, near the sandy spit, hundreds, possibly thousands, of huge elephant seals rocked and swayed as if moving in time to some macabre demonic orchestra as the screeching wind whistled across the black sandy spit, dragging the sand into the air and hurling it against and along the steep, jagged cliffs, creating its own hellish music on the hundred foot high ice pipes.

Billy Smith looked along the rail to where Billy Lanne was staring at the shore. For once, he was glad he was only a ship's boy and wouldn't be going ashore. For Billy Lanne though, there was no such luck. Captain Robinson had addressed the men and the mates had drawn up the rosters of those who would go ashore and begin the killing whilst the Offley would head to desolation Island in search of the Elizabeth Jane. The Offley could only get about a mile from shore in the best of weather and place, and even then, she had to be ready to get away from the land lest the wind get up from the wrong direction and drive her on to a lee shore.

All stores the whale boats could carry were ferried ashore whilst the weather was reasonable and a beachmaster, Lucas, was put in charge until the Elizabeth Jane could be contacted and the rest of the shore materials, including the lighter and the huts, could be ferried ashore.

The two Billy's gave a thumbs up to each other as Billy Lanne went over the rail and down into the first whale boat. Within two hours, all stores and forty men were heading ashore to bump on the rocky bottom of the wide open bay and the Offley was making sail and moving to the south, away from this bleak and dangerous place, then to turn north west, to Desolation Island, in search of whales and the Elizabeth Jane.

The men stood on the shore and watched the Offley depart. She had well cleared the headland of the sandy spit and was almost out of sight, but already the wind was beginning to change direction into the south and the sea was making.

It was a four mile trek across the black volcanic sand and ice, to a rocky outcrop where it seemed the Americans who had come before them had set up some semblance of a camp. With no hut or solid walls to provide a windbreak, the men were left to gather stones to erect rock walls and lay the driftwood poles they found on the beach, across the piles of stones, and cover these with a sail. They managed to find planks from a wreck washed up on the rocks and stitched these into the side of the sails to form some semblance of a roof against the makeshift stone walls, then packed the cracks with moss and covered the sail with flat stones to stop it from blowing away. The highest point of the hut was just four feet, as to lift it any higher, the screaming wind would simply hurl their primitive hovel up onto the ice cliffs.

They had a small wood stove in their supplies, but what good was a wood stove without any wood? At Lucas' instruction they scraped lichens and peat from between the rocks and broke open some crates to provide some heat until they could get some seals killed and blubber to burn.

With just ten hours of sunlight at that time of year, the men split into three parties. The first party would continue to bring supplies up to the make shift camp, another would begin killing what seals they could, which didn't take long. This group, the second party, were only gone a short time before they came back with some strips of blubber for the fire. Billy Lanne had been used to making fire since he was born and surveyed the whaler's hovel and fireplace with dismay. Forty men would have to crawl through the narrow opening into the cramped low hovel, there to endure the suffocating smoke from the burning blubber and peat, while they tried to cook, eat and sleep. There was no room for their supplies, which had to be left outside at the mercy of the elements, and whatever else was foolhardy enough to exist in this freezing hell. He didn't know it then, but hell would be an improvement on what these men were about to face.

Chapter 17

Desolation Island (Kergulen Island)
3rd Oct, 1858

The Offley had reached Desolation Island in just four days. As she moved into Christmas Harbour, there were a number of American barques mustering there. Most of them were full of elephant oil and were preparing to return to New Bedford or whatever port they had sailed from. Captain Robinson duly noted the Elizabeth Jane was not among them and knew they were in trouble. To make an attempt to anchor at Heard Island would be foolish and without his tender he would not be able to retrieve any oil from the island and his men would have no shelter or transport from the island.

He spoke to a number of ships and managed to pen a letter to Doctor Crowther in the faint hope of knowledge of the Elizabeth Jane. He had called on the bull horn to any ship that might be approaching Van Dieman's land and the reply from the Salsette, a new Bedford whaler, gave him hope the expedition could be saved.

He decided to keep whaling in the hope that the Elizabeth Jane would somehow arrive to save the expedition. The feeling aboard was one of dismay. Billy lay in his bunk that night and listened to the wind in the rigging. He had just come off his shift at the tryworks and galley and was still warm from the heat of the hearths. As he climbed into his bunk, he ran his hands over his new ditty box and thought of Billy Lanne, four Hundred and fifty miles away on the shore of that god forsaken mountain of ice. There would be no trees to cut the timber to line the ditty box on this trip.

The next day dawned cold and bleak over Desolation Island and already some of the American ships were readying to depart for home. With half of her crew on Heard Island sealing, the Offley had only a depleted crew and no tender to serve her. Captain Robinson decided the Offley would continue whaling in the hope they could at least fill the ship with sperm oil while the crew on shore would fill as many barrels of seal oil and blubber as they could during the summer and with Doctor Crowther's help, maybe a schooner would arrive in time to get the oil off the island and save the season.

With a short crew, Billy was pressed into service in all manner of works, at dawn, he would be stoking the fires in the hearths, cooking and serving breakfast, washing pots as fast as he could before the hot sea water cooled and froze in the tubs. Then to the cooper's room to help place the steel rings over the barrel staves and ensure they were water, or in this case, oiltight. From there he would be peeling spuds, breaking ice off the gunwales, climbing into the rigging to break ice of the yards, ensuring the falling ice didn't hit anyone as it crashed to the deck.

And after all this, he was also expected to take his place in the freezing cold tops for two hours every day, on the lookout for whales. He carried a seal skin over his oil skin coat, tied around his waist and completely covering his head. It was heavy and unwieldy climbing with the thick blubbery skin but at least it was bearable when the screaming winds threatened to tear him clear out of the lookout and fling him far out across the sleet lashed white caps. Cramped and freezing in the tops, the seal skin keeping just enough body heat in to enable him to function, although he had to continually brush the ice off his peek hole in the skin by raking his forehead against the mast stays. On more than one occasion, as the ship broached coming off a large wave, he had to hold on for dear life until the Offley righted herself and then brace his legs against the mast to stop himself being catapulted out of the lookout to the deck below as the ship ran into the back of the next wave. On these occasions he would reach up inside his clothes and press the leather thong around his neck so hard he could feel the coin beneath the skin of the caul, all the while peering out into the sleety gloom in search of white puffs of spray, in a veritable sea of spray.

His vigilance and tenacity paid off one morning, not long after he had settled in for another uncomfortable ride. The weather had eased and the white caps and rollers changed to a sloppy grey sheen, with long lines of thin, white, foam zig zagging before the wind, and as he scraped the sheet of ice off the sealskin blocking his view, he saw not one, but a whole pod of sperm whales off the port bow, running with the ship but much slower. He coughed up a throatful of spittle and ran it around in his mouth and swallowed it to lubricate his throat, before bracing himself against the mast and the rigging and screaming out as loud as he could, 'Thar she blows!'

Instantly the deck came alive and he was looking down into a dozen or more grizzled, frost covered faces staring back up at him and turning to follow the direction he was pointing. He looked to the poop deck where captain Robinson and his wife had come on deck to search back and forth from the tops to the vast expanse of sea, a number of times before the captain threw up his arm exclaiming, 'Yes, I see there!' Before calling up to him. 'Well done, that man Billy!

Billy remained at his post and like all the men on deck, the cold, and their predicament, was forgotten. There were whales to catch!

Already the boats were being swayed out in their davits, harpooners were loading the tubs of rope and everyone, from the captain to the cook and the cooper, was busy preparing for the chase ahead. The captain was pulling on his oilskins even as he hurled orders to the helmsman to get the ship as close as he can without spooking the whales. He didn't want the oarsmen to have to row so far, the ship would lose sight of them before they even lanced a whale. In these parts, just a few miles would put them out of sight and out of earshot, with the chances of making it back to the ship with a whale in tow before the wind got up again, becoming very slim.

Billy could see the whales up close, now there were three bulls and two cows in total with the bulls encircling the cows, although there was about a hundred yards distance between each monster and as each whale surfaced for air, at least three spouts could be seen, in close succession. The ship was now abreast of the pod and he could feel the ship slowing as the sails began spilling air. He saw, rather than heard, the mate call to him to come down and he stiffly stood up, shaking one leg, then the other to get the blood flowing, then began swinging down the stays to the rail.

The boats attacked in pairs once they'd picked their target. Each boatsteerer selected a bull whale and homed in on him. Getting slightly ahead of the whale while he was submerged, and allowing for his speed, they turned as one, coming abreast of the beasts just as they surfaced. The harpooner could see the alarm in the beast's eye as he hurled the lance true and let the warp run. The other boat was already in position and two more lances were thrown to each whale, each one hitting home.

Then began a mighty chase as the whales never even slowed, but instead, began to turn away to the north. With the captain and the first mate commanding two of the whale boats, they couldn't see which because of the distance, it was up to the second mate to command the ship and he gave the order to turn the yards and get under way in the hope they could keep the boats in sight at least until night fall.

Luckily, it was just before dark when the Offley came up on the boats. Each one had killed a whale and the oarsmen were labouring under the tow against the wind. The Offley hove to and the grateful oarsmen pulled the first whale alongside as the staging was lowered down. Billy and Mrs. Robinson, as well as her seven year old son, Alfred, were ready with warm clothes and hot drinks for the boatsmen to consume before the flensing began.

All night the Offley tried out. Billy tended the hearths and stirred the oil in the trypots, the roiling smoke from the tryworks funneled up into the rigging between the sails before being swept away by the gusting wind that had got up just after the whales had been secured alongside.

The pink and red glow of the hearths flames mixed with the glow of the lanterns that hung from the yards, and the shadows of the yard wide strips of blubber that were constantly being hauled over the bulwarks to be chopped into manageable chunks and carried to the tryworks or booking boards, had the ship looking something like a scene from Dante's Inferno, Billy listened to the calls and curses from the crew, as they slipped and slid on the grease, blood and ice that covered the deck in the shadowy darkness, and the shrieking wind through the rigging only added to the bedlam that was whaling in the southern ocean.

As dawn broke, the weariness set in. Legs and arms began to drag and heads began to droop, Billy was scrubbing the last of the blood and slime from the area around the tryworks and he felt himself beginning to nod off. A hand on his shoulder steadied him and he managed to stay upright on the heaving deck. It was the cook.

'Breakfasts ready for the men, Billy.' He said as he took the scrubbing broom from the boy's hand. 'You're one of the men now.' He paused. 'Get some grub into yerself and grab some sleep, lad, they'll be plenty more of this goin's on before we're done with this trip.'

Billy forced a meal of potatoes and beans down his throat with a mug full of hot tea and went below and climbed wearily into his berth. He ran his hand across the rough top of the ditty box and pressed the caul around his neck between his thumb and forefinger in thanks for spotting the whales, before drifting into a deep slumber.

Chapter 18

Heard (Heard's) Island, Southern Ocean
December 28th 1858

It had been two months since the Offley had dropped them off and still no sign of her or the Elizabeth Jane. Billy Lanne and some of the crew abandoned on Heard Island had made the best of a bad situation. They had scrounged what timber and driftwood they could from the parts of the island that were not covered in snow and ice. With the summer, at least some of the ice had melted, exposing bits of timbers of wrecked ships that could be used to shore up their meagre hovel. The hovel had been extended to accommodate the men and some of their supplies and Lucas, the beachmaster, kept a close eye on how the food was rationed out. It wasn't as if he was miserly with the tucker, it was just that some of the men felt there seemed to be an abundance of food and gear, so why not help themselves to whatever they felt like?

With Christmas just gone and no sign of savior, there was a general feeling that the Elizabeth Jane had met with misfortune and they had been left to fend for themselves. Some of the men, including Billy. had begun to ration the foodstuffs and clothes in an attempt to eke out their provisions for the longest possible time, and as they were being paid on the lay system, and seals being plentiful, there was no shortage of work. As long as their food held out, they could continue to kill, flense and stuff the barrels with blubber for trying out aboard the offley when she arrives, *if* she arrives! At least there was no problem keeping most of the food preserved, although the flour was mouldy due to the damp air and all the greens had begun to sprout. The elephant grass that grew in abundance on the exposed parts of the island made an excellent salad vegetable and once the men saw Billy and a couple of Islanders eating the seal blubber, the men began chewing on it as a source of vitamin c to avoid the debilitating effects of scurvy.

Each day the men would separate into three groups, one for the killing party who would go out with lances and short guns, a rifle no longer than two feet in length, for easy carrying, which could be placed against a sleeping elephant seals head and fired.

Each elephant seal would yield two or three barrels of oil but, having no tryworks ashore, the second party would have to flense up the seals, cut up the blubber and stuff it into barrels. At times the seals would be too far from where the cooper was constructing the barrels, near the hut. So, the men would roll the barrels to where the largest number of sea elephants had been killed and flense and pack the barrels there on the beach. Once tried out, a barrel of blubber would make about three quarters of a barrel of oil.

Increasingly, Lucas, the beachmaster would arrange himself a job near the camp and would disappear into the humpy once the work parties had left on the pretext of cooking for the men. On a number of occasions, the work parties had returned to some feeble excuse as to why the meal hadn't been prepared, and had to cook up their meal in the dark. One particular freezing evening, the men returned to find not only their food still frozen in their boxes and the fire black out, but when they finally did locate Lucas in the rear of the hut, under a pile of blankets, to their disgust the man that was supposed to be leading them and looking out for their welfare was dead drunk. Once roused from his drunken slumber, the beachmaster became belligerent and abusive, threatening to charge the men with mutiny if they didn't accede to his demands for more drink. The rum barrel was checked and it was found Lucas had been stealing rum on a daily basis since Christmas and there was very little of the one comfort they had to stave off the cold and miserable conditions, left in the last barrel.

The men were incensed! Lucas was dragged out of the humpy and beaten to the ground. He struggled to his feet and ran towards the beach amid a storm of sleet and punches. Billy stood aside, as did the other natives in the group. It did not pay for a native to intervene in a white man's fight. They let the white men take out the frustrations on the luckless drunk all the way down to the beach, until the cold and wind tore away their curses and Lucas' cries of pain. Billy and a sandwich islander, named John Mohee moved to the fireplace and began to stir life into the cold coals and with the talents inborn to most natives, soon had cheery blaze warming up the humpy. When the men returned, Billy was not surprised to see Lucas was not among them, but a tall man McCall, pointed to John Mohee, 'From now on, Mohee, you will be beach master, in charge of food and drink.' Not willing to be a native in charge of a gang of desperate and unruly white men, but having no say in the matter, the sandwich islander nodded and began getting the stores out for cooking. That night the men feasted on everything that was likely to spoil over the next week or so and drank the rest of the rum. It was not enough to get them all drunk but it managed to raise the spirits of most of the men, including Billy. That night, the wind got up again and Billy could have sworn the canvas roof of the humpy would have been torn away in the gale had it not been for the sheets of black sand being hurled on to the roof, forcing the men to brace the ceiling with planks and broken oars in an effort to stop it from collapsing in on them. At the height of the storm with the wind blowing at least sixty knots, Billy peered out from under his oilskins and rug to see Lucas crawl in under the flap of heavy sealskin that served as a semblance of a door, and move to his usual corner of the cramped hut. The alcohol had worn off and Billy could see the first signs of frostbite on his nose and battered face. He nodded at Billy and Billy nodded back, he was glad they hadn't killed him or left him out in the storm, where the effect would have been much the same.

With the storm still raging, the next day was declared a rest day. Lucas had been accepted back into the gang, albeit much farther down the pecking order, and Mohee began organising the food, telling the men they could have whatever they wanted, or needed from the stores. This would have been fine if they had some time limit on their stay on the island, but nobody knew when, or even *if*, there would be a ship coming for them.

Chapter 19

Hobart Town,
Tasmania
February 2nd 1859

Doctor Crowther had received two letters this week, both of them alarming him to a great extent. The first was from Mauritius announcing his schooner, Elizabeth Jane, had been condemned and sold at auction in Mauritius after springing a plank on her way to Desolation Island. The second letter, from Captain Robinson of the Offley, requesting news of the Elizabeth Jane and informing him of his being unable to offload elephant oil from Heard Island without a tender to support him.

Captain Robinson declared he had fifty two tuns of sea elephant oil and three tuns of sperm oil stowed down and another forty Tuns ready for shipment on the beach at Heard Island.

Doctor Crowther immediately set about organizing a second tender and purchased the Flying Squirrel, another schooner lying at Sydney Cove. The schooner was fitted out and set sail for Heard Island via Cape Horn but after months of sailing across the Pacific, she failed to make even that leg of her journey when the crew, after battling heavy sea trying to 'round the horn', put into Valparaiso, Peru and it was there the crew mutinied and refuse to man the ship. Frustrated, captain Ledwell applied to the consul of the port to have them punished, but was refused. He then had to wait at the wharf in Valparaiso, as he attempted to hire a new crew, but after a month's wait and nothing forthcoming, he was forced to admit defeat and sixty nine days after leaving Sydney, the Flying Squirrel sailed back through Sydney heads leaving the men on Heard Island stranded a second time.

During this time however, Captain Robinson had an idea that might save the voyage after all. On two occasions, on the rare calm days whilst travelling from desolation island, he had sighted a schooner making her way to the island. At first there was great joy on the Offley when the sail appeared on the horizon, as they believed it could be the Elizabeth Jane finally come to relieve the men on Heard Island but as they neared the schooner it became apparent it was an American boat looking for her missing mother ship. In January, 1859, the Offley was entering the mouth of Christmas Harbour, Desolation Island, when she chanced upon the American schooner once again.

After speaking with her through the bull horn, Captain Robinson discovered she was the American schooner, Mary Powell, come to the island for the same purpose as the Elizabeth Jane should have, as tender for a mother ship. Unfortunately, her mother ship had obviously been waylaid and she was a tender with no ship to tend.

There was much rejoicing at Heard Island when not one, but two, sets of sails were seen approaching the island. The first and largest was a square rigged barque, and obviously the Offley, as she was the only square rigged barque to have entered these waters, but the second set of sails was the one the men on the island had been waiting for since October, never mind, she wasn't the Elizabeth Jane, the men didn't care. They just wanted to go home!

Much was their disappointment when Captain Robinson addressed the crews of both ships and informed them of their commitment to their contracts. Thus, the crews would be split up and the Offley would overwinter at desolation island and the Mary Powell would go black whaling and use whatever calm weather was available to get as many barrels of oil transsshipped from Heard Island aboard the Mary Powell for shipment to Desolation Island and loading onto the Offley as was required to fill both boats. The land crew of forty men, eighteen from the Offley and twenty two from the Mary Powell would be landed to kill and try seals over the winter.

Billy Lanne was selected to return to Heard Island, a decision he took with his usual shrug of his shoulders, even though he was fully aware the conditions would be even worse over the winter months, whilst Black Billy was chosen to help crew the Mary Powell. Once the men were fed and revictualled aboard the Offley, and they were made aware there were now two ships' not just one, to look after them, their mood changed from one of desperation to acceptance, especially knowing there was finally to be a reward for all their hard work.

As they lined the rail to transfer to the Mary Powell, the captain Robinson called Billy's name and waved him over that imaginary line behind the foremast to come to his cabin. Not sure what to expect, Billy followed the mate down the steps into the captain's cabin, under the poop deck. Once there, the captain pulled a sheet of paper from a stack of the same and passed it to Billy with the words, 'There you go son, something to put in that sea chest of yours, it wouldn't do to send you to do a man's job on the Mary Powell as a mere ship's boy.' He smiled at Billy as Billy took the sheet of paper. 'You'll be going as an Able Seaman, and a well deserved lift in pay, as well.'

Billy hurried down the deck to the foc'sle. The men were already climbing down the ladders into the Mary Powell and Billy Lanne grabbed his shoulder as he went past. He recognized the piece of paper for what it was and nodded. 'I'll see you when we you come to pick us up. We should have plenty oil for you, young'un.'

Chapter 20

Spit Bay, Heard Island
February 9, 1859

Spit Bay was a hive of activity as goods were again loaded from the Mary Powell onto a raft and towed ashore with whale boats. Teams of men dragged goods and gear in sleds and wheel barrows up the black sandy beach and out onto the eight mile long spit to the hut. On reaching the hut, the cooper, carpenter and cooks would drop out of the line of men to begin organizing the camp into something more habitable than it was. Many jokes and wisecracks were levelled at Billy Lanne, John Mohee and the previous crew who had constructed the humpy. These jibes would later be retracted when the sixty mile an hour, sleet filled winds would come shrieking their vengeance at these human interlopers and the efforts of the expert carpenters and builders were reduced to little more than the original humpy and forty freezing cold men huddled together trying to stay warm around a blubber fire, praying the sail cloth roof would stay until daylight.

Four miles out to sea, on board the Offley, there were more pressing, never before experienced, needs. Captain Robinson had fended off his wife's entreaties to come on the voyage with him, for months, but had finally relented at her insistence, believing they would be home in Hobart in seven months and here it was, almost nine months at sea and no sign at all they would be home this side of Christmas.

He had watched his wife's midriff swell and wondered just when just when she would break the news to him. He had also noted the first mate's querying glance as his wife struggled to get up from her chair following dinner each night. At last, it was too much for him and he broached the subject as they readied for bed and to his horror, was informed it could be any day now. His wife was a strong woman, she had to be, to endure the rigors of life aboard a whaling vessel, especially in these latitudes, and especially with two young children in tow, but of all the calamities he had experienced in his years at sea, he had never heard of a birth on a whaling vessel before. The more he thought about this predicament, the more his mind conjured up things that could go wrong. There was no way they could return to Hobart in time, and there was nowhere closer, and as well, there was no one with any experience in childbirth aboard either ship. The safety of his wife was paramount and he decided to sail to Desolation Island and stay until the baby was born, or, he shook his head, the alternative was simply too hard to think about.

The Offley sailed for Desolation Island.

They had been there two weeks when the Mary Powell arrived. She had completed loading the barrels from Heard Island and came alongside to offload the thirty tuns of sea elephant oil to the Offley.

The Offley saw the last barrels of whale oil and blubber come over the rail when the captain was called to his cabin by his eight year old son. There was silence over the two boats as all labour stopped and men sat down to await the outcome of Mrs. Robinson's labour.

The first mate was first to enter on deck and as he put his hands together in applause, both crews jumped to their feet and looked to the captain as he came on deck. His beaming smile of relief was shared by everyone as the good news was relayed to all.

The captain addressed the men and informed them that the new baby was a boy and would be named James Kergulen Robinson. A sailor called out, 'Three cheers for Kergulen Jim!' Kergulen being the recent official name of Desolation Island, but a single call of an unknown sailor would have the name Kergulen Jim applied to James for the rest of his relatively short life. He would be born on the eleventh day of March, 1859, surrounded by cold freezing water, and yet die of thirst in the Australian desert, surrounded by dry, arid sand at the age of fifty four.

The Offley stayed in Christmas Harbour, Desolation Island, for the next seven months whilst Billy Lanne and the beach crew hunted and killed sea elephants, and the Mary Powell hunted black whale and the occasional southern right. William made sure he gathered all the experience he could while he was on the schooner. They had no tryworks aboard so all blubber had to be taken to the offley for trying out. This meant more voyages from island to island and even though it was relatively calm and comfortable in Christmas Harbour, they would much prefer to get a larger load out to the Mary Powell than make extra trips back and forth to the island.

After many weeks of hard slog under the most trying conditions, the men felt they had at last turned the corner of the voyage, and as October rolled around, and with hundreds of barrels of blubber and oil stowed on board the Mary Powell, it looked like a November date for leaving this accursed place, and a return to civilisation.

This would be the last load, the Mary Powell hove to and made ready to signal the shore she would be sending the boats in to begin towing the loaded raft out to her. Captain Nash kept a weather eye out and at the first sign of trouble he moved further offshore and ran a Morris line from the anchor to ride out the storm. The storm hit the Mary Powell about ten o'clock that night and captain ordered more line put out in an effort to make the boat stay.

All night the wind screeched through the rigging and the Mary Powell ducked and plunged as the waves threatened to break her anchor line, A heavy snubber was hung on the anchor in an effort to keep the anchor on the bottom and halt snatching of her cable. No one, not even the captain could imagine the line gradually reeling out over the bitts with each heavy wave that collided with her bows.

It was about eight in the morning of the twenty third of October, 1859, the last of the Mary Powell's anchor cable slipped over the bitts and fell to the ocean floor, rendering the little schooner helpless and being driven on to a lee shore. The wind had eased slightly but as the ship turned beam on to the waves, it was apparent to everyone on board what had happened. With nowhere to turn and no sea room, the schooner was doomed.

Each man, including Billy, was on deck in an instant, staring at the towering cliffs of ice a hundred feet above them. Every now and then one of the men would look over his shoulder towards open sea in the hope of a boat that might save them, but every man knew there would be no escape by sea and if by some miracle, they did manage to get to the narrow strip of wave battered rocks on the shore, there was no safety there. To a man they would be battered to death by the heavy seas crashing against the cliffs or frozen to death clinging to the wreckage of the Mary Powell.

By now the ship was right under the cliffs and her keel had hit the bottom more than once. It was over, there was no hope now as the ship heeled over and the top mast yardarm crashed into the wall of ice. The captain steadied himself by holding onto a stay as one young seaman tapped him on the shoulder. He turned and saw a fresh faced American crewman facing him. Thinking this man might be looking for absolution he was about to shake his head when he noticed the lance warp curled about the seaman's shoulder and the pick in his hand.

'What is it?' Captain Nash asked.

'Beg pardon, captain.' The young man replied rather hurriedly. 'I reckon I may have a way out for us.' He explained to the captain he could climb the mast and walk out on the yardarm, and when the yard crashed against the wall of ice, he could jump onto the ice and using his lance as an anchor he could hack steps with his ice axe down from the top of the ice cliff. He could then use the rope to help haul the men up from the rocky shore one by one, taking the smallest first, and as each one clambered up to the top of the ice cliff, they could help haul the next until they were all out.

The captain new it was a suicidal mission but they had no other way out of this predicament. He readily gave his permission.

Billy and all on board watched as the young seaman, carrying his load of rope, his axe and his lance climbed through the swirling rigging, already some of the ropes had broken under the strain and were lashing about in the wind, threatening to tear him from his lofty perch. He reached the tops and began walking out on the yardarm just as the ship lurched towards the cliff again but, instead of holding back and waiting, the young man made a dash for the cliff face and leapt from the yardarm just before the end of the yard smashed with splintering force against the ice face.

Billy had visions of watching as the young seaman plummeted down the ice face to his doom, but as he looked up past where the yard arm had hit, he could see the young man sprawled against the face of the mountain, his lance driven firmly into the ice. Within seconds, the man was digging furiously and climbing by lifting the lance and plunging it into the ice time and again, gaining height up the cliff wall each time he did.

Finally, he was at the top, calling for another man to follow. The captain looked around for the lightest man in the crew and his eyes fell on Billy. Billy needed no second bidding, he was at home as the next man when he was in the rigging and almost ran up the shrouds. He got to the yardarm at the tops and could see it had splintered on the end and almost come away with the impact of hitting the cliff. He stopped and made fast the flying ropes around the yard to stabilise it, before dashing out and jumping the gap between the end of the yard and the cliff. He was only a couple of seconds in the air, but the gap across to the rope seemed to take an eternity before his hands closed around it and he gained a foothold in the axe steps the young seaman had dug. Both young lads stood at the top of the snow covered cliff and watched as the crew made their way to the shore, via the boats, holding their breaths as the boats rolled and struck bottom in the wild surf. Thankfully, the Mary Powell provided a modicum of shelter from the wind and apart from getting soaked from the freezing surf, there were no broken bones as they clambered up the shore to huddle like a flock of bedraggled penguins, at the foot of the cliff.

Billy was only young but he was very strong and between them the two men began hauling the others up to the top of the cliff. When it was over there was no rejoicing as they stood and watched their gallant little ship and four hundred tuns of seal blubber being bashed to pieces on the rocks below. Then they turned away and headed towards spit bay, some ten miles away. It would be dark on the second night, before they reached within sight of the camp and although they could see the glow of the fires at the camp, they were still too far away for anyone to hear their calls for help. Even though it may cost them their lives, they knew they would have to spend another night on the ice. They would still have to dig ice caves and huddle together to stay alive.

Using the lance the young American had with him, as well as a short flensing blade Captain Nash had the foresight to grab, before he was the last to be hauled up the cliff, they chopped and cut their way under a ledge to create an ice cave of sorts, into which they climbed and huddled together, penguin fashion, the warmth from their collective bodies creating an increase of heat towards the centre of the group and after a time, those on the outside of the group, when the cold got too unbearable, worked their way to the core in order to stay alive.

This process managed to keep all of them alive for three days. Even so, by the afternoon of the third day, the frostbite had taken its toll on those who stayed to long on the perimeter of the group, or lifted their heads in the few moments of sleep, they could manage in their frozen state, thus exposing their skin to the frozen air. As Captain Nash looked around in the grey of dawn, he could see there were noses, cheeks and fingers that would never recover from the effects of this journey and could quite easily contribute to the deaths of these men, if they didn't find help soon.

He roused the men and they shuffled out among the snow flurries and down the hill towards the camp. The lights that seemed so close during the night were gone, faded into the first rays of daylight and the camp that seemed so welcoming last night was just another tiny black blob among the ice sheets of Spit Harbour.

The wind that had caused this calamity had eased to just a few light gusts, increasing visibility for those at the camp as they headed to work in the direction of the shipwreck survivors. Billy Lanne stared at what he thought was a line of elephant seals coming down the long slope towards them and stopped. He couldn't understand why the seals that had now become wary of men and their camp, would move towards the obvious danger the men presented. John Mohee moved up to stand beside Billy. He too could not make out just what was happening, until one of the survivors stumbled and fell in the snow and the others moved to help him.

At Billy's and John Mohee's calls for help the entire camp rushed out across the snow, some having the foresight to grab the sleds and drag them towards the men who were beginning to mill about as they lost orientation and the direction of the camp.

Billy Lanne saw Billy Smith as soon as he got to within fifty yards of the men and realized what had happened. Billy Smith was in better condition than most, and helped put the more infirm survivors on the sleds before taking a hand to help drag the sleds to the camp. Once there, the fire was increased to a blaze and two more were lit to encircle the men and heat the melted snow for warm drinks that would help replenish their body heat. A call from the beach had them turning their heads towards the sea, a sail had appeared out of the mist and was making its way into spit harbour. Once at anchor, the timely arrival of the schooner, Cornelia, which was on its way to inform the men on shore of the loss of the Mary Powell, her wreckage at the bottom of the ice cliffs, being noted three days ago.

The loss of their tender and all her cargo meant the voyage was over. The only chance of any earnings from this horrendous ordeal was the forty tuns or so already stowed aboard the Offley. The Cornelia took the crew to Christmas Harbour and broke the sad news of the Mary Powell's loss and their dramatic rescue by the ingenuity and bravery of the young American sailor.

At least ten of the crew from the Mary Powell had suffered severe frostbite and Captain Robinson had the unenviable task of having to amputate a number of fingers from at least four of the men, as well as the tips of two noses with a sharpened flensing axe.

Captain Robinson was thankful that all his charges had survived, including his wife and new born son, and he thanked the men for their service. He knew there would be an inquiry and possible legal action against the company but for the moment he declared the voyage a failure and turned his ship for Hobart and home.

The Offley sailed into Hobart on January 10, 1860, three years since she was first fitted out for the Desolation Island voyage. The fitting out had cost Doctor Crowther an estimated five thousand pounds and had returned less than two thousand pounds in revenue, a loss of a more than three thousand pounds with the crew receiving no wages for the whole three years of the voyage.

For the two Billy's it had been a voyage to remember. Their dreams of making a fortune from Heard Island voyages were dashed, but their dreams of whaling for a living were far from finished.

They were both respected able seamen, with the experience and papers to prove it, and though each of them went their different ways on other ships, they would remain firm friends for life. Billy Lanne, the aborigine, would go back to crewing on whaling ships for Doctor Crowther and be known as 'King Billy' in acknowledgement of his being the last man of his people, ironically, he would become more famous in the events of his death, that he ever would be in life, whilst 'Black Billy' Smith, half caste, would spread his career over many ships out of Hobart, including the Calypso, Flying Childers, Maid of Erin, Highlander and the Othello and the Marie Laurie, (pronounced Marii Lowery) moving from able seaman through the mate's classes to master, later becoming a well respected ship's captain in his own right and the title of 'Black Billy' would disappear and he would become Captain William Smith, but not before encountering more adventures and ordeals on the high seas.

Chapter 21

March 2nd, 1869
Offices of the Anglo Australian Guano Company,
Salamanca Place,
Hobart, Tasmania

Doctor William Lodewick Crowther sat behind the desk of the Anglo Australian Guano Company, in Salamanca Place, poring over the notices of the company's affairs. Despite the somewhat grandiose name he had given it when he had founded the company, the entity had failed to live up to its expectations and now that his ships were returning from the so called guano filled islands of the pacific with little more than sandy soil in their holds, this company was promising to become as much a financial failure as the desolation island voyage, nine years ago.

He stood up from his desk and moved to the window. He could see his carriage driver chatting with a constable in front of his building and as the constable moved away, he looked about the office. Although not nearly as ostentatious as his doctor's suite in the city centre, he was comfortable in these surroundings, he liked the smell of oiled rope and tar coupled with the sight and smell of the many different timbers stacked and ready to be loaded aboard his ships for supply to the islands across the pacific. He was fully aware that his businesses were, for the most part, responsible for the activity that he saw on the streets and wharves below him, but whaling was becoming more and more marginal these days, and trading with the islands of the pacific was the new direction his ships would go, shipping goods and timber to the islands and returning with holds full of valuable guano. Well, that had been the plan anyway, he mused.

With his sawmills and trading business interests still successful, it wasn't that he would end up in the poorhouse should the Anglo Australian company be wound up, but it wouldn't do for a person of his standing in both the English and Tasmanian community, to be heading a company that was about to go under. He resolved to transfer his shares to his fellow board members as soon as practicable and distance himself from any enquiries that might arise from the liquidation of Anglo Australian Guano. He was a prominent surgeon, a successful ship owner, benefactor to the poor and a politician whose star was definitely on the rise. His mind drifted back to his days in London. The last thing he needed was to fade into obscurity in the wake of a business collapse on this far flung antipodean shore. No, what he needed now was recognition in circles far beyond the shores of Tasmania. Recognition from his peers in London that would flow back to Hobart, convincing the small minded people of Tasmania's so called Royal Society, that they could not compare to the greatest city in the world. In this backwater, twelve thousand miles from civilisation, it would be so easy to fade from people's minds and remain in obscurity forever, and he wasn't about to let that happen if he could help it.

A single heavy knock at the door stirred him from his reverie and he turned. 'Come', he called, but to his annoyance, the door was already opening. It was his secretary, followed closely by his driver, and Crowther wondered what it was that had his carriage driver climbing the stairs of the warehouse to see him.

'Beg pardon, Mister Crowther,' The driver had removed his cap and waited for Crowther to invite him to go on. Crowther gave a curt nod, and the driver spoke.

'Young Billy Lanne has died, sir.

Crowther stared at the man, puzzled. He cocked his head to one side. 'Who, or what, pray tell, is young Billy Lanne?'

The driver stumbled over his words. 'The young darky, the aboriginal, the, the last native you were wanting to keep an eye on.' His voice trailed off as he waited for the information to sink in to Crowther's otherwise distracted mind.

It took just a few seconds, but when it did sink in that William Lanne, the last male Tasmanian aboriginal had died, Crowther's features were transformed from one of annoyance to one of stark realisation that here was possibly his chance to immortalise both himself and the young aboriginal. Like all people of this island, he was aware the aboriginal was fast approaching extinction and although he had already recovered a number of skulls as well as a comprehensive collection of bones of various body parts, to be able to present Sir William Flowers, the curator of the Royal College of Surgeons Hunterian Museum, a fresh, perfect specimen of a full grown aboriginal man for display within the hallowed walls of that famous of all societies, would certainly cement his own place within that society. He mused at the irony that Billy Lanne and his young half caste friend, had once collected specimens for sale to him and was now going to be the most famous of all these specimens, on display for all to see.

Crowther's mind began to race and he drew his eyes away from the two men, feigning calmness. He needn't have bothered, both his secretary and his driver were aware of his determination to collect the best and most rare of specimens for display in London's best museums. Doctor Crowther had been good to both men, as well as their friends and neighbours. Providing employment and affordable health care when their children were ill. They were both prepared to spring into action at his smallest request.

'Where is he now?' He whispered, quietly.

'The Dog and Partridge ale house on Barrack Street.' His secretary answered, then added, knowingly, 'Unattended.'

At his secretary's last word, Crowther immediately stepped over to the desk and grabbed a quill from its stand, holding the sheet of note paper on the blotting pad with his left hand, he dipped the pen into the ink well at the top right hand corner of the desk and pressed it lightly to the paper. He quickly wrote two letters, one to the premier of Tasmania, Richard Dry, requesting that as honorary medical officer of the general hospital, he be allowed to take charge of the body of William Lanne. He was fully aware that, being a political opponent, Dry disliked him, and would most likely refuse his request in favour of Morton Allport, the vice president of the Royal Society and George Stokell, the house surgeon, but his ploy would be, if he were unable to be contacted by the return letter, it could be argued that his belief in being granted permission would possibly imply permission to carry out his plan. It was a long shot, but who was he if he wasn't a man used to taking risks. He knew the premier was a deeply religious man, as opposed to the scientific man he was. He also believed, as many eminent scientists did, that white European's were far advanced in knowledge, and the sciences than the cannibals and native breeds of the islands. It seemed obvious these races of the islands were fast becoming extinct through their lack of ability to accept change and the lack of churchmen to acknowledge scientific fact. Wasn't it only last year, the eminent scientist, Thomas Huxley, Charles Darwin's closest friend and ally, referred to Tasmanian aboriginal's skulls as proof of Darwin's theory of evolution. He believed studies desperately needed to be carried out to prove this theory, before these races died out altogether. He was sad about the death of Lanne, he was a good chap, but now that he's gone, he would be doing a far greater service to humanity and evolution than simply rotting in the ground, and if the church fanatics had their way, we would all be stuck in a mire of religion and misbeliefs. Someone needed to take charge and it seems it was up to him. He had a plan that would usurp that upstart, Allport, and deliver the prize to Sir William Flowers, and of course, the prestige of delivery of the last available skeleton of this, so very rare, prize, would no doubt be shared with himself.

The second letter he addressed to the person at the dog and partridge in charge of the corpse, if there was one, ordering that, as honorary medical officer of the general hospital, the body of William Lanne be removed to the morgue of that hospital and be placed under his supervision until he arrived there.

He blotted the ink dry on the letters and studied them for a few seconds. Satisfied he had worded his requests strongly enough, he passed a letter to both his secretary and his carriage driver. He stared hard at his secretary and tapped his forefinger on the top letter.

'You will take this letter to the Premier's office and hand deliver it to his secretary. Don't wait for an answer.' The secretary nodded his understanding, as Crowther turned and placed the second letter in the driver's hand. 'You are to go directly to the Dog and Partridge and hand this to the person in charge of the body of William Lanne,' as both men turned away, Crowther added, 'and should you see my son, Bingham, on your way, tell him to attend my office immediately!'

He heard the footsteps of the men retreat down the stairs towards the open doors of the warehouse, before hearing muffled voices followed by the heavy clumping of his son's patent leather shoes as they met the dusty oaken boards of the stairway. As he entered the room, Crowther motion him closer and confided in him a plan to remove the body of Lanne, the aboriginal, and ship it to London in a cask of brandy aboard one of his ships.

Bingham shook his head, 'I've just come from the hospital, there are two police constables, as well as a full staff there.' He shrugged, 'We would have to walk the body through the entire length of the hospital. He shook his head. 'We have no hope of removing a fully intact body from the building without being noticed.'

'Damn Morton Allport,' his father cursed.

Bingham stared at his father. 'I think I know of a way that might work, but we need to get Stokell away from the hospital somehow.'

His father returned his stare. 'You devise a plan to get the body out of the morgue and away, and I'll take care of Stokell.'

George Stokell had been a friend of Morton Allport and a political ally of the premier of Tasmania, Richard Dry. He was aware of Allport's penchant for digging up aboriginal skeletons and selling them to museums all over Europe, but he had little problem with that practice, providing it was sanctioned by the government and there could be no accusations of grave robbing from the general public which might harm his career as general surgeon. He was also aware Allport had commandeered, or disinterred, at least one hundred and fifty aboriginal bodies and skeletons and had them shipped to various museums around Europe. Lanne's corpse would certainly arouse interest and he resolved to keep it under surveillance until Premier Dry had made his decision to give the remains to the Royal Society of Tasmania for study and exhibition.

He had intended to go to the general hospital that evening but was met in the street by Doctor Crowther and invited to Crowther's home for dinner and a discussion. An unusual request considering the circumstances, but seeing as how an amiable discussion over dinner might resolve the issue of Lanne's body, he nonetheless, agreed. Besides, if he had Crowther across the dinner table from him, how could the good doctor perform any of his nefarious tasks he might be wont to do.

Assuring Morton Allport, he would be in Crowther's company for the best part of the evening, George Stokell set off for the Crowther residence from the hospital, arriving there promptly at eight.

He was met at the door by Mrs. Crowther, with profuse apologies that the good doctor had been slightly delayed and would be attending dinner in just a few moments.

The fact that Doctor Crowther's good wife had assured him that Crowther would be attending them soon, put Stokell's mind at ease, and as the staff busied themselves setting his table and pouring his brandy, he could not let his unease show and embarrass the good woman by taking his leave before he had eaten.

Chapter 22

Hobart General Hospital,
Liverpool Street,
Hobart,
2nd March, 1869

Crowther and his son, Bingham, had the carriage driver drop them off around the corner from the hospital's main door in Argyle Street and ordered him to proceed to the wall adjacent the dead house building. They moved quickly and unobtrusively through the stone pillars of the main gate and along the long corridor towards the rear of the building. They entered the morgue area just before eight, satisfied that Stokell had been diverted from his task of overseeing the charge of the morgue. The attendant in charge, recognising the two prominent surgeons, quickly withdrew and left them to their own devices, but both men were aware that a removal of the corpse of Billy Lanne would be impossible without bringing a good deal of attention to themselves and their nefarious acts. Nevertheless, Crowther was not to be outdone and came prepared for such a development.

Closing the heavy door behind them, both men walked through to the main two rooms of mortuary area, Crowther pulled back the sheets from the corpse of Billy Lanne whilst his son walked through to the adjoining room to survey the second body. Crowther was pleased to see the two corpses were the same sex, and build. Bingham checked the morgue's log and identified the white man as one Thomas Ross, a school teacher who had presumably died of unknown causes, the other was definitely an aboriginal man, undoubtedly, Billy Lanne.

Crowther placed his valise on the bench, near Billy Lanne's head and laid his surgical tools on the tray atop the dumbwaiter trolley. He looked to where Bingham was following his lead 'Don't be too particular about that one', indicating Ross' body, and Bingham nodded as his father began to remove Billy Lanne's scalp from his corpse by making a cut along each side of his head from his right eye brow, around the back and base of the skull to the opposing eye brow. Whilst he was doing this, Bingham went to work on the second corpse, the body of the young white school teacher.

Crowther had made the incisions around both sides of Lanne's head and down to the base of the skull. He began lifting the flaps of Billy's scalp from the base of his skull exposed by his scalpel and began forcing his right hand up under the fold of Billy's scalp, the skin and fatty tissue creating a slurping sound as he worked his hand forward, tearing the scalp away from the shiny, white skull beneath.

Williams facial skin contorted and folded forward in a heavy frown, as if in complaint of the atrocity being committed on his person, before tearing away from his facial bones to reveal his upper jaw. With a few deft slices of his scalpel, Crowther cut through the sinews of Billy's cheek, neck and lower jaw, the flesh of Billy's ears and neck proving quite stubborn, forcing the doctor to heave on the folds of skin and flesh to expose the skull. The effort of cutting through the sinews that held both skulls to their respective head and spines, together with the knowledge they might be discovered at any moment, had both men sweating profusely. Crowther pushed Billy's now bared and bloody skull forwards against the folds of skin and flesh that was once the young man's identifying features, and pushed his scalpel repeatedly between the base of the skull and the spine. He gave a final cut and the skull separated from the body of what was once William Lanne.

Pleased at his success of obtaining a fine and possibly the only, specimen of Darwin's missing link, complete with brain intact, Crowther heaved a sigh of relief before taking the skull that Bingham had removed from the other corpse, that of Thomas Ross, a white school teacher, and roughly forcing the bloody white orb into the cavity where Billy's skull once had been, pulling the folds of Billy's skin and flesh over and around the skull of the teacher, Billy's now distorted and sagging features looking more like a bloodied and battered leather sack than the face of a human being.

Bingham placed the claws of the surgical tool into the flesh on either side of the folds of skin, pulling the them together and allowing his father to stitch the cuts roughly together, resewing the skull inside the head cavity, whilst he wrapped Billy's skull in muslin cloth and placed it in a sack bag before walking quickly out the back door. He crept silently over to the wall and offered a low whistle, his whistle answered, he swung the bag up and over the high brick fence for his driver to pick it up and place it safely under his seat in his carriage.

Doctor Crowther wiped the blood and gore from Billy's now unrecognizable visage and pulled the sheet over what was once the corpse's head, he stepped over to the porcelain hand basin and began scrubbing the blood and fatty tissue from his hands and forearms, he turned and stared at the body shape beneath the stained white sheet, his only regret of his actions, was being unable to remove the whole of Lanne's body for the scientists in London to study and place on exhibition in those hallowed halls of the Royal college of surgeons in Lincolns Inn fields, London. Instead, he was forced to leave the remainder of what was perhaps the only specimen of an aboriginal man left on earth to the likes of Allport and Stokell and their friends at the Royal Tasmanian Society. 'Bloody disgrace.' He commented as he and his son opened the door to the main hall and left the building.

For almost an hour George Stokell had tolerated Mrs. Crowther's banter before he became suspicious that this had been a ploy to delay him from his duty. As he stood up from the table, Mrs. Crowther had dropped her head in guilt and he knew he had been duped. Still, he made his polite excuses towards the good lady and hurriedly descended the front steps and climbed into his carriage, noting angrily that Crowther's carriage was still nowhere in sight.

He alighted from his carriage outside the hospital at nine o'clock and headed directly for the mortuary building. There was no sign of Crowther, or his carriage, so it was entirely possible his suspicions were unfounded, and he was relieved he had left the Crowther residence on good terms. Much was his ire when, after being told that both the Doctors Crowther had been in attendance at the mortuary that evening, he demanded the key from the attendant, and took in the terrible sight that lay beneath the bloodied sheets of the stretchers.

He stared at the bloodied and mutilated corpses of both Ross and Lanne, one with its eyeless sockets and displaced lower jaw, creating a hideous caricature of a human head, the other completely headless, save for numerous, rumpled folds of skin where the young school teacher's head used to be, yet failed to acknowledge the despicable act that had been perpetrated on these two young men. He saw only that he had been duped, and that prized possession, a fresh aboriginal skull, complete with brain intact, had been stolen from him. No doubt the brain would already have been extracted from the skull and both placed in respective preservative jars for dissection at a later date. As he drew the sheets completely from the bodies, he noted there was little other disturbance to the body, but suspected Crowther would return and offer some ploy to add further insult by removing the complete corpse. Recalling premier Dry's promise to allow ownership of the body to the Royal Society, once the formalities of the funeral were completed, he personally locked the door of the mortuary and swore the attendant, John Greaves, to secrecy, and promised to reward him handsomely to guard the door until he got back.

Stokell alighted his carriage and set off for the house of the Royal Society of Tasmania Secretary, Doctor James Agnew. Fearful of losing his position as recently appointed, house surgeon, George Stokell was a worried man. He knew both Premier Dry and Agnew would view this extraordinary event as his fault. He had failed to adequately protect and prevent the mutilation of two corpses, although in his favour, almost every surgeon and honorary medical officer in the city had access to the mortuary for the purposes of dissecting corpses. Still, when it came to the overseeing of the dismembering and removal of a body without full permission, George Stokell decided he would let the warring parties fight it out. He needed support from these men, particularly when Crowther was most likely to point the finger at him for the illegal dissection, thus diverting blame from himself, and then rely on Allport and Agnew to throw him to the wolves for failing in his duty as house surgeon. Unlike Crowther, he was not a risk taker, but he could not stand by as Crowther lorded his position in Hobart society over appointed men. He wanted confirmation his actions would be sanctioned by both the Society and Morton Allport, and above all, by the premier, thus ensuring his position as house surgeon would be safe should all go wrong with his plans.

After calling at James Agnew's home, the men set off to join Morton Allport, and following a short discussion during which the indignant Stokell described the removal of Lanne's skull, without bothering to even mention the mutilation of the body of John Ross. Allport was incensed at the affrontery of Crowther to believe his should be the right to purloin the last specimen of an intact aboriginal male when they all knew the corpse was the property of the Royal society. James Agnew suggested the premier be informed at once, but loathe to disturb the premier at such a late hour, Allport decided Stokell and Greaves should attend the morgue to ensure the corpse was kept safe pending the premier's advice, and to use this time to remove any further articles from Lanne's corpse the Royal Society of Tasmania would deem appropriate.

On arrival at the mortuary, Stokell called John Greaves into the morgue and closed the door behind them. He didn't trust Allport and knew he was in danger of losing his position should the other attendants witness him removing Lanne's body without permission. Crowther could even be waiting somewhere within the hospital building for all he knew, just waiting his chance to accuse the hospital surgeon for the removal of the aboriginal's skull, thus diverting attention from himself.

Swearing Greaves to secrecy, and intimating his actions were to prevent Crowther from committing any further acts of theft from the hospital, Stokell began removing both feet and hands from the mutilated corpse. When finished, he washed the blood and tissue from the articles and wrapped the individual pieces in cloth. At Greaves inquiring stare, he stepped over to the body once again and deftly lifting Billy's penis to one side, he pressed thumb and forefinger into his scrotum and pulled down as he carefully flensed the scrotum from Billy Lanne's lower body, leaving the testicles still attached to their respective vas deferens, as the scrotum came away in his hand.

He held the now limp sac towards Greaves. 'You now own a tobacco pouch made from the very last Tasmanian aboriginal, a very unique artifact indeed.'

As his words sank in, Greaves smiled, and stuffed the offensive item in his pocket. Stokell was aware he would be questioned and probably even searched, as he left the building, particularly if Crowther was about. But Greaves could move about the building as he saw fit and later make his way to a rendezvous with Allport and his cohorts, thus avoiding Crowther altogether.

Confident Greaves was committed to his plan through the acceptance of the scrotum, he placed the wrapped bundles of Billy Lanne's feet and hands within the deep inner pockets of Greaves' coat and patted the coat down before instructing him to leave quietly and without drawing attention to himself.

Chapter 23

Hobart Cemetery,
Early hours of Sunday, March 7th, 1869

The two constables leaned against the taller gravestones adjacent to the earthen hump of soil that marked Billy Lanne's grave. Occasionally, one would walk over and pick a faggot or two from the woodpile and drop them into the brazier that served to keep the frost off their long serge coats.

The thick fog that rose from the river and settled over Hobart Town deflected the light from the fire in the brazier, creating shadows that reflected off the standing gravestones, adding to the already eerie atmosphere in the graveyard, and both constables, although glad of each other's company and the warmth created by the fire, would much rather be home safe in their warm beds than be exposed to the elements and evils of the shadowy burial ground in their dreary mission to keep watch over a worthless pile of dirt.

The men had exhausted their meagre supply of conversation hours ago, and as the long hours after midnight dragged on, they stared into the hot coals of the fire, each willing the welcoming light of dawn to approach. But it was not the dawn that awoken them from their reveries, a dancing lantern coming down the centre lane of the cemetery had both men standing upright and coming awake as the man approached. Their fears allayed as the buttons from the constable's uniform and hat reflected the light from the lantern he was carrying, informing them he was one of their own, still, they enquired as to his business on this night and were satisfied when the junior constable handed over a note from the chief constable, informing them they were to stand down and return to their homes.

Needing no second bidding, and not even bothering to question a direct order from their superior, lest the order be rescinded and they be forced to stand guard in this lonely outpost on their own, they left for the comfort of their own beds and the brazier stood alone, its welcoming warmth shared by others who moved from among the grave stones to begin their ghoulish task.

Chapter 24

March 7th, 1869

Hobart, Tasmania

Returning from a second voyage on the Flying Childers, sixteen months at sea under captain McGregor, where the returns were certainly not as good as the last voyage, William had stepped down off the gang plank onto the new wharf only to be told his old mate, Billy Lanne, had died and had been buried only yesterday.

William was devastated to learn that 'King Billy' had returned from a voyage in his favourite ship, Runnymede, very unwell and had visited the doctor on two occasions feeling and looking decidedly worse each time. On the morning of the third, he was persuaded to go to the general hospital, when he collapsed on his bed in the Dog and Partridge pub and died.

'They say he died of Cholera.' The barman at the Dog and Partridge, told William after he had hurried up to the corner of Barrack Street and Goulburn streets and entered the bar. There were still a few men in the pub, leftovers from the funeral which they said was the biggest send off for an ordinary seaman they had seen. William was glad for that at least, and gave his most profuse apologies for not being there, which were accepted gracefully, given he had no choice, being at sea.

A soft tap at his shoulder caused him turn and face Captain Bayley, one of the most respected sea captains in the colony. Bayley, a quietly spoken man and another man, a sandwich islander, by the name of John Bull, called William aside and described the 'disgraceful happenings' of the past week. They moved to a corner table and Captain Bayley began by asking William if he and Billy had ever gathered artifacts for Crowther. The omission of the prefix, Doctor, or even mister, surprised William as he knew Captain Bayley to be a very polite and respectful man, usually. However, as the captain and John Bull went on, William could feel the muscles in his face tighten. The captain must have noticed it and explained that the only reason he was bringing the subject up, was that he believed the same events could transpire and happen to any islander or person of colour. William sat back in his chair and listened as Captain Bayley went on.

'Billy Lanne had died on Wednesday last. The doctor said it was choleraic dysentery. However, some hours after he died, Doctor Crowther and his son, Bingham, had entered into the death house where Billy's body was kept and mutilated his body by cutting his head open and removing his skull.'

'His skull!' William exclaimed, 'Why would he do such a thing?'

Captain Bayley went on, 'Doctor Crowther is a man of science, or claims to be.' John Bull interjected. 'That gives him no cause to mutilate a man's body.' He looked William straight in the eye, as was his way, when wanting someone to understand just what it was, he was politely trying to say. 'Not in the way THEY did.'

Captain Bayley lifted his hand above the table, to call for calm, and went on, 'The story is, Crowther had been collecting pieces of aboriginals and sending them to the Royal College of Surgeons. In return they would look favourably on him by bestowing some sort of medal, or honour, on him.' The captain took a breath and went on.

'Everybody is aware that Billy Lanne was the last male, full blood Tasmanian aborigine on god's earth, and scientists, looking for the link that might prove, or disprove, mister Darwin's theory of evolution, will stop at nothing to say they own a part of that missing link.'

'How would stealing someone's head prove where he came from?' William asked. 'And why wasn't they stopped?'

'Your guess is as good as mine to the first question, and I'll tell you the story I have heard from many sources in the last couple of days.' Captain Bayley replied, before going on.

Doctor William Lodewick Crowther was seated in his office when his secretary walked in. 'That man, Lanne. The aboriginal who worked for you.'

'Yes, what about him?' The eminent surgeon asked.

'He's dead.' The secretary replied.

Crowther put down his pen and stared at the messenger. 'Dead, how? He was only a relatively young man.'

'Thirty four. Too much drink and too much hard living, I suppose,' the secretary was about to go on when Crowther stopped him, abruptly.

'Tell Bingham to come through.' He demanded, brusquely. The good doctor was normally politely spoken to his employees, but on a subject this close to his heart, he was known to be demanding, even arrogant.

His son, Bingham, entered the room and Crowther instructed the secretary to go and find out as much information on Billy Lanne as he could, especially who was in charge of the body and where his body was taken.

This was his one and last chance to get a complete specimen of an aboriginal off to Sir William Flowers, curator of the Royal College of Surgeons Hunterian Museum, and finally circumvent Allport's numerous attempts to own an aboriginal skeleton for that impudent Royal Society of Tasmania. He was well aware Allport and his cronies had stolen many bodies and native artifacts and arranged a meeting with the premier of Tasmania, Richard Dry. As an honorary medical officer at Hobart's General Hospital, Doctor Crowther obtained a coroner's order, and had the body of William Lanne sent to the hospital dead house.

Much was his ire when the Premier informed him that 'King Billy's' body would be buried first, then exhumed and placed under the care of Allport's Royal Society for scientific study.'

Crowther was incensed. 'Who the hell to these colonials think they are?' He ranted. 'Believing an insignificant little backwater like Tasmania could compare with London as a centre for scientific studies! Preposterous!'

On Thursday, the fourth of March, Premier Dry instructed Doctor George Stokell, the house surgeon, not to permit any mutilation of Lanne's body and after telling this to the steward, the attendant, and Charles Seager, a storekeeper, George Stokell left and met Doctor Crowther in the street.

Crowther told Stokell that the premier had given Lanne's body to him and he intended to have it, but Stokell informed him of the premier's orders to him, that the body should not be touched. Doctor Crowther then changed his attitude and invited Stokell to his house to discuss the matter.'

This time it was William's turn to hold his hand up and interject, 'Why would two men argue over something so terrible and then decide to hold a meeting at one of their homes?'

'To get Stokell out of the way.' One of the men answered, angrily. And John bull tapped the table with the point of his finger.

'And pay him to stay out of the way, I'll bet, while the two Crowther's did their dirty work.'

The captain went on, 'The story goes, Stokell arrived at Doctor Crowther's house promptly at eight o'clock, but Crowther wasn't home. His wife had an excuse, that conveniently, no one seems to remember, she explained he wouldn't be long and kept him chatting there for about an hour. During that time, Crowther and his son, Bingham, had entered the hospital's dead house, cut the skin off Billy Lanne's head and removed his skull.' The captain sighed and shook his head at the callousness of the crime, and continued, 'Young Billy's skull had then been replaced by that of an unknown white man and his scalp sewn back up.'

The barman approached the table with another round of drinks and the room went quiet for a while, before John Bull took up the story. 'They then put Billy's head in a bag and threw it over the bloody hospital fence! They knew they couldn't get his whole body out without someone noticing it, so they decided to take his head and come back for the body later.'

The bar seemed to be overtaken by a morbid sadness, these men were tough and had seen many privations and atrocities inflicted on themselves and others, but for an eminent member of Hobart to commit such abominations, and to someone they all knew, was almost unbelievable in this day and age.

'And that's not the whole story,' John Bull went on. 'Apparently, Stokell got scared and told the secretary of the Royal Society, James Agnew, of the mutilation and he then told Morton Allport and John Greaves. They claim they tried to prevent the Crowther's from getting any more body parts by cutting off Billy's hands and feet, AND his scrotum.'

'His WHAT?' Asked Billy, never having referred to his private parts in medical terms.

'His ball bag.' John Bull said sadly. He looked around the room and spoke as if the removal of Billy's manhood was the ultimate insult to the last male full blood Tasmanian aboriginal male on earth. 'They claimed they were keeping them safe from Crowther's clutches, but that's a load of bullshit. They're every bit as corrupt as Crowther, not one of them volunteered to pay towards his funeral expenses, Captain Bayley paid for all that!'

'Bastards!' John Bull spat noisily into the spittoon between the window and the table and took a deep breath. All in the room waited for what could be more news of this sordid affair.

'And this morning,' John Bull said loudly, 'This morning, when the grave digger went to the grave, he was gone!'

'What? They all exclaimed, 'Who was gone?'

'When the premier found out what had been done to Billy, he had two policemen stand guard at the graveside, but someone had sent them home late on Saturday night and when the grave digger arrived at the cemetery at nine the next morning, the grave had been dug up, the coffin exposed and a trail of blood leading to the gate of one of the warehouses of the Anglo Australian Guano Company, which is owned by Doctor Crowther.'

This last comment was obviously an exaggeration as there would hardly be any blood flowing from a three day old corpse which had been thoroughly exsanguinated, still, William couldn't believe it! No story of cannibalism from the islands could be as bloodthirsty as the story they were all witness to right here and now, and this quiet and pretty little city of Hobarton, supposedly full of caring and concerned citizens was moving on as if nothing happened!

This macabre tale of a friend, mutilated by people who claimed for years, they cared for his welfare, and all they were after were his bones!

After shaking hands with his fellow whalers, William walked with captain Bayley to his carriage. As he was about to step up into the carriage, captain Bayley turned to William and spoke, 'You know, William, it won't be long before you will be a master of a ship in your own right, and I wish you well in your endeavor's, you deserve it.' He hesitated, then went on, 'The aboriginal is almost gone, and it will be a long time before people change their attitudes towards half castes as well. At sea, or in the company of seamen, you might be respected in your position, but once you hit this city's streets, to them,' he nodded towards three ladies who had just crossed the street near them. 'You, and those like you, will never be quite human' He shook his head sadly and seated himself in the carriage. 'Mind how you go, William.' And the carriage drove off.

As he walked down the street towards the lodging houses of Wapping, William promised himself never would he allow himself to be taken in by members of the establishment or allow himself cause to rely on the authorities for his care.

That night, he reflected on the sad demise of his friend and recalled how Billy had related the plight of his people to William. 'If they would attack us, then we could defend ourselves, or at least, run away, but they simply ignore us, as if we don't exist, except as a nuisance to them,' Billy shook his head sadly and took another swig from the rum bottle and rolled it around in his hand, before going on, 'they give us all things that are bad.' He sighed heavily. 'My people can't fight back, when they don't know what we're fighting against.'

Both William and Billy had heard of the atrocities committed by both the whites against the blacks and vice versa, but if they believed only half of the rumours that abounded throughout the bars and streets from time to time, then the colony would be in a constant state of war. No, it wasn't the hatred for each other, or even the dislike, it was the indifference, a total disregard for their future and lack of care for the welfare of the family groups, or tribes, from whites and blacks alike. Some black tribes, or individuals, would take advantage of others of their colour with the support of white groups, or individuals, each with a selfish bent in mind, the result being that weaker groups would become more and more disenfranchised. An unintentional, disorganised, destruction of a race that had no idea how to collectively defend itself. William could still hear his friend's words as he had placed his hand on Billy's shoulder in sympathy for his plight. 'I need to go back to Oyster Cove and look after my people.' Billy whispered drunkenly, but William knew he never would.

Offices of the Anglo Australian Guano Company
Salamanca Place
Hobart

William Lodewick Crowther stood at the window of his office and looked out over the new wharf and the river Derwent beyond. The usual hustle and bustle of the waterfront area was his favourite scene, a reminder of the dramatic and modern changes taking place in the little colony. As he concluded each deal, or signed off on a new and successful voyage from one of his ships, he allowed himself the luxury of taking in his favourite scene, watching as the bustle of the wharves and surrounds epitomised man's triumph over adversity within the once poor and decrepit convict settlement.

But the main object of his triumph was not the ships unloading their cargo at the wharf, it was a rapidly disappearing, London bound clipper, Wagoola, her sails blossoming out from her yardarms in time with the white 'bone in her teeth' as the westerly winds took hold and she gathered way down the Derwent.

This would be one of his greatest triumphs, he had beaten Morton Allport, he had beaten George Stokell, and not too far into the future he would beat that upstart, Dry. Allport must have placed the hands and feet in a secure place within the colony, but where? He had no doubt there would be an inquiry, but far from Allport, Stokell, and the Royal Tasmanian Society being able to accuse him of impropriety, by removing the hands and feet from Billy Lanne's corpse, they had hamstrung themselves from demanding answers that would quite possibly incriminate themselves. He had no doubt, Billy Lanne's appendages would reappear sometime in the future and by then he would, have been instrumental in proving to the world, Darwin's theory of evolution. He smiled, safe in the knowledge most people of the colony would be too intent on their own survival to continue dwelling on the events of the past couple of weeks. Certainly, there would be an inquiry, Allport would make sure of that, but he was confident he could weather the storm, and with his position among the people needing medical help within the colony, he had no doubt he would soon be elevated to the position of an eminent man of science within both London and Tasmanian Society, and in death, Billy Lanne would cease to be the unobtrusive black man who disappeared into history without a murmur, instead he would be lauded as the Tasmanian aborigine who proved to be the missing link between modern man and his ancestors.

Deep within the dark hold of the Wagoola, lay row upon row of wooden tuns, each filled with two hundred and fifty six gallons of whale oil bound for the oil markets of London. That is, all except one. One barrel, carefully placed in a far corner row, identical to all other barrels, except for the small, white cross on top and bottom and an identifying number addressed to Sir William Flowers of the London Hunterian Museum.

The cloying smell of tar, timber and whale oil permeated the airless hold, easily disguising the faint, almost imperceptible, hint of surgical spirit, embalming the mutilated body of Billy Lanne in that single tun. The headless torso cradling its own head in its lap as it made its journey into obscurity.

Chapter 26
Somewhere in the South Pacific
1870

William had attained the position of first mate, aboard the Maid of Erin, a tidy little brig, owned by Olaf Hedberg, of Hobart, on the ninth of April, 1870. Mister Hedberg was thinking of taking the Maid of Erin out of whaling, due to poor returns, and offered William the chance to take her to see if he could 'find some fish'. William jumped at the chance to captain his own vessel and after organizing his crew, the 'Maid' set sail for south west cape and Pedra Branca. His trusty Ditty Box, now half full of papers and almost completely lined with slivers of the timbers of the many places he had visited, now took pride of place on the captain's table in the stateroom.

After only two short trips, one of less than fourteen weeks, they had succeeded in stowing sixty three tuns of sperm oil, which had been shipped to London aboard the Wagoola.

On the third, and most successful voyage, the 'Maid' left Hobart on November the sixth, 1871, and with the friendly rivalry that was beginning to grow between the Maid and the Offley, William's old ship, the skipper decided to venture further afield, sailing to the middle grounds between New Zealand and Lord Howe Island and almost all places in between. He would have liked to sail towards his old home, Navigator's Island, but even as the name of his home island had changed, it now being called its original native name, Sa'moa, there would be little left for him after all this time. Besides, the scarcity of whales didn't allow for the luxury of gallivanting about the world searching for your past. He reminded himself that he had a job to do and the owners would be hanging their hats, and their pride, in him bringing home a good haul of oil.

The maid had caught two whales off the north coast of New Zealand, both spermaceti, and with six tuns being cooled in the copper drums alongside each of the trypots, and the remainder stowed in their tuns below deck, she turned and once again headed north, in search of the elusive wisps of vapour that marked the trail of the spermaceti.

Again, the whales surfaced with a regularity that suited William. It wouldn't do for a brig the size of the Maid to be surrounded by the giant sea creatures, with only three boats and a spare, most of the whales in a large pod would be gone to the far corners of the Pacific by the time she had tried out the first two whales. No, it suited William, and the crew, to capture enough spermaceti at a regular rate to make it worth their while, as well as giving the crew a rest from the dangers that abounded in the hunt.

After four months at sea and two and a half thousand gallons of spermaceti aboard, the ship was looking slightly weather beaten. She had not made land for supplies since New Zealand and the men were starting to grumble at the rations of bully beef and weevil infested hard tack. William was in the chart room, which doubled as his cabin, looking for somewhere among all that great expanse of ocean, to secure a port that might supply them with fresh meat and vegetables and hopefully, fresh fruit, to stave of that most dreaded of seaman's disease, scurvy, when the first mate knocked, then entered, 'Beggin' pardon, captain,' The mate said quietly. 'The men have been askin' where we are, and when we might get some fresh food.' He hesitated. He didn't like asking these 'questions of comfort' from the men. Questions that would raise the ire of most captains when they are more engrossed in finding whales, than finding food. But William too, was more than sick of ship's biscuit you had to bang the shit, or at least the weevils, out of, before you dipped them in your tea to soften them lest you break your teeth. He nodded to the mate and picked up the chart from the table. 'Call the crew to the poop deck.' He said, and followed the mate to the steps. Once on deck, he called the men in close and smiled at their uneasiness. Every man knew the station of a seaman was before the mast not aft of the main mast and certainly not on the captain's deck, unless you were the helmsman.

They were not suited to being at this end of the ship, that was obvious, but the captain had wished it, and whatever the captain wishes? Not wanting to hold the chart up to the stiff south easterly breeze lest it be torn from his hands, captain Smith told the men to gather round and form a wind break and he will lead them to fresh food.

The men shook their heads in disbelief that this black man, captain though he was, could point them to land anytime soon, while with their very eyes, they could all see there was nothing that even resembled land, or the ships position on the sea. What they didn't know was that William was trained from a baby to recognize the signs of land and the foibles of navigation in the Pacific Ocean. He laid the chart out on the deck, so all could see, and traced a line with his thumb from the northern most tip of New Zealand to within one hundred miles of Lord Howe Island. 'Gentlemen, he said as he placed his thumb hard down on to the chart just to the left of the island, 'We are here!' He moved his thumb across the chart, towards a tiny speck of ink on the map. 'And by this time tomorrow, we will be here!'

Once again, he drove his thumb hard onto the chart, on the tiny speck on the chart that marked the island. If any man was not convinced, they didn't say, and the first mate smiled as they went back to their stations but secretly, he hoped against hope the captain would be proven right.

Thus, it was when the two large rounded peaks that marked the northern tip of Lord Howe Island hove into view at day break the following day, the men were ecstatic. Captain William Smith had navigated himself into folk lore. The incident with the thumb and the chart, to be told and retold for more than a hundred years to come.

The Maid sailed around the island until she finally found a bay she could navigate and entered in. Putting down both her anchors in the calm blue waters, the crew marveled at the beauty of this place. His memories were very worn, but something about this place reminded William of home. Perhaps it was the beautiful, white, sandy beaches and coves between the rocky headlands. Or was it the low shoreline, gradually rising to green, verdant peaks of lush rain forest and somewhat forbidding valleys.

There were a number of timber huts and what looked like vegetable gardens just off the sandy beach in front of the ship and at least two canoes heading out to greet them, peacefully, he hoped. He needn't have bothered, Lord Howe Island had become a resupply station for ships travelling to Norfolk Island and back to the Australian mainland and after talking to the natives, many of whom could speak at least some English, two boats were put down and William dipped into the cash box and the carpenters tool box to replenish the much needed stores.

The Maid stayed only the one night. Enticing though the calm, crystal clear waters of the bay might be, it was obvious the bay was an open roadstead and it wouldn't do for a sailing ship to be caught on a lee shore in a south easterly blow, William had experienced that before!

With a fully victualled ship and a now happy crew, the Maid of Erin made her way north, around the island or should that be, islands, as there were at least three islands and a series of large rocks, making up the group, and probably more they could not see from the deck of the ship.

She travelled slowly, lines strung from her stern in the hope of a fresh fish supper, before a call from the tops had them hauling in their lines and looking seawards for another whale. But it was not to seaward the crewman in the tops was pointing, it was towards the shore, and when they looked, the crew could see a man running down a very narrow inlet towards the shore, waving his arms frantically.

Cautiously, William had the Maid hove to, and with the northern tip of the island on her windward side, she was almost stopped dead when the yards were turned but still, they were too late. The cove had disappeared as the ship's forward motion obliterated the narrow opening to the beach. William ordered the ship back her sails and she began moving ever so slowly in reverse. The helmsman replied to the captain that he had no control but William held up his hand. He knew they had plenty of water under her keel and a calm sea, apart from the crew needing to keep manipulating the sails, it wouldn't hurt to be uncontrollable for a short time.

The call came from the tops again, 'Man on Beach!' Then, 'Man in water!' The cove had opened up again and they could all see the man wading and reaching out as if he could get to them. William was wary, from here he could see the man was an islander and was obviously running to them for help, he had no obvious weapons, so what was he doing here? The young man dived into a wave and then surfaced again and a memory of when William was a young man frightened and desperate, also surfaced, and he ordered a boat swayed down.

Ordering the lookout to keep an eye for any pursuers to the man, he ordered the second mate into the boat with four other crewmen with two lances between them. No sense going light handed, especially if there did happen to be aggressive islanders. Besides, the practice of black birding had not yet ceased in these parts and William had first hand knowledge of that practice.

The man was still swimming strongly and the boat was almost to him, he was obviously very fit and strong, not unlike himself, mused William as the man lifted himself on his own arms and swung his legs over the gunwale of the whale boat. The men made room for him on the mid thwart and the mate turned the boat back to the ship, giving a wave of his arm to signal William all was in order.

With the Maid under way again, the captain and first and second mates were seated around the chart table in the captain's cabin, maintaining their silence, whilst the man tucked into his first decent meal in months. The man surprised William and both the first and the second mates with his clear spoken English, he explained he was Cabo Verdean, a Cape Verde Islander, his name was Domingo Jose and he had been a harpooner aboard a whale boat that had lanced a whale, and when the whale ran, he had been tipped out of the boat within sight of the island and the boat was taken by the whale in the darkness, he knew not where. He kept swimming all night until he reached the island and washed up in this little cove. The cliffs were far too high to climb and from what he'd seen from the whaleboat, the country was far too rough to walk, and even if he did, he knew there were blackbirder's in the area, and cannibals in the hills behind the cove, he could hear them of a night, as he tried to sleep. Many ships had passed the opening to the cove but with its narrow opening, the ships were too far out to see him.

All he knew of his ship was she was a Nantucket whaler that had picked him up at the Cape Verde Islands off the west coast of Africa, in the Atlantic and he had no wish to go back, 'And anyway, I've been here for over a month now, they would have given me up for dead along ago.'

He stared William in the eye. 'What will become of me?' he asked. Then shot his own question back to the men when he suddenly realised William was the same colour as himself. 'Where are YOU from?'

William was aware he was of the same colour as the man and the question was quite legitimate, given this man had never seen a black Captain of an English whaling ship, or any English ship, in his life!

The parallel to his own experience was not lost on William as he explained to Domingo that he was welcome to work his passage, but before they docked at Hobart, he would have to be a registered member of the crew, otherwise he wouldn't pass customs and would need to go back to either Cape Verde, or Nantucket. Domingo's face dropped and William quickly assured him that Hobart was a long way off and if he was as good a crewman as we think you might be, he would think of something before that time arrived. Another call from the tops came through the jalousie, 'Thar she Blows!' and this time it *was* a whale.

On deck, they could see the whale spout as it broke the surface, a white spurt of warm mist that lingered just above the creature in the light breeze. The ship had well cleared the northern tip of Lord Howe and the south easterly, though lighter than William would have liked in a chase, filled her sails and pushed her along, slightly faster than the whale, a bull spermaceti.

William ordered two boats swayed out and told the mate to be ready with the other two in case another whale showed up. Sperms usually travelled in pods when there were females around, but this one seemed to be a lone male, about forty feet in length and seemingly oblivious to their presence.

The Maid lowered two boats as she drew as near as she could without spooking the whale and William noticed the new man, Domingo, was in the lead boat as harpooner. 'That was quick.' He said to himself.

Already, the crew were lowering the scaffold platform, even before the boats got away from the side of the ship and William could smell the smoke from the tryworks as the fires began to increase in the hearths. He watched the young ship's boy feeding the fires under the direction of the cook and could recall just a few years ago that was himself. It didn't seem so long ago, but a lifetime of living had gone into those few years since the Offley voyages. Anyway, looking over the deck at the crew in their jobs and the second mate barking orders, he was pleased that confidence was high, as the boats pushed off and headed for their prey.

The boats caught up with the whale about a mile distant from the ship, so it was hard to see just what was going on at the kill site, the wind had eased even more and although William had crammed on full sail and what breeze there was, was coming from behind, the crew could feel the Maid was not keeping up with the whale chase.

At the kill site, the first mate's boat had moved alongside the whale and was about to turn at right angles, coming up just in front of the whales left pectoral fin. Sperm whales had smaller pectoral fins than humpbacks, but they were still capable of sweeping a fully loaded whale boat back along its side and under its mighty tail which could deliver a crushing blow, sending the boat and its crew, to eternity.

The second boat, with Domingo at its prow, held back, as the second mate's boat touched the side of the whale and the mate hurled his lance into the back of the whale as close as he could to the blowhole. As the lance dug deep into the thick blubber the whale shuddered and with a downward push of its tail, accelerated to an enormous speed and the mate was catapulted into the boat backwards, unable to use his second lance head. The boat was sliding along the whale's side and under the left pectoral fin as Domingo called to his crew to get closer to the whale, and within seconds had hurled his own lance into the whale's back. By this time, the two boats were being dragged along the side of the whale, banging against each other's gunwales, and the oarsmen that still had their oars, had to ship them aboard, or have them batter their own crews. The lance heads were buried deep and the men were powerless to do anything and the whale lifted its tail high, ready to batter these puny humans to death. Both the mate in the first boat and the oarsmen in the second boat were desperately trying to tie off the lines around the logger heads in the stern in order to avoid being dragged under and crushed by the tail but each man knew they were much too close to the whale. If the whale sounded, and it would certainly do so as soon as it discovered it couldn't reach the boats with its tail, it would sound, diving deep and taking the two whaleboats and the crew's, miles deep beneath the waves. Each man was preparing to abandon the boats as the second boat brushed against the whale's side but instead of jumping over the side, Domingo jumped up onto the whales back and ran along the barnacled covered back of the whale and drove his lance with all his might, deep into the whale's vitals. Instantly, a geyser of blood erupted from the whale's blowhole that could be seen from as far away as the Maid, each man in the boats was blinded by the fountain of blood and waited to feel the bows of both boats being dragged under to their doom. But it never happened. Splashing water on their faces to clear their vision from the continuous spurting of the whale's vital fluids, they could see Domingo, atop the whale, working the lance back and forth in an effort to shred the whale's vital organs, but he needn't have bothered, the whale was dead. Domingo's first thrust with his lance had not only severed the whale's artery it had also penetrated the whale's brain stem, paralysing the leviathan, making it unable to sound.

From the shouts and screams of the panicked men and the banging of oars and gunwales, an eerie quiet came over the scene, the only sound, the watery hiss from the whale's blowhole as the life ebbed from its body and each man listening to his own heartbeat as he thanked his god, and Domingo, for his quick actions that had undoubtedly saved their lives.

By the time the men had collected themselves, and the oars that had been thrown into the water, the maid had almost caught up to them. Ropes were fixed around the tail of the leviathan and both boats began rowing to the maid. There followed a frenzy on the deck and sides of the Maid of Erin, with pink and red smoke roiling through the sails and rigging, reflecting all the flickering lights and shadows, like a giant circus tent on the open sea.

There would be more whales to follow as the Maid worked her way down the middle grounds of the south Pacific Ocean until finally, she arrived at the mouth of the river Derwent. During the voyage Domingo had not only proven himself to be a more than adequate harpooner, he was an exceptional deck hand as well, and William found himself warming to the man. He was not sure whether it was because they were of the same colour or it was simply Domingo's personable nature, but it was certainly the colour that gave William the excuse to get Domingo into Tasmania without him being arrested by customs and William having to explain his actions to Olaf Hedberg, the owner.

William called Domingo to his cabin and had the first and second mate, as well as Domingo, swear that Domingo was, in fact, Domingo Jose Evorall, half brother to William Smith, the captain of the Maid of Erin. Signed affidavits would convince the authorities, and their colour would put paid any likely objections. After all, who knows, or can prove, where these heathens really come from?

The Maid entered into port on October, 27, 1872 after eleven months at sea with ninety tuns of sperm oil, worth approximately six thousand, three hundred English pounds.

On inspection by the port authority, William explained to the authorities that Domingo Jose Evorall was his half brother, and given they were both coloured, and of similar looks, the authorities never questioned the word of a ship's Captain.

Domingo had a new home, as did William, and as they walked along the wharf, looking to find new lodgings as whalemen did, almost every time they came into port after a long trip. After all, there was no point keeping lodgings rented when they would be at sea for up to two years.

The two men were in high spirits as they headed for town, Domingo had borrowed a little suit from William and although hatless, this handsome Cape Verdean looks didn't fail to catch the eyes of two red headed girls, walking with their parents along Castray Esplanade in the opposite direction. William nodded to the parents and doffed his hat to the girls in a cheeky display of introduction. The girls laughed and Domingo, not to be outdone, held his hands up and pointed to the milliner's shop along the street. Motioning them to stay where they were, he ran to the shop, purchased a fedora style hat and ran back to where William Tedman his wife, Mary, their two daughters and William Smith were waiting. As he reached the small group, he stopped and doffed his hat in an overdramatic display of introduction. This well dressed, dark skinned gentleman with a gold earring in his right ear, certainly took the girl's fancy. The girls both laughed, William grinned and even Mister and Mrs. Tedman smiled at the antics of these two friendly islanders.

'Where do you come from?' The eldest girl, Sarah, asked. Domingo answered quickly before William could. 'Tasmania,' He answered, and looked first at William, then back to the girls. 'Domingo Jose Evorall Smith and captain William Henry Smith at your service. We are both Tasmanian, eligible, bachelors.'

This statement caused laughter from all four of the Tedman family and when William invited them to share lunch at the nearest tea room, they accepted.

Mister Tedman neglected to mention he had been a convict, and explained he was a timber worker, more specifically, a splitter. Splitting shingles for roofs and palings for houses and fences, at a place called Recherche Bay.

'I know of that place, I've sailed past it and even anchored there in the Flying Childers.' William stopped short of mentioning the Lallah Rookh, and even his time at Oyster Cove. The feelings of most whites, even those who accepted islanders, rarely extended to aborigines and he didn't think it was worthy of muddying the waters to overexplain his situation. 'It looks to be a beautiful place, from a ship.'

'It is a beautiful place,' Bill's wife, Mary, spoke up. 'And with the timber industry thriving there, they say it will rival Hobart as a city, one day.'

'Some of the biggest trees in the world.' Bill added. 'And plenty of work for two young men who are not frightened of hard work.'

The girls, who had introduced themselves as Sarah and Rosetta, then turned to their father with entreaties of, 'Why don't we show them our place, dad?' 'I'm sure the men would love to see the Bay.' 'This will be the only chance to visit Recherche, they must see it.'

Bill Tedman had a wry grin on his face when he invited the two men to visit their place at Recherche Bay. He knew his daughters were smitten with these two handsome islanders, and they didn't seem to be bad sorts. Who knows, the girls might have found themselves a catch, or two.

The brothers spent four days at Recherche, travelling by ketch, with the Tedman's from Hobart, and seeing the land being opened up in the hills beyond the shores of D'entrecasteaux channel. The channel was calm and peaceful with sandy bays and inlets carved into the shore, very much like his distant memories of Samoa, although William's thoughts turned to Billy Lanne and the atrocities that had been committed against him and his people, as Sarah pointed out the old aboriginal settlement on the shore at Oyster Cove.

It was twenty years since he had walked up to this very shore as a young, frightened, boy, now here he was, captain of a whaling ship and as he caught Sarah looking at him from the corner of her eye, it seemed his life was about to take another turn.

Both William and Domingo thought Recherche was a great place! It was no wonder everyone said it would rival Hobart as the centre of commerce. There were sawmills and sawpits, with logs being split and shaped and sawn by axe, adze and crosscut saws on shore and in the hills around.

Shoe roads, with bullock and horse teams, snaked from the forest to the ends of the wooden tramways that led to the wharves. There, the coastal barges and ketches loaded with billets of timber, plowed to and from Port Davey on the west coast with boat timber for the shipyards of the Huon and Derwent Rivers, to the north. Huge hardwood trees that sometimes were so big, it would take teams of men, days just to fall them, and when they were down, men would swarm over them, driving wedges and chocks into the cracks with heavy hammers, in an effort to split them and scale them down to at least be manageable for the tramways and sawmills to handle them.

The men both noticed that work had begun on a post office, three stores and the Domeney's had begun to build a boarding house on the shore, in a place the girls called pigsties bay, and least three more sawmills and talk of steam sawmills, were under construction. It was a thriving community, just as Sarah and Rosie had said.

There were a number of white, sandy beaches with crystal clear waters lapping their shores between the rocky bluffs, most of them with wharfs and rickety piers with men either loading or unloading timber, or repairing boats and nets, and although they discovered they would have to walk a distance to find a secluded bay that suited them, this never deterred the foursome as they swam and dived into the waves being generated by the ketches going past

The couples paired off and swam and dived the reefs and beaches for shipwreck treasures and shell fish. The temperature of the water, although not as cold as it could get, was far colder than the two men were used to, especially Domingo, but in the spirit of bravado, they would never let on to the girls that the goosebumps that covered their skin might be the result of their being unused to handle the cold Tasmanian waters.

More than once, William caught the others looking at the caul pouch that hung on the leather thong around his neck and was ready for the questions that he knew for sure would be asked. The skin of the caul had hardened and tanned over the years and he had to reluctantly replace the leather thong at least twice. Once, as his neck grew in his teenage years and again when the leather had frozen that many times in the voyage to Heard's island, it had begun to chafe his skin. But it was the outline of the coin that had formed an imprint through the skin of the caul as the weight of ropes, crates, barrels and timber pressed against his chest in the course of his work, that had the question asked by sailors and townspeople alike. 'What is that around your neck, William?' The same question that Sarah asked now.

William explained to the other three of the circumstances of the caul and after each had felt the outline of the silver coin, Rosie stood back and spoke. 'Well, here we have two dark, mysterious, gentlemen, one with a silver coin around his neck, and the other with a gold ring in his ear lobe!' The two girls laughed, and Rosie went on. 'You always said you would like to meet a mysterious, dark gentlemen, Sarah, and now we have both met one each and THEY couldn't be more mysterious!'

It was time for all four of them to laugh, but neither William, nor Domingo volunteered any further information about their past, they decided their position as stateless islanders was still precarious in this young colony, and more information would have to wait until later.

After four days, the men said their goodbyes amid promises to visit the next time their ship came in. They thanked Bill and Mary Tedman for their hospitality and boarded a ketch to Hobart.

Chapter 27

17th July, 1873
Hobart, Tasmania

William met Olaf Hedberg at the agent's offices and was disappointed when Mister Hedberg advised him that, although William had two very profitable voyages that he was most grateful for, the Maid was in sore need of a refit and he was even thinking of fitting her out as a cargo vessel, Tasmania was becoming more productive as a colony and there were a great many goods that required larger ships than the coastal ketches could handle. He apologised to the men, he did, however, introduce both William and Domingo to Captain Copping, whom William had met before.

Captain Copping informed them he was offered the position of Captain of the Othello and invited William to be his first officer. William accepted on the proviso that Domingo Jose Evorall would be second officer. Captain Copping, knowing, as all whaling ship's captains did, that a good crew was the key in productive whaling and having heard of their reputation in the Maid of Erin, readily agreed, and together with a crew of twenty four, they proceeded to the south seas in search of the great cetacean.

The captain had agreed to follow in the path of the last voyage of the Maid of Erin, and the ship shaped a course for the south west cape of Tasmania. The Othello made a beautiful sight as she passed Recherche Bay and the men stood in the stern of the ship, near the wheel, hoping to catch sight of the girls. The men wondered if the Tedman family were aware they would be on the ship. They knew that any news from Hobart would travel fast in the tiny community of the channel area and any one of the tiny cutters or yawls could have passed on the news of their being aboard the Othello.

The ship had opened up the bay and was about to clear fisher's point at the western end of Recherche Bay when a small cutter steered out from the land and almost into the path of the Othello. Although well clear of the ship, the cutter was almost abeam when William spotted both Sarah's and Rosie's red hair. Although they couldn't make out their facial features, at this distance, there was no mistaking that fiery red hair of the Tedman girls, and both men waved and cheered as the Othello began to draw away from the little cutter that had the two girls waving madly as they recognised William and Domingo.

For five weeks, the Othello cruised the grounds of South West Cape until it became clear the whales had moved on. Captain Copping then shaped a course for New Zealand and agreed to follow the Maid's course to the middle grounds.

Day after day, the Othello moved through the waters of the Southern Ocean, sailing along the north coast of New Zealand, before turning north. In almost the same position where the Maid caught her whale, almost within sight of Domingo's cove, the lookout sighted another sperm whale. The boats were lowered, and with William in one, and Domingo in the other, the first whale caught was text book whaling. The captain hove to alongside the forty five foot leviathan and the flenser's began their gory task. Carefully, the whale's head was removed and lifted into the ship. But not before William and Domingo had bailed the spermaceti out of the head case. With the whale firmly anchored to the side of the ship, the junk, that part of the head just behind the case, was cut away from the body and lifted over the gunwale and onto the ship. The junk was like a honeycomb, with hundreds of large pores and cavities filled with oil, the instant it was lifted, the weight of the junk itself, forced the oil out through the pores in the flesh and bone, bringing much cursing from the men as they slipped and slid in the oil, trying desperately to stop as much of the greasy substance as possible from oozing onto the deck and being lost.

The rest, commonly called the body, was then left to the flensers to do their work. It was just as the flensers were about to start, when a call came from the top's 'Thar she Blows.' Immediately, the deck became a frenzy of men running and climbing over the long strips of blubber to hook into larger strips and haul them over the rail. Boys were busy trying to keep the fires in the hearth from getting too hot and burning the oil whilst being yelled at to hurry up and get the trypots cleared to make room for more. William and Domingo were already in the boats that were still in the water, alongside the rapidly disappearing carcass of the first whale and men were climbing across the carcass as they tried to get into the boats, slipping and sliding as they did so, with the Othello beginning to get under way again.

Over it all, Captain Copping stood immobile alongside the helmsman, then realising they were short of men, he motioned for the helmsman to join the deck crew, and took the wheel himself.

The whales were about two miles distant, dead ahead. The scaffold was hauled clear of the whale and both William and Domingo pulled to the front of the carcass and tied on to the ladders that hung down the side of the ship. The ship was listing under the drag of the whale carcass and William climbed out of his boat and began cutting the whale clear. Domingo motioned to two other men to do the same and the carcass began sliding along the ship's side as the Othello began to make way.

By the time the carcass had cleared the stern, it was already under water and sinking fast. A brief nod from the captain told everyone he was satisfied they had recovered all of the oil they would get from that whale, and it was on to the next, but it was not to be.

The whales had sounded and resurfaced so far away, it was clear to all the Othello could not catch them with the two whale boats dragging alongside. The captain called to heave to and complete the trying out of the whale that still covered the deck with its bones and blubber. The solitary whale yielded ten tuns of oil and it was a case of what should have been, on the way down through the latitudes towards Tasmania without sighting a single whale, until they reached Recherche Bay on Christmas eve, 1873.

Great excitement prevailed in the Tedman household as the barque moved slowly up the channel, children ran along the shoreline and out along the piers and wharves, to wave as the Othello made her way into the bay. A whaling barque was a common sight in the channel as the big ships passed by from Hobart to the whaling grounds, but not so common was the sight of one of these one hundred and fifty foot monsters, made all the larger in full sail, as she made her way into Recherche Bay, turning to port as she came past pigsties bay and furling all her sails as she came abreast of Adams point. With her yardarms turned and both anchors let go, taking care to keep pearl rock well off her starboard beam, the captain declared her snugged down and the crew made preparations for revictualling.

With the ship at a complete stop, William and Domingo climbed the shrouds until they reached the lookout. The view was breathtaking and without the pressure of having to sight whales, the men could take their time to scout out their surroundings. To the east, they could see far beyond pigsties bay to a strip of gleaming white sand and what looked to be a lagoon beyond that. The Actaeon islands stood out from the shore further out, and in the distance, Bruni Island rose from the sea to form the eastern side of the D'entrecasteaux channel.

To the west, South East Cape formed the final barrier against the prevailing westerly winds that could devastate even the largest of the world's navies, should the roaring forties escalate to their worst. Even here, in Recherche, the Othello would have no choice but to make sail and run for the safety of ports further north and captain copping knew he would not be taking any chances with the fickle weather in these parts. He would get all supplies aboard and have the crew stay aboard, to prevent any deserters leaving the ship in a vulnerable state in the event of a blow.

To the north, the huge mountains and walls of giant forest gave the impression of Recherche Bay being an oasis between the edge of impenetrable forest and equally impenetrable ocean, with access to the outside world and civilization only by the narrow channel of water between Bruni Island and the mainland and totally reliant for the means of life, on the little ketches and watercraft that plied these waters.

From their lofty perch, the men could see the townspeople gathering on the shore and the piers that dotted the white, sandy beach, and it didn't take them long to identify two shocks of flowing red hair, standing in a small ketch, holding on to the mast as the little craft made its way towards the ship.

The Ripple same alongside the Othello and the genial captain Copping welcomed Rosie and Sarah aboard. Once over the rail, William and Domingo took them by the arm and led them away from the hustle and bustle of resupplying the ship.

Normally, it was the job of the first and second mate to organize the resupply, but captain Copping was aware of his mate's interest in these two young ladies and volunteered to organise the resupply himself.

In the relative quiet of the bows near the foc'sle jalousie, the girl's invited the men for Christmas dinner at the Tedman's, explaining they had already booked two rooms at Mrs. Domeney's boarding house. The men had to break the sad news that no one was allowed on shore, as the ship would be leaving for the great Australian bight whaling grounds at first light in the morning.

The girl's faces dropped. 'But it's Christmas.' Sarah held her hands clasped in front of her, whilst looking towards the poop deck where captain Copping was directing the resupply. 'Surely the captain will let you have one night off?'

Rosie broke in. 'What if we invite the captain too?' She asked. 'He can stay ashore and we can bring you back to the ship straight after lunch.' She lifted her arms in triumph as if she had solved the problem, but William shook his head. 'Sorry girl, but by the time we get everything stowed away, there will be just a short sleep and we'll have to get the ship under way.'

All the plans the girls had made since they saw the ship coming into the bay, dissolved into despair, to lighten the moment of sadness, Domingo broke in. 'We shouldn't be gone too long, this trip is half way through.' He drew a deep breath and went on. 'What if we have a really good trip and we come back and ask you to get married,' The girl's stared at him, shocked, as if he was trying to make light of a very serious situation. Sarah looked at William. 'Do you mean that?' William didn't know what to say. He looked accusingly at Domingo for talking too much, but when all was said and done, marriage to this girl certainly wasn't the worst thing that could happen to him. He grinned. 'Why not?' he asked. Then he added. 'But it could be a while, and what if we don't have a good trip?' He looked at Domingo as if to disclaim his brother's statement, but Domingo shrugged his shoulders, and in an effort to placate Sarah and Rosie, went on in his usual, inimitable, Cabo Verdean style. 'We have love, now all we need is luck, and we can all be happy.'

'Is this a proposal?' Both of the girls asked, not sure whether to believe the two men or not.

'Only if we can afford it.' William answered, and Domingo nodded.

'Like I said, Domingo replied. 'If we have luck with the rest of the trip, and we come home with plenty of oil,' he shrugged again, 'Then we would be in a position to ask your parents for your hands in marriage,' He shrugged again, 'Why not?'

The girls still didn't know what to think. They looked back and forth from each other to the men.

'Well then,' Rosie said, at length. 'We will just have to rely on luck, won't we?'

The girls were still disappointed the brothers weren't coming for dinner, and they would have to cancel the rooms at Mrs. Domeney's but, on the possible proposal of marriage, the wait might just be worth it.

Sarah and Rosie stayed aboard the Othello until the very last boat was leaving for the shore. Then, as they reached the rail, they each held their hands up to the men's lucky charms, Sarah grabbing first William's hand in hers before placing both their hands around the caul on the leather thong around William's neck and Rosie rubbing Domingo's earring between her thumb and forefinger. 'You will have luck! You will have luck! You will have very good luck!' they exclaimed together, as the crewman from the ripple reached out and held their hands in turn as they stepped down the gangplank.

Chapter 28

Recherche Bay
December 25th
1873

By the time the sky in the east over Bruni Island turned grey with the dawn, the Othello was already moving out of Recherche Bay, towards Fishers Point and open sea.

She would sail for five days without seeing a whale of any description, and although the proposal of marriage had been a secret between them, everyone knew there would be no secrets kept aboard a deck of just one hundred and thirty feet long and twenty seven, gossip starved, men.

The crew had kept shtum until each and every one was fully aware of William and Domingo's promise, then the good natured jibes came thick and fast. And that was fine with the brothers, but after three months of cruising the waters off western Australia, with a dearth of whales sighted, the good natured jibes began to turn into taunts, with one crew member suggesting the girls had cursed the voyage with their antics and they would forever be wandering the seas until the brothers could fulfil their promise. Domingo was about to put him in his place, threatening to 'shake him till he rattled' both men knowing that any violence would be met with harsh penalties for both of them, until William intervened.

William offered to take bets on the question of whether the Othello would stow whales or not and the crewman, put on the spot by his own words, had no option but to bet a portion of his 'lay' which was one, one hundred and fiftieth of the profit from the catch. Over the coming weeks as the empty sea provided the rest of the crew with more confidence, and believing they would have nothing to lose if the voyage was a failure, the crew began to place bets with William and Domingo, to the point where the two islanders, if they lost the bets, would not only lose the chance of marriage but would be in debt for a considerable amount of their lives. Captain Copping was aware of the bets and called William aside. 'To resolve this incident, and dissolve the bad blood, not just between the crew, but to your betrothed as well, William, YOU HAVE to find me some whales.'

William went to the chart room and took the relevant map to the deck and pored over it. There was silence on the deck as each man from the captain to the cook, pretended not to be interested in what the Samoan was thinking, as he ran his hands over the charts. As seamen, superstition was the controlling nature of these men. Being uneducated and ignorant of the sciences, and certainly lacking in godliness, it could take only a few words of a disgruntled crewman to foment an argument, or even a mutiny. In their reasoning, there had to be a cause of luck, whether it be good or bad, and at the moment, theirs was bad.

William took a gamble and approached the captain. 'There is no life here, captain,' he said, flatly. 'We need to go where the big birds are, or at least, where they've been.'

'Where they've been?' captain Copping questioned. William spoke of the frigates and albatross that wing endlessly over the oceans, searching for the food columns that rise from the deepest depths, providing an abundance of food for every sea creature imaginable. 'We've been chasing whales and as long as we're chasing them, we are never going to catch them. He stared the captain in the eye. 'We have to get in front of them, and let them catch us.'

Captain Copping nodded in agreement. What William was saying made sense, he knew the whales, sperm whales in particular, fed in the deep water about one hundred and sixty miles off the continental shelf, in over fifteen hundred fathoms. The giant squid they feasted on followed the food column from that depth to the surface and if the whales had to come up for air, then that's where they would surface.

William had two men in the lookout sighting for birds, any birds at first, then the petrels, gannets and albatross that would signal a food column. Once sighted, the Othello would clap on all sail and get in front of the columns of smaller fish and seabirds and hopefully meet the whales head on as they moved throughout the Australian bight.

It was just two days later, the call came from the tops, signaling the arrival of two albatross' and the crew stood at the rail and watched as these solitary birds dipped and swooped gracefully, barely clearing the wave tops as they made their way north. The helmsman was given his orders to follow them and the Othello took up the pursuit. Many times, the birds flew out of sight but managed to return to swoop around the ships stern and move off once again, as if, like a sheep dog in trials, directing the barque and herding it where it needed to go.

For four days and nights, the Othello travelled in a straight line and when dawn broke on the fifth day, the lookouts hadn't even reached their post when the call came.

As William and Jose came on deck the Othello was surrounded by seabirds and seals, a million whitecaps from the stiff southerly breeze, and whales! William didn't wait for the captain's orders, he knew what he would want and ordered the boats swayed out. All four boats were swayed out in their davits and began dropping towards the water. There was no need to heave to or change direction, as the Othello must have passed the whale pod in the night and the whales were just astern of the ship and travelling at the same speed. There seemed to be dozens of them, and the boat steerers hardest job was deciding which whale to go for, as the harpooners rose to their feet in the bows of each whaleboat and prepared to launch their lances.

Captain Copping was bracing himself against the wheel and holding it steady with one hand, whilst craning his neck to see what was happening astern of the ship. Some of the whales were so close and there were so many of them, he could smell the stinky vapour as it was blown high though their blowholes.

Two of the boats were running now, each had lanced their whale and he could easily make out the harpooners changing places with the steersmen, the latter running the warp around the loggerhead and letting it run through the block under pressure, trying to slow the whale. By this time, he could see the other two whale boats had also lanced their whales and were doing the same. He ordered the topsails blown and the yards turned, slowing the ship to the same pace as the lanced whales. No point in getting too far ahead of her own boats, besides, four whales was excellent catching and there would be a lot of work trying out before she could get under way again.

With the fires in the tryworks lit for the first time in months, the Othello sat with two whales either side of her and lookouts still pointing to the pod moving away in the distance.

Captain copping was ecstatic and called over the loud hailer to all the men working, to remind them he was making a note in the slop's chest that the bets the naysayers laid against William would be honoured from the lays of each man that laid a bet. There were some grumbles among the crew but with oil bubbling in the trywork cauldrons and the knowledge they were at least going to get paid, and possibly, if William's good luck held, it would seem the marriages were back on.

Captain Copping was a smart man, he was aware it was not all about honour, he knew these men would remember for a long time to come, the time they lost wages because of their mistrust in the captain and the mate, and hopefully their punishment would serve to remind them to have faith in the hierarchy of the ship and the talents of the captain.

All night the smoke roiled from the tryworks, up through the rigging and furled sails, to be swept away by the southerly wind, and by morning the four whales had been tried out and the oil cooled and funneled into the lower deck. The cooper had complained to the captain over the breakfast, about the lack of materials to build more tuns, 'We've probably got enough staves for about fifty tuns, captain, no more.'

'If running out of barrel staves is a problem, mister cooper,' The captain laughed. 'Then it's a bloody good problem to have!' 'Now then, William and Domingo, get some sleep and I'll have a look out posted for more of your whales, William.'

As William and his brother climbed into their bunks, Domingo turned to the other man. 'Do you realise, William, we are going to get one fiftieth of the lay each, as well as guaranteed payment of the bets laid against you,' He paused. 'If we get enough whales to fill those last tuns, we are going to be rich men.' He laughed. 'Rich, married, men!'

The Othello cut westward across the great Australian bight, keeping in the deep water and off the continental shelf and encountered the whales on two more occasions. She spoke to the whaler, Flying Childers, on the twentieth of March, 1874, and reported forty eight tuns stowed and running out of staves for tuns. She would need to return to Hobarton.

The Flying Childers returned to Hobart, and on passing Recherche Bay relayed the message that the Othello was having a successful voyage. At the Tedman's house this news was received with much glee and excitement and preparations were begun for the ship's return.

After spending two days washing down at Barnes Bay in the river Derwent, and then to the new wharf for offloading, Captain Copping suggested William and Domingo get lodgings close to ship so they might get cleaned up and rid themselves of the cloying smell of burning blubber and whale oil. He also informed them of the Othello going to McGregor's slipway for a refit, so they had plenty of time for a wedding to happen, if it was going to. The men agreed, a good bath and scrub up was in order, but as they were coming down the gangplank onto the wharf, an excited squeal arose from the other end of the pier.

It was the Tedman girls, and although they weren't running, for it wouldn't do for young ladies to run into a man's arms in public, they were certainly walking fast. More than slightly embarrassed at not having properly cleaned up for the occasion, although they were acceptably attired, William and Domingo pretended to be indifferent, and the girls slowed to a walk as they approached. Then, just as the girls got within a few steps of them, the men each suddenly dropped down on one knee and removed their hats in preparation of asking their hand in marriage.

Bill Tedman and his wife stood back while the couples hugged and kissed, then graciously accepted the men's request for their blessing.

Both couples were married in a double ceremony on the 30th of September, 1874, in the congregational church in Burnett Street in Hobart, Tasmania. And where would two half caste islanders take their wives to honeymoon, why Recherche bay, of course.

With their payment for this voyage of forty five pounds and ten shillings each, plus more than ten pounds in betting money their unfortunate crew members had grudgingly relinquished, the men, together with their wives, boarded a ketch for Recherche.

The four had booked into Mrs. Domeney's boarding house at Bennett's point, and during long walks, picnics on the rocky beach at quiet cove and pony and trap rides, courtesy of Mister Domeney, planned their futures.

Each day, when the boat was available, the foursome would board Mister Domeney's boat, the Ripple, and travel across the bay to the sandy beaches of Cockle Creek. It was whilst picnicking near the mouth of Cockle Creek, Sarah noticed two men surveying blocks of land along the foot track, with the somewhat grandiose name of Esplanade, west of the mouth of the creek. When asked, the men said they were surveying land for mister Bolton, a well known land and mill owner in the district.

Sarah asked just what it would cost to have a plot of land surveyed, and the man replied, 'Why don't you ask him yourself?' and pointed to a fellow entering the esplanade from the bush beyond.

John Bolton was an entrepreneur who owned land in Recherche and settlements along the D'entrecasteaux channel. Mister Bolton could see the potential in the area around Recherche, and was keen to see families move in and begin to develop the area.

Both he and mister Domeney were very keen to see new families buy and settle into the district and although it was some distance from Bennett's point, requiring a boat trip across the bay, the blocks of land at Cockle creek were cheaper and, according to mister Domeney, it wouldn't be too long before the whole foreshore of Recherche Bay, including the settlements of Leprena and Catamaran would be one small city. Sarah's enthusiasm was infectious and by the time the afternoon was over, William and Sarah's new address, minus their house, was a five acre, double block at Esplanade, Recherche, facing across the bay, past Mott's beach to Domingo Evorall's block, on the point that would be forever known as Evorall's Point.

Neither Sarah or Rosetta, or their parents, could read or write, and there being no schools of government offices in the area, William, still aware he was officially an illegal citizen, and fearful that if some office johnny in Hobarton checked on his ownership of land whilst not registered as a legal citizen, they might risk losing their property and all they owned. Unlike Domingo, with his devil may care attitude, William was a careful man and concocted a plan for Sarah to bring the papers to him to check and make sure everything was in order, then she would buy the land in her name, a common practice in the young colony. And so it was, that the land was entered into her name and remained in the name of Sarah A. Smith until many years after they both died.

William and Domingo continued to serve as first and second mate respectively, aboard the Othello and helped her become known as the 'Luckiest Whaler of that season,' taking ninety tuns of whale oil, worth more than nine thousand English pounds in that year of high oil prices, and on the fourth of March, eighteen seventy six, William placed his certificate of 'master of foreign grade ships' in the Ditty Box atop the deeds to the land in Recherche, his references from Olaf Hedberg and Edward Copping, and other papers he had gathered over the years, before he and Domingo went to join his new ship, the whaling barque, Marie Laure.

Chapter 29

Henry Street,
Strahan, Tasmania
1939

The old woman smiled as the tiny grandchild at her side fell asleep, still clutching the whale's teeth, one in each hand. It was the name that almost caused her to choke as she was telling Wacky the story. Although she often thought about it, she hadn't spoken that name in almost fifty years and when she mentioned it, it was if someone else had spoken the words. She whispered it softly to herself, 'Marie Laurie.' Many people mispronounced the name, calling the ship, Marie Lorrie, instead of the correct pronunciation, Marii Lowery, the name of some long forgotten Scottish maiden. But Mary Ann would never forget the name of the most beautiful ship in the world, a ship she spent the first four years of her life, learning how to walk on her rolling decks, with her father, the Samoan, laughing at her struggles to stand, scooping her up into his strong, dark arms as the green sea rolled over the ship's bulwarks and out through the scuppers, bragging to everyone how she had no fear and was as brave as any seaman he had ever known. She remembers snuggling into his thick, woolly, coat as the freezing winds of Dutch Harbour whipped ice flurries off the water, and waking in her gimballed crib, the ship's carpenter had constructed for her. She vaguely remembered the warm sunshine streaming through the sails as the Marie Laurie passed through the islands of the tropics and remembered vividly the stories her father and uncle Domingo told of her father passing her on to the back of the giant sperm whale, while she tried to hold onto the gigantic wooden box, he gave her. She recalled her childhood days of swimming and fishing after school at Recherche. As well as the first and last wedding to ever take place in Recherche at the newly built Congregational Mission Hall, just a week after the hall opened and just two weeks after her eleventh birthday, in eighteen eighty nine, and just a month after her poor sister, Sarah Jane was born. Mary Ann could recall it as if it was just yesterday. All the ladies, most of the men, and certainly all the children in the area were present at the marriage of mister Mark Clark to Ethel, the only daughter of mister Oldham, the sawmill foreman. Newspapers ran the story of this thriving area of the state and with whaling, sawmilling, coal mining and fishing providing work for all of its young men, the sun certainly shone on Recherche that year.

Where did it all go? Mary Ann lay in the dark, listening to the breathing of the only precious thing left in her life, her granddaughter. She loved her children dearly, but they had all grown and moved away, the only thing she had to tie her to a past that had already faded away, was this small work box, a pair of whale's teeth and, she smiled, a girl that seemed to love them and her memories, as much as she did. Unfortunately, with the good comes the bad, and as if some unseen power decided that life was just too good in their tiny world, it all seemed to come crashing down.

She couldn't recall the death of her brothers, William Domingo, at age five, although she vaguely remembers the sadness that pervaded their lives, and after Thomas Alexander and William Domingo died tragically from scarlet fever, less than one day apart, never really seemed to leave them.

Just one year after the hall was built, her sister would die of unknown causes at only six months of age and although her mother had another seven children, including herself and Jim, she never seemed to get over little Sarah Jane's death and her dad never spoke about it, although she often caught him in a quiet moment softly rubbing the caul between his thumb and forefinger as a tear trickled down his cheek.

She had never even given a thought to the fact she was black, the kids from Recherche played together regardless of the colour of their skin and it wasn't until she was twenty two years old that she was even aware she was different to some of the other people of the area.

Her world had suffered a cataclysmic blow that day in eighteen ninety eight, on a day that seemed like any other. She had gone for a swim off the pier near Planter's beach and was waiting for her thick, dark, curly hair to dry in the sun, before walking home.

She had watched the fishing boat pull into the pier where she sat, watching the seagulls crowding around the mast and stern of the boat in such numbers, she wondered how they managed to avoid each other in the maelstrom of wings and feathers. The man stood on the gunwale of the boat, painter in hand and not holding onto anything but his balance as the little craft drifted slowly into the wharf. He stepped lightly from the gunwale onto the wharf as the boat bumped gently against the timbers. 'Hello,' He called to Mary Ann. 'You live around here?' She replied by waving her hand in the direction of the houses along the esplanade, behind a thicket of trees. 'Over there.' She got up to go and realised he had made up the distance between them in a few short steps.

'Would you like a job?' He asked, and she turned to face him. 'My name's Harold Glover, and I've got a hold full of fish that needs cleaning, and I can't do it alone.'

The old lady screwed her eyes shut, trying not to remember that part of her life and the horror that followed as she innocently went to help, with the promise of pay, only to be punched to the deck of the boat and repeatedly raped until the man, Harry Glover, had finished, and then added insult to injury as he pushed her onto the pier, telling her to 'Get off my boat, you black bitch,' and calmly stepped back on to his boat and sailed away.

Mary Ann recalls how she half staggered, half ran, down the dusty track and stumbled into her mother's arms inside the kitchen of their weatherboard house and her mother's screams of anguish when she told her what had happened. With her father away at Port Davey, Constable Driscoll was sent for and within days, the fisherman was arrested and held at the Port Huon police station. She recalled constable Driscoll talking with her mother at the kitchen door, their voices were kept low to avoid her overhearing that Glover had claimed the sex was consensual and given she was only a black girl with no witnesses, it was unlikely any charges could be proven. Her mother nodded and saw the constable out, before collapsing to the kitchen floor and sobbing hysterically as her daughter tried to console her.

The trauma of her ordeal was exacerbated when the throes of morning sickness began to intrude on her life and nine months later Lydia Lucy Isobell Smith was born. She would be three years old when Mary Ann married an old friend, Harry Doherty, who adopted Lydia as his own. It finally occurred to her that if she had been a white, English girl, then Glover would have certainly gone to jail for a very long time, but her dad being half caste, regardless of his standing in the whaling community, relegated her to being the daughter of a half caste, and not quite human.

She reached out and took the whale's teeth from her granddaughter's hands and placed them on the table near the bed. She lay back on her pillow with a sigh and tried to remember happier times.

Chapter 30

Port Davey,
Tasmania, 1877

William had been offered the job of chief officer of the whaling barque, Flying Childers, captained by Alexander MacGregor, a well known ship owner and trader of Hobarton.

The Flying Childers was a three boat ship, named after a famously undefeated race horse and had herself, developed a reputation as a thoroughbred in whaling circles.

She had caught a *'twelve tunner'* whale off the west coast of Tasmania and was moving, albeit very slowly, into the bay at Port Davey. With the whale lashed alongside, she moved towards Breaksea Island, at the mouth of the Davey Channel, before turning to port and moving up into Payne Bay and letting go her anchors.

Captain McGregor had seen the dark clouds forming to the north and had guessed a storm was brewing. William had tapped the barometer in the chart room and pursed his lips as the needle dropped suddenly to almost nine hundred and forty millibars. He climbed the steps up to the deck and informed the captain, before ordering the three planked platform to be swung down onto the whale, and kicking off the special leather boots most whalemen used to walk safely on the barnacled covered skin of the whales back. He reached into the hole cut in the whale's head and began bailing the spermaceti from the head and passing it up to the men on the platform. Already, the flensers were at work, they too could feel the motion of the waves turning from a light westerly push to an oily calm, 'the calm before the storm' the old sailors say.

The case empty, the crew began cutting the head and lifting it over the rail, while the deck boys swept up the oil that oozed from the hundreds of tiny cavities in the flesh and bone of the junk and fed it into the trypots.

Captain MacGregor was keeping a weather eye out, and although there were no men in the crosstrees, as all hands were engaged in getting the whale tried out, both William and the captain could imagine the storm activity that was bearing down on the little settlement, from the north west.

With the deck squared away and only the cleanup in progress, the whale carcass was cut free and the 'Childers' moved up to the head of Payne Bay, a safe berth in all weathers except hard southerlies.

The wind, when it did come, was a stiff gale from the north west, which caught them by surprise and had the ship dragging both anchors to rest on a sandy bottom just off the eastern shore of Payne Bay. Undeterred, captain MacGregor had reckoned that the squall, stiff though it was, would blow itself out in a day or so, and to be sure, ordered the foremast and mains yards be sent down in an effort to halt the wind resistance these huge baulks of timber and sails could create under the wind. He also ordered all the crew, except himself, William Smith, the chief officer and four hands, to shore. This done, and with the vessel quiet, the crew and the people of Port Davey settled down to wait for the weather to ease, so that they might refloat the ship that had served them so well. It seemed luck was on their side when the Maid of Erin, William's old ship, sailed on up the bay and dropped anchor in the lee of the western shore. Captain Curphey of the Maid and MacGregor were good friends and no doubt the capstans of the maid would turn the Childers into deeper water as soon as the weather cleared.

For seven days they waited, before a boat was put down from the Flying Childers and ferried captain MacGregor, William Smith and the four crewmen, ashore. The captain warned the barometer had signaled an impending storm and advised no work could be done until the weather cleared. William and two men took a boat out to the Maid of Erin and advised Captain Curphey of the impending storm. Curphey informed them he was aware of the barometer's reading but assured them the maid was well snugged down and safe where she was and would be better suited to be close handy at the first sign of a break in the weather as soon as the storm had passed.

The storm, when it did come, was far fiercer that any of them thought it would be, a screaming northwesterly gale that tore sheets of spray from the lee of Kelly Basin and hurled it into the rigging and into the faces of the deck crew. Captain Curphey stood at the watch until four o'clock in the afternoon of the twenty sixth, then shaking his head at the sheer ferocity of the storm, he ordered a second anchor let go. 'No sense waiting until she starts to drag, mister mate,' He yelled above the wind. 'Might as well bed her down comfortably and hope that bloody wind doesn't swing too hard to the south.' He knew that, even in this gale, the north and western shores of Payne Bay would give enough degree of shelter to prevent the ship from dragging anchor, and even if that did happen, the wind break provided by the western shore would be enough for the Maid to get under way and sail back across the bay to the shelter of the furiously waving trees on the western shore. But the south was an open roadstead, the only resistance to a southerly wind was a low line of hills about ten miles away, providing no shelter at all, for their position. He was only too aware that should the howling gale beating down on them from the west, swing and come from the south, they could be in real trouble. With nothing but surf and shore behind and on both sides, the Maid would have no option but to rely solely on her anchors holding firm, and try to ride the storm out. An option he did not relish.

With seventy five fathoms of cable on her starboard anchor and thirty on her port, the Maid seemed to be riding comfortably and captain Curphey retired to his quarters.

At three am, he was called up by the watch and as he climbed to the wheel house and looked blearily out on to the scene before him, his worst fears were realised.

The Maid no longer had her head high to the west. Instead, she was riding heavily, plunging deep into the troughs coming up the bay from the south. The wind had shifted and was increasing. 'Get all hands dressed and ready for work.' He said, calmly, almost jokingly, and the seaman spun on his heel and disappeared down the hatchway.

The captain noticed the helmsman eyeing him nervously and he grinned. The seaman relaxed noticeably. 'Pretty stiff blow, sir. The Helmsman said, squinting his eyes as he tried to see through the blackness to the point where the anchor cables disappeared over the bows. 'She should be alright, though, eh?' It was more a question than an observation, and even the captain felt his stomach tighten with apprehension as they each felt the sickening jolt of the ship as she snapped back on her cables, waiting for that feeling of helpless terror as the anchors tore free of the bottom and allowed the ship to turn on her beam ends to the mercy of the waves.

But the anchors held, the Maid riding high and tearing at the straining cables like a rebellious dog at an uncomfortable leash. Before plunging deep into the troughs behind, tons of water cascading over her bows and flooding across her deck.

Within minutes, the crew had mustered in the wheelhouse, awaiting the captain's orders. Each and every man aware of their precarious position, each and every man bracing themselves, tensing as the ship jerked and tossed, each and every man willing the anchor cables to hold fast, then relaxing as she straightened up for the next briny onslaught.

'Well lads,' The captain grinned, 'There's little we can do until daylight, we'll just have to sit it out and see what we can do then.'

The three hours until daylight seemed like an eternity, and even though not one man ventured out on deck, all were tired and sore from the strain of trying to stay upright and alert in the tiny wheelhouse, daylight itself giving little solace to the frightened crew as the true horror of their predicament was revealed.

During the night, the Maid had shifted, slowly inching her way across the bay until her anchors had found rocky bottom, exposing her to the full force of the terrible tempest that tore into Port Davey on that terrible day in Eighteen Seventy Seven.

The seas in the normally calm anchorage had become very heavy, the cold southerly gale dragging the caps off the waves and turning them to slivers of ice as it tore them away into the gloom. Looking astern, the captain could make out the dim shadow of the Flying Childers, she was less than a mile away, but she might as well as been on the far side of the world.

Through the sleet and spray, he could make out the movement of her fore and main masts. At first, lifting in unison, then independently of each other, as the surf lifted her and slammed her down on the reef, time and again, tearing her bottom open and smashing her beautiful lines to matchwood. The flying Childers would sail no more, he mused, and if God didn't lend a hand soon, the Maid would come to the same end. As he turned back to face the storm, he had to assume that God wasn't looking to Port Davey that day.

Hour after hour, the waves and wind continued to batter the little ship and from their position in the wheelhouse, the crew sensed she was beginning to labour under the strain, mountains of water that at first, burst against her bows, were now coming over her bows, sending spray high in the air, and holding her under for just that little bit longer each time.

As she lifted high and threw tons of water of her deck, she seemed to shudder wearily, before once more plunging deeper into the next onslaught. The men began to wonder just how long she could keep up the battle before her decks were punched open by the massive seas.

At ten o'clock that morning, the captain ordered the topgallant and royal yards sent down, and the crew to a man, heaved and dragged at the heavy ropes, at times up to their waists in water as they lowered the heavy timber booms to the deck. He contemplated sending the mains down as well, but he decided he would need sail for steering if the anchors should fail, a decision that wouldn't have made any difference either way.

Huddled in the deck house, wet and shivering, the crew watched as their world blew apart. At first, it descended on them like a bright, silver mist, closing in around the vessel and making visibility outside the gunwales and around the boat non existent. Even the brilliant white tops of the foam streaked waves tearing past almost at arm's length disappeared into the whiteness. Then it began.

Like a screaming banshee, the wind turned into the south and blew a hurricane force, hail and sleet tearing open the white mist like a curtain and hurling tons of water across the deck of the Maid. Within seconds, the starboard cable had parted and the ship veered to port, threatening to go beam on as the remaining anchor fought to keep its tenuous hold on the rocky bottom.

From where he stood, the captain could see the anchor cable had jumped off the bits and was beginning to saw through the bow, tearing chunks of timber from the bow as it sawed back and forth under the strain. He immediately ordered a stream and kedge anchor over the side in the hope it might catch a reef and hold. The six inch plaited rope was quickly bent to the steel and wooden anchor and let go. What was left of the port cable was then paid out to the end, the hopes of all on board going with it.

The six inch diameter rope lasted all of two hours, and at three o'clock in the afternoon, snapped, sending the ship end whipping across the deck to wash uselessly back and forth in the swirling water.

With no anchors left and relying solely on the port anchor, the captain ordered all hands to get ready to make sail in a last ditch attempt to save her should the cable let go, but even as he spoke, he knew she could not hold on one anchor alone, all they could do was to hope for a break in the weather before night fall so they might try to sail her back across the bay, to the safety of the western shore. But it was not to be.

For two long hours, the Maid held against all the sea could throw at her, then, at five o'clock the sickening jolt as the final strands parted, convinced the captain the battle was lost. Within seconds, he realised trying to make sail was futile, the ship had already turned and was running for the shore. He ordered all hands into the rigging, but he needn't have wasted his breath, already the crew were holding on for their lives as the stricken ship hurtled shoreward.

She struck about two hundred yards offshore, her speed sending her high over a reef and heeling on to her port side, threatening to capsize her and bury all aboard in the swirling foam, but at the last moment, she righted and settled upright amongst the reefs and pounding surf.

The first mate and three others immediately swung a boat away and lowered it to the water and began to clamber down the stays towards it, when the captain gave a shout to come back. All four men grabbed for the stays and held on for dear life as a huge torrent of water completely covered the ship, tearing away their only means of safety, and they could only watch in dismay as the still upright whaleboat ducked and dived its way out of sight towards the breakers.

The captain stared after it, certain now that all lives were lost. He looked past the fast disappearing dinghy to the shore beyond, his mind racing, trying to find a way to deliver his men up from their perilous predicament.

At first, he blamed the runnels of water pouring across his face, and shook his head to clear his vision. He was only seeing things, wishful thinking. No, there it was again. He pointed shore wards and all eyes followed the direction of his arm.

'There!' He screamed above the howling wind. 'There, a boat! God help them they're coming to save us!'

A cheer went up from the wet and exhausted men as each one of them sighted the tiny, dark, speck as it lifted on the crest of a wave, the oars lifting and falling in almost precision timing as it made its way between the reefs and waves towards them.

The gale that had rattled the walls and roofs of the little settlement and sent dogs inland to huddle together under whatever shelter they could find, had shown no sign of abating. In fact, by daylight, when Thomas Dougherty arose, the flapping of the scrim and paper that covered the walls of the front room of the little house, as well as the sheets of rain that beat against the tiny panes of glass, gave indication there would be no work done today. Still, instead of climbing back into bed, he loaded kindling and an armful of wood into the brick fireplace and lifted the heavy cast iron kettle, from the hearth to the middle and lowest of the three hooks that hung down from inside the chimney.

He placed the back of his hand against the dungarees that hung inside the massive eight foot wide chimney, and satisfied they were dry, lifted them down from the hook and moved to the table and put them on.

He had no sooner finished buttoning his braces, when there was a loud knocking at the door, followed by the distant barking of one of the dogs from the comfort of its warm lair.

He opened the door to see both Tom Heather and 'Black Billy' Smith, chief mate of the Flying Childers, and Bill Ferrer, bosun of the same ship, standing on the back porch. He ushered the men inside. 'What is it, then?' He asked, grabbing a towel from its hook near the back door and passing it to the man in front, knowing that men the calibre of these, would not be out in such weather, without something being amiss.

Tom Heather spoke first. 'It's the Maid of Erin,' He breathed heavily, wiping the water from his face and passing the towel to William, who with water dripping from every exposed point of his clothes and body, was obviously drenched to the skin. 'She's dragged during the night and she looks like she's in trouble.'

'How close is she?' Asked Dougherty, looking towards Billy, chief mate of the Flying Childers, and who, just a week ago was in the same predicament as the men aboard the Maid.

Bill Ferrer broke in, 'She's still a fair way out, but she's plunging deep and the winds coming around to the south in a gale.' The bosun coughed and went on, taking the towel from William and wiping his dripping face. 'The chief's been 'round to the far end of the beach, past the Childers, she's wrecked, and it looks like the Maid's going to go the same way if this wind doesn't ease.' The respectful term of chief, by another seaman, instead of the derogatory term, 'Black Billy' bestowed on him by townspeople and bushmen, in reference to his Samoan heritage, was not lost on Dougherty, but here, in this tiny outpost of humanity the term 'Black Billy' was a term of endearment. They all knew Billy, as his reputation as a navigator and whaleman as well as his feats of strength, had preceded him, something that these people of one of the most isolated places in the world, respected.

Little did either of the two men know that their as yet, unborn, children would meet and marry and begin a line of descendants that would someday, allow this story to finally be told.

'She's in real trouble, alright. I've been looking to see if she would put a boat down, but I suppose captain Curphey's hoping this wind will ease.' He frowned, then added, 'But I can tell you here and now, that it's only going to get worse as the day wears on.'

Dougherty had donned his boots and oilskins and was moving towards the door. Agnes, his wife, had dressed and came through to the front room, 'Go and see from the beach, Tom, I'll get some dry clothes for Billy.'

As the men moved towards the door, she added, 'I'll have food and hot drinks when you get back.'

Outside, the squalls had eased slightly, but the sea was as rough as Dougherty had ever seen. As the men broke through the tree line to the beach, it was like running into an invisible wall. Shards of sleet drove at their faces, causing them to duck their heads and cover their faces with their hands. Out in the bay, line upon line of breakers stretched into the distance, finally disappearing into the grey rain squalls that reached from sea to sky, marching like an endless army of giants across a maelstrom of foam and white water.

The Maid of Erin was but a darker blotch among the waves. At times, her masts were the only part of her visible from the shore, behind the walls of grey water and foam. The walls of water rushing over and around her, giving the impression of speed, but with her back to the shore and a hurricane in her teeth, this maid was going nowhere.

Dougherty studied the scene before him for a few moments, unsure, at this stage, of what to do. He turned his back to the howling wind and cupped his hand to his mouth. 'What do you think, Billy,' He yelled. 'She's too far out to get a line, and anyways, a punt will never survive in that sea.'

Tom heather broke in, 'Billy's got a whaleboat off the Childers, ready for sea if we need her. Do you think we can make it, Tom?'

William had risen before daylight. The noise of the storm had kept him awake all night. Unknown to most of the crew, who were snoring noisily, William could hear the branches of the trees banging against the shed walls, signifying a wind change. This time it was more to the south, and getting stronger. The last thing they needed.

He dressed, and waited near the fire pot, lifting the vent on the stove to increase the heat and loading a few more dry logs into the fire. He could feel the cold permeating the shed as the wind backed southerly and blew harder.

At daylight, he made his way through the rain squalls to where the whale boat was tied up on the tree line, just off the beach. The tide was full in and the storm surge had the waves breaking over the stern of the whale boat, it was full of water and the coils of rope, normally neatly placed in their boxes had tipped over and tangled around the loggerhead as he had suspected they would, but he was relieved they had not been washed out of the boat altogether and he grabbed a bailer and began scooping the water from the boat.

It took about half an hour to get the boat back where he could rock it back and forth enough to slide it onto the couple of small logs he had placed under the keel, and using a cant dog he had found near the side of Tom Heather's house, he managed to slide the boat up the beach and under the edge of a skillion normally used to protect the firewood pile. Wringing wet, but satisfied the boat was safe and would stay relatively dry, he made his way back to the shed and let Tom Heather know the boat was safe should they need it.

Dougherty shook his head and motioned for the men to go back in the trees, out of the wind.

They moved behind the line of trees and backed against them for protection as another rain squall pelted them with rain and sleet. 'I think the only thing we can do at this time, is wait and see if her anchors hold. If they fail, I don't think there's any way she can make sea room in this wind.' He paused and looked in the direction of where the Maid was struggling to survive. 'I think we'd better wait and see, in the meantime, you'd better come up to the house.' He looked again in the direction of the struggling ship, and added, 'I think it's going to be a long day.'

By the time they arrived back at Dougherty's house, they could see people coming from all directions, all worried for the safety of the crew of the Maid and all willing to help in any way they could.

Joe Page, George Rayner and Bob Woolley were all standing under the skillion woodshed of Dougherty's place, sheltering from the torrents of water that cascaded down from the shingle roof and off the already full water tank, to be grabbed by the wind and whipped first this way, then that, causing the men to dodge back and forth, under the cover of the shed roof.

Dougherty motioned them inside.

The kitchen of the house was, by now, warm and inviting. Agnes, together with two other wives had made numerous cups of sweet, black tea, and the men gratefully scooped up the large tin pannikins and slurped noisily to the disapproving looks of the women folk.

Joe Page broke the silence.

'What about ropes?' He asked, looking about the room at the men's faces.

Tom heather again related the story of Billy Smith and the whale boat from the Flying Childers, adding, 'She's up in the scrub behind the Childers, rigged and ready for sea, should we need her.'

Tom Heather had invited the crew off the Childers to stay in his boat shed, where there was a fire pot and plenty of hay filled chaff bags to sleep on. Tom's wife and two other ladies had cooked them up a feed of scones and jam, which Captain MacGregor and the crew of the Childers had eagerly washed down with copious pannikins of post and rail tea. There was also a cauldron of kangaroo tail stew, which was replenished each time it dropped to a certain level in the pot. With almost all of the comforts of home, the captain and crew settled down to wait out the storm until, with the help of the Maid of Erin, the Childers could be refloated and they could return to sea.

The men looked to Billy, somewhat drier, but with sand and leaves still sticking out of his curly black hair, it was obvious he had been working hard while most of them had been asleep. They knew it must have taken a massive effort for one man to shift and ready a whaleboat in these conditions.

Joe Page spoke again. 'I think we should post a man or two to keep watch on the maid, and take shifts. No sense us all standing out in this weather, if we did that, we'd all be worn out and no good to anyone should she go up.'

'You're right, Joe,' answered Dougherty. Some of us will go along to the Childers and watch from the shore, the rest of you stay here and keep warm in *case* you're needed. Me, Harry, Tom and Billy'll go first, the rest of you, take a spell and we'll send for you if we need you.'

The second mate off the Childers spoke up. 'It's no good like that, Tom. You'll need four men and a steersman, if'n you want to get a boat out in this weather,' He added, I'd better come with you.'

'Alright,' Said Dougherty, 'It's five a shift then.'

The first five oilskin clad men set off along the beach, heads bowed and turned to the left to avoid the biting sleet and wind blown grit. It had been some hours since daylight, and as they were forced to walk along the soft sand at the tree line to avoid the curling waves, they knew it would be some time before they reached the point opposite the stern of the dark shadow that heaved and plunged on her cables, just a mile from shore and safety.

It took about half an hour to reach the wreck of the Flying Childers and they made their way up to where the whaleboat lay between two piner's huts. They bailed the last of the water out and turned to watch the Maid of Erin.

From their vantage point outside Tom Heather's house, they had a better view and could actually see the waves breaking over her and forcing her bows under. They could see both her cables, as taut as bowstrings, whipping through the surface of the water as she lifted high through the backs of the waves, hurling tons of water from her decks and over her stern.

The flying Childers was fast becoming a wreck. Her back had been broken and her main mast had torn from its step, laying over and tearing a gaping hole in her port side through which water surged and heaved, spreading her contents along the beach to become yet another hazard for any would be rescuer.

A shout from Billy Smith brought their heads up and they could make out the shapes of men moving about the deck of the Maid, and a little while later, as their relieving party was moving up the beach towards them, they stood in silence as they watched the uppermost yardarms being lowered to the deck.

Leaving the other five men to look out for the maid, William, Dougherty, and the rest, made their way back along the beach, to a hot lunch back at his house. They sat around the fire, talking and telling yarns until around one o'clock, when one of Tom Heather's sons came running in to inform them of the Maid losing one of her anchors. The men grabbed for their oilskins and once again set off along the foam covered beach.

The weather had worsened and the wind tore at their clothes and threatened to blow them off their feet, the rain and sleet forcing the men into the cover of trees, there to turn their backs and get their breath, before setting off once again in the direction of the Maid.

Occasionally, they would chance to look out to sea and relief would be profound when they would see the dark shape of the maid rise again from the foamy depths.

The storm was now almost hurricane force, and as they reached the track leading up to Tom Heather's house, they could see the Maid making heavy weather of it. She had drifted even further across the bay and a closer look revealed that the storm was gathering even further, they knew she would never see the night out if the storm worsened. Dougherty and Billy moved to where the whale boat was lying and with the help of the rest of the men, they rolled it down to a spot, just above high water, then retreated to the shelter of Tom's shed to watch and wait. They didn't have long to wait. At around three o'clock they saw the Maid's stern veer suddenly to port, the starboard cable had parted, leaving but one cable to hold and the worst of the storm far from over.

The men stood facing out to sea, eyes fixed on the Maid, oblivious now to the storm that raged around them and wondering what would be the next move of Captain Curphey, if indeed he had any more moves left.

At five o'clock, the decision was made for them, as the port cable finally succumbed to the overwhelming strain and snapped with a sound like a cannon firing. Immediately, they could see the ship turn shoreward and begin running before the wind. As she sped down the waves, they could see the crew climbing into the rigging, hoping the power of the wind and waves would now turn its power to good and drive her safely up onto the sandy beach and deliver up her crew to the safety of those waiting on the shore.

But it was not to be. A mere hundred yards from safety, the Maid of Erin struck and heaved skywards before heeling over, the boiling surf covering her decks completely, before she managed to right herself and wallow heavily among the jagged reefs and boulders that surrounded her.

'Come on,' Yelled Billy Smith, and began heaving at the gunwale of the whale boat, gone the black fella half caste, looked down on by decent white folk, in his place the renowned ship's captain, capable of navigating these small craft through huge seas to hunt the giant quarry of the southern oceans.

Every man deferred immediately to this dark skinned savior, and began dragging the boat to the water's edge. Inside a minute, the boat was in the water with Dougherty, Heather, Page and Smith rowing for all they were worth and Chief William Smith standing tall at the stern with the rudder in both hands, directing their oars with shouts of, *Hold*! As the boat crested the wave and, *Pull!* As the boat broke through the backs of the grey walls of brine.

As they passed the wreck of the Flying Childers, they could see over their right shoulders, the crew of the Maid frantically trying to lower a boat and hopes were high they might clear the wreck in their own boat before the whale boat was forced to close with the foundering wreck. But, as their boat lifted once more from the foaming troughs, they saw to their dismay, the ships boat being borne away from the ship as the crew clung desperately to the rigging of the stricken whaler.

At the shout from William Smith, each man turned his back on the Maid, and began to heave on their oars, thankful not to have to view the scene ahead of them, concentrating only on the depth of oar blade in the water, as the whale boat drew near the ship.

The evacuation of the crew took two trips. By the time they reached the shore the first time, the first crew were spent. It took all hands to turn the whale boat around and another crew piled in to grab the oars. William Smith again took the steering oar and nobody argued. The boat once again plied out through the breakers and slammed into the side of the ship. A rope thrown by William was caught and made fast by Captain Curphey and the oarsmen shipped their oars as the whale boat was drawn alongside. Within seconds, the crew, including the captain were bundled into the whale boat and William, sensing the Maid being lifted high off the bottom by the next set of rollers, brought his knife slashing down across the light manilla painter and roared at the oarsmen to pull for their lives.

They needed no second bidding, as the masts, with their yardarms hanging askew, came soaring over the top of the little boat, threatening to crush them and drive them beneath the water forever.

Their journey back to shore was as hair raising as the first. Overloaded and with a following sea, the whale boat became unstable and threatened to capsize on more than one occasion. Only the expert efforts of the dark skinned boat steerer, hauling on the long rudder oar and shouting orders at the frightened oarsmen, brought them through and around the jagged reefs to the safety of the beach. As the boat hit the sandy bottom, men piled out, willing hands grasping the gunwales and hauling the boat far up the beach.

The women and children had all gathered and blankets were thrown around the shoulders of the grateful seamen as they were led to the warmth and safety of Tom Heather's home. The captain of the Maid of Erin, before accepting any help, took each man by the hand and thanked them warmly, especially William Smith, and swore that he would mention their bravery and hospitality in his report.

On the following Thursday, the day dawned clear and bright. The sea had flattened off and the wind that had raged about the little settlement for the last week was reduced to a light breeze from the southwest. Dougherty had brought his ketch, Emerald Isle, out of the Davey River and the crews of both the Flying Childers and the Maid of Erin, said their goodbyes and thank you to the people of Port Davey. As the ketch sailed down Payne Bay, to a man, they stared at the broken spars and masts of the two, once proud ships, that would never sail again.

William had been both seaman and master of both ships and as the wrecks were cut off from his view as the Emerald Isle turned to open up Davey Bay, he wondered if this was an omen for the whaling industry. Two ships lost at once, a big hole in the Hobarton shipping industry and no more ships to fill their place. He turned and looked forward once again. He had a little seven month old boy at home in Recherche he had never seen, and was looking forward to seeing.

It was reported at the inquiry that followed the wreck of the two ships, and in the Mercury newspaper in Hobarton on the 26th June, 1877, that, Captain Curphey had stated, *'a great deal of thanks and gratitude for saving the lives of my crew was owed to William Smith, the former Chief mate of the Flying Childers and to the hospitality of the people of Port Davey for their kindness and bravery.'*

Chapter 31

Wednesday, July 4th, 1877
Recherche Bay,
Tasmania

William could see Sarah, Rosie, Domingo and the Tedman's on the wharf at Recherche as the Emerald Isle moved slowly into the wharf. He laughed as Tom Dougherty called to Sarah, 'No need to stop and offload his gear, love,' they all laughed when he added, 'It's all at the bottom of the ocean.'

William thought of his Ditty box and all the work he had put into it, not to mention his papers, cash, and personal items kept safe within the locked box. Sarah's face fell as she saw the look of sadness on William's face, she loved the Ditty Box and as well as his life, she had hoped he would save the box with its many timbered facets. It was as though the work box brought them luck, as well as the caul, and as long as they had both, they could achieve anything.

Skillfully, Thomas Dougherty had set the ketch into an arc, moving as close to the wharf as possible, and as she drifted past the end of the wooden pier, William stepped off the rail and into the arms of his wife and new baby son and amongst waving and well wishing, the Emerald Isle kept moving in the same arc and out into the channel, on towards Hobarton.

Firmly ensconced at Mrs. Domeney's boarding house, William heard all about the birth of his new first born, James Henry Smith, and how Mister Domeney had lost his boat the Ripple, and almost his life, off flat witch island and had to row home in a dinghy. He felt sad for mister Domeney, when he discovered that neither the boat, which he built himself, nor the cargo, was insured, and the loss would have to be incurred by the Domeneys.

Then, they all demanded he relate the tale of the two ships lost. They were all familiar with the Maid and the Childers, as well as their captain's, and thanked their lucky stars all of both crews were safe.

William related the tale of the Flying Childers and The Maid of Erin shipwrecks as it happened, and silence fell on the dining room at the boarding house until he finished his story. Each person taking a moment to relive the terror of those men aboard the Maid, and forever grateful to those at Port Davey who had participated in their rescue.

Mister Domeney said the townspeople of Recherche and the authorities held grave fears for the Ketch, Ethel Cuthbert. Apparently, she had left Launceston on the 22nd of July, bound for Port Davey, and there has been no news of her since. They were hoping she could have made Macquarie Harbour for shelter, but there was no news as yet.

As they readied for bed that night, William and Sarah both stood over baby Jim's cot and wondered what the future might hold, what with the dangers of being a whale man. Sarah was worried, and considering the events of the past month, with good reason. 'What will we do now, William?' she asked quietly.

'What do you mean?' asked her husband, but he knew what she meant. There were three of them now and if William could lose not one, but two ships, in a matter of a single week, and with the men on the Ethel Cuthbert's safety in doubt. Maybe it was time to start thinking of a new occupation, a safer one. Sarah's whisper broke into his thoughts. 'Now we've lost the Ditty Box, maybe our luck will run out.' William thought for a while and murmured back, 'We'll sleep on it and talk about it in the morning,'

Although a fine morning in Recherche, the wind was still a cold southeasterly, and William, Sarah, Rosie and Domingo were suitably rugged up as they sat on the verandah of Mrs. Domeney's boarding house when captain Lloyd of the ketch Coral, walked up the track to the house.

He informed the group that his boss, Mister Woolley, had purchased the wrecks of the Childer's and the Maid and was offering work to William and Domingo, recovering salvage from the wrecks. He had heard of William's bravery at the sight of the wrecks and wondered if he could go back and direct operations. The little group on the verandah of the house nodded solemnly when he also reported that he was the father of the captain of the Ethel Cuthbert and he was hoping for some good news about his son and the crew.

Both William and Domingo jumped at the chance to make some money while between whale cruises and took just two days off to spend time with their families, before boarding the Coral and heading back to Port Davey.

The two men spent the next two weeks cutting out the rigging and blocking the yards and spars from what was left of the maid on to a lighter, so they could be transshipped aboard the Coral and her sister ketch, Bertha. It was on the last day of the job, as both boats were preparing to leave Port Davey, a call of nature had Domingo wandering into the scrub near the shoreline. An excited yell had William thinking his brother had chanced upon a snake or some other danger in his efforts to find a quiet space out of the wind. William walked slowly towards the sound and was surprised to see Domingo digging frantically at spot near the base of the wreck of the Childers, laughing and calling to him to help. William ran to see what the commotion was about and couldn't believe his eyes when his brother scooped the sand away from a spar to reveal the triangles of mahogany and Huon pine on the top of the Ditty Box lid. Hardly daring to believe the box could have survived, William fell in beside his brother and began scooping the sand and rocks away to reveal the work box, still intact and still with the tiny brass key inserted in the lock.

The other men couldn't fathom what all the commotion was about and stared from their positions on the boats, until William stood up and walked towards them, the work box held high above his head and a smile on his face from ear to ear. The Ditty Box had survived, and once captain Lloyd had seen the name on the papers inside, although some of them were water damaged beyond recognition, he conceded the Ditty Box was indeed William's property and congratulated the men on finding it.

Sadly, all the news was not good. The men would learn later, that the Ethel Cuthbert had foundered in the same storm that wrecked the Flying Childers and the Maid of Erin. The North Star had sighted the wreck, nine miles north of the Pieman River heads, some fifty miles distant, and although an intensive search was raised, no survivors were ever found.

The Coral and the Bertha arrived in Recherche on the twenty second of July, 1877 and with the two ketches carrying on towards Hobarton, both William and Domingo, were pleased to be home, William carried the Ditty Box proudly under his arm, impatient to show Sarah that their lucky charm had survived, of all things, a shipwreck, and there would be better news waiting at the at the Domeney's. Sarah and Rosie met them at the door of their lodgings, astonished the Ditty Box had survived and apologising for not meeting them at the wharf on account of the baby being asleep and not wishing to wake him. Sarah was waving a letter she had already opened, but because neither the girls, nor their parents, could read, and she didn't want to embarrass herself by asking Mrs. Domeney to read it to them. 'I just know it's good news, I just know it is!' She exclaimed, as Rosie spoke over her in their excitement. 'The letter came the same time as you found the Ditty Box, I'll bet.' The girls squealed with delight. 'That means our luck has changed.' Sarah reached up and rubbed the caul between her thumb and forefinger, as William did, and Rosie reached up and did the same to Domingo's golden earring. Then both girls placed their hands on the Ditty Box in Domingo's arms, for extra luck, as William opened the letter.

William frowned and his face looked serious enough for the girls and Domingo to stop talking, before William smiled broadly. The letter was from William Sherwin a whaling ship owner of Hobarton, congratulating William on his bravery at Port Davey and offering him the position of Captain of the Barque, Marie Laurie. The excited laughing of all, brought Mrs. Domeney running to hush them before they woke the baby.

Chapter 32

Whaling Barque, Marie Laurie
New wharf,
Hobarton, Tasmania, 18th September, 1877

The Marie Laurie was built in the Seychelles Islands in Eighteen Forty, the same year William Smith was born, using identical methods of construction as used in the Elizabethan era, and forgotten by many shipbuilders by the time of the twentieth century. For many years the Marie Laurie sailed the northern grounds from Greenland to the Bering Strait in search of whales, until she was purchased by captain William Sherwin of Hobarton.

William and Domingo stood with their wives, on the new wharf, and looked over the Marie Laurie as if she were their own. A typical whaling barque, bluff bows and heavy timbers, she was built for working the heavy seas of the northern and southern latitudes but with her square rigged fore and main masts, and fore and aft rigged mizzen mast, she was much more agile when steering in close and confined areas near a lee shore and head winds, than the standard square riggers. The term barque refers to a particular sail-plan, with three masts, fore-and-aft sails on the aftermost or mizzen, mast, and square sails on all other masts. A major advantage of the barque's rigging was that they needed smaller crews and were therefore cheaper to run.

Whaling barque's averaged between two hundred and fifty and four hundred tons, and were little more than 100 feet in length on deck. The Marie Laurie was two hundred and seventy eight tons, a good manageable size for the Tasmanian whaling grounds. The whaler was built for stability, not speed. It carried a large amount of specialized equipment, such as the heavy brick and iron tryworks. She held two boats each side of the superstructure and one on the roof as a spare. The whale boats were suspended from iron davits, swung inwards, over the gunwale. The hearths and tryworks were ahead of the main mast as in most whalers, and round the base of the try-works was a low wooden framework, a foot or so in height called the goose pen, kept filled with sea water. Two small deck houses were built on the stern end, one for the cook's galley and the other to store the cooper's tools and supplies. The two cabins were connected overhead to provide shelter for the helmsmen at the steering wheel, in the 'hurricane house'. Aloft, the Marie Laurie, like other whaling Barques, kept a lookout from the time she left port until the time she returned from her voyages, the lookouts had no protection from the elements and instead of a crow's nest, differed from other ships only in that it had masthead hoops, a set of spectacled shaped, iron hoops, inside which the lookout stood and held the hoops to steady himself, whilst bracing himself on a wooden plank nailed to the mast, by the strength of his legs alone. Forrard of the foremast, near the foc'sle jalousie were the animal pens and stalls. Although empty now, William and Domingo joked that it wouldn't be long before goats, pigs and chickens would be cackling, bleating and grunting as the ship made her way across the oceans.

Sarah and Rosie climbed aboard and began familiarising themselves with the boat, whilst William and Domingo set off for the agent's office to organise a crew for their first voyage. Sarah sat the Ditty Box on the right side of the captain's table, and both girls tapped it for good luck. Like all seafarer's, they were beginning to embraced the superstitions and charms that they hoped would keep the ship, and their husbands, safe from harm's way.

Within a day, and with the help of the agent, mister Sherwin, Domingo had signed a full crew aboard after cajoling, threatening and stopping just short of accusing them of downright cowardice, as he walked among them in the bar of the Nautilus Hotel, demanding they sign on for what he promised would be a short and profitable voyage. It was late in the afternoon by the time the ship's manifest was submitted, and at six pm, the Marie Laurie had cleared the channel and was anchored of crayfish point, Taroona, awaiting the dawn.

The next day, with a crew of twenty four, including William Henry Smith as Captain, Domingo Jose Evorall Smith, as first mate, and five passengers, Sarah Smith, master James Smith, Mister and Mrs. Tedman, and Rosetta Evorall, the Marie Laurie set off down D'entrecasteaux channel towards their first port of call, Recherche Bay.

At Recherche, the girls spent their last night with their husbands at the Domeney's, and the Tedman's said goodbye. At dawn, the Marie Laurie shipped her whale boat, hauled anchor and moved off towards the western whaling grounds.

Within sight of south west Cape, and in company with the Aladdin, they sighted their first whale. It was getting dark, and with not enough light to catch the whale, the Aladdin signaled she would heave to, in the hope the whale would stay around. William decided to move farther west, in the hope the whale would travel in the same direction where they could see it should it rise on the morrow. At dawn the Aladdin's choice proved correct. Just outside Port Davey the whale rose, and was sighted. Two boats were put down and within hours, the crew of the Aladdin had a twelve tunner in tow to Port Davey for trying out.

The Marie Laurie continued her quest further west and was rewarded by a sighting just before dark on the eighteenth of February. William used his old whaler's trick again and pressed on until it was too dark to see, then hove to and used his sails to continue to drift in the direction he hoped the whales were going. The Nineteenth of February dawned clear and crisp with at least two whales within sight of the mast head and another two possibles off in the distance. William clapped on all sail, overtaking the hindmost whales and proving up the existence of a further three to the west.

William positioned the Marie Laurie just ahead of the foremost whales, hoping there would be time to get these giants alongside the ship, before the following whales could be headed off as they approached from the south. The plan worked. Domingo had his whale harpooned and killed within minutes of approaching the beast. Then, knowing the sperm whale would float, he bent the rope to a large wooden block that would float behind the whale and act as both a drogue and a sighting buoy should the whale float beneath the waves. Then he turned his boat to where the second mate was struggling to kill his whale. The second mate's harpoon had hit bone, bending and lodging in the spine of the giant thirty ton leviathan. The whale was thrashing about, trying to rid itself of the painful lance and threatening to sound, taking the entire crew of the whale boat deep into the briny depths. Domingo had his crew pull along the port side of the whale, and taking his spare lance, he leapt onto the whales back and ran forward. The whale was angry, trying to swat the first boat with its pectoral fin, rolling from side to side as it did so. If it had sounded immediately, the lance head would have been jerked out of the bony plate in its back and it would have been home free, but in its desire to retaliate against the puny humans, it hesitated, and Domingo was able to brace himself over that part behind the head, about five feet behind the blowhole which was the thinnest part of the skull covering the cerebellum, that part of the sperm whale's brain that controls movement, sensory information and motor action. Domingo knew that a lance passing through the thin bone at the back of the skull and entering the cerebellum would instantly paralyse the forty foot monster, rendering the giant cetacean harmless. He balanced on the balls of his feet, almost toppling off the back of the whale to he did so, and lifted the lance high above his head, before thrusting it full length, deep into the body of the whale. The lance head passed through the rear sinus passage of the blowhole and continued down through the soft blubber and frontal sac of the rear part of the blowhole, before striking and penetrating the skull and entering the cerebellum. The whale ceased breathing and went limp, sagging in the water like a giant rubbery mat, its heart was still beating, pumping its life blood away on the waters, but for all intents and purposes, it was dead.

This time, it was the second mate who was ready with the drogue and had it tied off around the tail fluke and dropped it into the water even before the dead whale had stopped shuddering in its death throes.

William had the Marie Laurie stand well off, away from the pod of young male sperm whales, he was well aware these creatures could reach speeds of more than thirty miles an hour, more than eight times as fast as his ship, if they were spooked and decided to run. He needed the pod to continue straight on into where Domingo and the other boats waited. The third whale boat was watching, biding his time as the whales approached, trying to present as small a target as possible by facing the oncoming pod and keeping their oars out of the water, so as not to deflect any of the whale's sonar clicks.

Then they were amongst them! Four whales spouting as they surfaced around them. There was no time to waste, the whales had already increased their speed to that which the whale boats could never hope to match, and each harpooner hurled his lance as the whales passed. Both lances struck and held, and the harpooners reefed their wooden staves out of the hilts and jammed another on the end, before sending their lances deep into the vitals of the great sea creatures.

Pandemonium ruled once again, as the harpooners ran back to the steering oars, tripping and sliding as blood and brine sprayed over their crew mates and thwarts. Both boats rocked and yawed, threatening to capsize and throw them all into the sea, until each steersman had settled on his thwart and had the rope securely wrapped around the loggerhead and was paying out steadily, slowing the whale down and giving the lance man time to drive their killing spikes home.

And then it was done, all aboard the boats, as well those on the ship, were more than surprised at how quickly the whales had died. The deck of the Marie Laure came alive as sailors rushed to get the securing chains out of their lockers, at the same time, the platforms were being swung down both sides of the ship.

'Four whales, four whales in one day!' William exclaimed as he walked around the deck of the Marie Laurie, clapping each man on the back and congratulating them. Darkness had overtaken the ship, and the last of the whale spouts had disappeared from the lookout's sight, rushing north into the gloom of twilight. Never mind, four whales in one day comes to about forty odd tuns of sperm oil and one hundred and thirty six teeth. not all big teeth of course, but still a valuable item for the manifest.

For the rest of that night, to an observer watching from a distance, the Marie Laurie looked more like a giant halloween lantern on the sea instead of a whaling ship. The flames from the tryworks hearths flared and danced their reflections on the smoke that swirled up through the sails. With two whales each side of the ship, and at the mercy of the wind and sea, all haste was made to break them down and get them stowed before the weather broke and put them all at risk. 'Many a slip 'twixt cup and lip.' Domingo would say to gee the men up as they worked in four hour shifts, with barely two hours sleep in between, and at the end of their stint, they would sluice themselves down with hot salt water and carbolic in an effort to rid themselves of the grimy, gelatinous oil, that clung as a film, to every part of their body, hair and clothes. Then, it was a meal of horse meat stew with ships biscuits and tea. Each man thankful they were still not so far from their last port and the meat was still reasonably fresh.

By the end of the third day of trying out, March fifteenth, 1878, the Marie Laurie had thirty Tuns of oil stowed and in the works. William ordered the last whale carcass cut free and with the tryworks still bubbling and the deck covered in layers of blubber, the ship set off to find more whales.

Satisfied he had made a good start, William was aware there would be no fresh supplies until the ship could make Recherche Bay. He conferred with his brother and they decided to fish their way back to home port, Domingo following another of William's mottos, 'Keep the crew well fed and happy, with something to look forward to'.

On March 31, 1878, Sarah and Rosie sighted the unmistakable shape of the Marie Laure, as she made her way past Fishers Point and into Recherche Bay. Both women grabbed up their bundles of washing and quickly pegged them on the long rope clothes line, Sarah grunting as she tried to drag the clothes prop into place, her growing belly getting in the way of the long manuka pole. Rosie laughed excitedly as her big sister stumbled around the pole. 'Leave that,' she said, taking the pole from Sarah's hands. 'You get the baby.' Sarah ran to get James from his cot, and together they headed off down the track to the pier, all the time keeping an eye out for what might be a wave or a hail from their husbands.

They knew the ship had only come in for supplies and would be leaving again, possible in the morning, if there was a chance of whales around, or if the weather suited, and they wanted to spend as much time as possible with their husbands. They could see other crew members wives and families coming out of their gates at the sight of the Marie Laure in all her glory as the morning sun gleamed off her brilliant white sails, the sun and salt water bleaching the once grimy streaks of oil from them on the way home and a shout from behind had them turning to see Mister Domeney, in his pony and gig, heading down to meet the ship.

They carefully stepped to one side as he reined up and motioned for them to climb aboard, he held his arms out to take young James as the two women, Sarah especially, gratefully clambered aboard.

With the ship snugged down, Domingo and William had to wait while the crew drew a percentage of their wages from the slop chest. They knew their families would be short of money and with thirty tuns of sperm oil stowed, they were pretty sure there would be money left over from their lays to cover an advance from their pay. Before they left the wharf, Mister Domeney assured those members of the crew who lived in Hobart, he would send word to the ship's agent in Hobart that the Marie Laure was having a good trip and it would be alright if their wives could draw on their lays, to tide them over. Over dinner that night at the Domeney's, Sarah informed William of her pregnancy and the possible need to have a home of their own, once their second child was born.

She reminded William of their plot of land near the mouth of Cockle creek and the small amount of money she had saved while he was away. Not nearly enough to build a home but it was a start, and the baby was due in July.

That night, William lay awake, trying to figure out how he was going to build a house in six months, and still be able to finish this voyage, which would take at least six more months. He lay in the dark for hours thinking about what to do while the Domeney house slept, and by morning, he had worked out a plan.

Three days later, on April 4th, the sails of the Marie Laure were once again disappearing behind Fisher's Point, bound for the western whaling grounds.

She would fish the western grounds, from Port Davey in south west Tasmania, to the edge of the Great Australian Bight, near Albany, west Australia until June 1878, with just fifteen tuns of sperm whale oil aboard, she turned for home in an effort to speed home in time for the captain to witness the birth of his second born.

From June until September every year, the roaring forties took command of the seas west of Tasmania and this year was no exception. Low pressure zones formed deep in the Southern Ocean and headed north from the Antarctic, sweeping across the great expanse of ocean, lifting the seas to unimaginable heights and hurling them against everything in their path. A ship caught in one of these frequent storms would be well advised to run for shelter and this is what the Marie Laure did. William ordered all topsails reefed and the crew stood craning their necks as they looked to the men high on the yards, swinging across a great arc, from port to starboard, as they scrambled to drag in and secure the huge sheets of canvas with nothing but their bare hands and sheer strength. William grinned as Domingo grabbed a rope and began swinging down off the foremast yardarm towards the deck, *'showing off, as usual.'* William whispered under his breath. His brother was about halfway down to the deck amid admiring grunts from the crew who witnessed his feat, as a large wave caught the ship under the stern and pushed her bow down to starboard. William caught his breath as the ship lurched to starboard and his brother swung out beyond the gunwale and over the grey, foam flecked water in a high arc, William could see the muscles in Domingo's shoulders and forearm become rigid as his brother fought to hold on to the wildly spinning rope. Gone was the broad grin and flamboyant waving arm, Domingo was holding on for dear life, to go overboard in this following sea would certainly spell his end. Worse, to come rushing back through the rigging like a pendulum on a rope, as the ship heeled to port, and be dashed against one of the masts or tryworks, could inflict terrible injuries that would mean certain agonising death. Domingo had cleared the starboard gunwale and was bringing his legs up under him in a futile effort to protect himself against the impact of whatever it was he was going to come in contact with, just as the ship righted itself and begun to heel in the opposite direction, nullifying the impetus his body had as the rope absorbed the centrifugal force and brought him to a slow halt as the deck rose to meet him. As the rope halted its swing and hung vertical, Domingo let go and stepped lightly across the deck and leant against the foremast in an effort to steady himself. To a man, the crew on the deck heaved a sigh of relief and applauded this foolhardy act of bravado, whilst William simply shook his head in relief at his brother's lucky escape from injury or a horrible death.

As the day wore on, the storm began building in the west behind them, the seas lifting the stern of the Marie Laure high, before rushing past on either side. William reckoned the ships speed at about nine knots, more than twice their normal speed and about as fast as their hull speed would allow. With a bit of luck this following sea and tail wind might keep them ahead of the worst of the weather until they could make Davey or even better, south east cape.

The lookout sighted what looked to be low rocky cape at 9am, the barely visible, long, low, grey line on the eastern horizon, distinguishable only as land to any except the most experienced seamen. Perfect! William had ordered the ship hove to for the night which slowed their approach to mainland Tasmania. The last thing they needed was to be pushed up on a lee shore in this blow in the middle of the night, forcing them to turn south, into the worst of the storm to avoid land fall at night. Even with sails and mostly bare poles, the ship had still carried more than fifty miles during the night and William had gotten little sleep, half expecting the scream of panic from the lookout as the monstrous breakers signaled the end for the Marie Laure and all aboard, for in this inky blackness, even the keenest eyes could never hope to sight the line of rocky shore until it was too late.

With storm sails and mizzen set and the ship rolling under a starboard quarter following sea, the Marie Laure inched her way south along the coast. William went aloft himself to try to get a bearing on where the ship was. He climbed the rigging of the foremast and hung on for dear life as the howling north west winds threatened to tear him away into the rain and wind. He stood on the two planks that were bolted to the mast and braced himself against it, worming his body up into the lookout station. 'Welcome aboard, sir.' The lookout in the other band of iron called loudly over the wind. William gripped his hands on the canvas covered cold iron rail encircling his waist and allowed his body to relax and move with the mast. He knew that trying to fight against the roll of the ship was futile and exhausting, he also knew he had to get this right. By his estimation, they were just ten miles from the breakers that hurled themselves against the rocky shore, one miscalculation and the Marie Laure would find herself among those breakers.

He peered into the grey mist ahead, thankful the worst of the storm was still behind them. To the north, he thought he could make out the long, thin line of low rocky point and tapped the crewman on the shoulder and pointed to the almost invisible hills in the distance, before quickly returning his hand to the relative comfort of the rail.

The seaman nodded. 'Low Rocky, I think.' William didn't admonish the man for not being certain, who could be certain, with certain visibility down to a mile and low rocky at least forty miles away. He turned his gaze to the land off their port bow. He could make out the tall hills behind the shore and what seemed to be a wide open bay on their port. He recognized it for Port Davey, but with the full force of the storm still to come and the memories of the Flying Childers and the Maid of Erin still fresh in his mind, also knowing that to stop over in Davey would destroy his chances of making it home for the birth of the baby, he decided against risking a delay of more than a week, in favour of heading for home. He nodded and patted the seaman on the shoulder in recognition of a job well done and began the climb down to the deck.

In the chart room, William wiped the rain water from his head and hands and bent course for Recherche Bay. With relatively clear daylight, and visibility to the south quite good, he ordered more sail so as to keep ahead of the threatening thunderheads to the north west and hopefully make home port this day.

The Marie Laure cleared south west cape and was making her way in heavy seas between Maatsuyker Island and De Witt island when the call came down from the tops. 'Thar She Blows!'

'Oh, No!' Domingo exclaimed, 'Not now!'

William shook his head and his eyes followed the lookout's out stretched arm. There were not one, but two whales, in the lee of flat witch island, they were young whales, the mist from their blow holes could be seen quite clearly as they rested out of the storm and the Marie Laure was coming into calmer water, out of sight of the spermaceti, yet advancing on them with every minute.

Most of the crew had come out of the focs'le and stood at the port rail, bleary eyed and shielding their faces against the wind and rain, they began looking back and forth from the whales to where William and Domingo stood near the helm, waiting for an order. William knew this could wreck any chance he had to be present at the birth of his child but he had a responsibility to the owners and his crew and didn't hesitate. 'Go get 'em.' He said to Domingo, and the first mate had no hesitation in calling the crew to stations.

William took the helm as his brother readied the tubs of ropes and called for extra harpoons to be added into the whale boats stores. He hoped to get this over with as soon as it was possible with no room for delays.

Then he had an idea! He ran to the wheel house and put it to William that they lash the whales alongside the ship, and taking advantage of the relatively calmer waters, tow the whales alongside the ship all the way to Recherche before the storm broke. They could see the whales quite plainly now, they were two juvenile sperm whales, lying in the lee of flat witch island, unaware the Marie Laure was bearing down on them. William nodded, if Domingo and the boatsmen could get the whales killed in one go, then it would be entirely possible, especially with a following sea, to tow two small whales, one either side of the ship, back to Recherche Bay.

The boats moved slowly up alongside the whales before attacking simultaneously. Being juveniles and with no adults around to guide them, neither whale could have had an inkling of what was about to happened and were overcome almost immediately. Utterly confused and disoriented by the iron lance heads being driven deep into their bodies, the young whales swum around in circles, dragging the heavy whaleboats filled with shouting men, each trying to gain help from its companion, to no avail, until the lance of the steersmen ended their struggles and it was over.

The Marie Laure had hove to in the lee of Flat witch island and instead of trying to beat up to the boats, William remained on station, the whales acting like drogues on the boats, steadying them whilst the wind which was swinging to the west, began pushing them towards her. In just half an hour of pulling, the boats had reached the ship and their relieved crews clambered aboard just as the full brunt of the storm came to bear.

Heavy chains were ready and flenser's cut deep notches near the tails to tow the whales tail first, the tail hauled up towards the bows evenly on both sides of the ship and iron hawsers ran around its head to hold the body of the whales against the sides of the barque. By the time they had the whales secured, the Marie Laure with her added bulk, had turned beam on to the waves and it took a great deal of seamanship from the captain as he heaved and dragged on the wheel, all the while yelling orders to the crew to haul the yards, first this way, then that. The ship laboured under the burden of the whales, wallowing and yawing as the seas began to build around her but in just a few hours, on July 9th, they had made Fishers point and the safety of Recherche Bay, just sixteen hours *after* little Mary Ann Smith was born.

Sarah had given birth at the Tedman's, and unlike James, Mary Ann was dark, just like William. Sarah's white skin and red hair contrasted deeply against this little dark bundle of joy at her breast and he couldn't help wondering if this would help or hinder her in her growing up years. Disease was rampant among newborns and infants in this far flung corner of the world and Mrs. Tedman ordered both William and Domingo from the house, and forbid them return until they were scrubbed squeaky clean with carbolic.

It normally took three days for resupply, but the same storm that had threatened to cost them their two whales, had continued to rage and William and his crew took every advantage of the few extra days in port. Each day for a week William visited his little 'dark eyed girl' and played with young 'Jim' while she was sleeping. A week later, the Marie Laure was ready for sea once again and for the first time in his life, William didn't really want to go to sea and leave his family behind. As the ship turned west from Fishers point, William took one last glance over his shoulder at Bill and Sarah Tedman's house and swore he would not be leaving them behind again.

It would be April 1879, nine long months of searching the vast open spaces of the Southern Ocean between Tasmania and the great Australian bight before the familiar sight of the Marie Laure would once again pass Fishers point inward bound for Recherche.

William's heart soared as he sighted his wife holding on to the handle of a baby carriage and her sister Rosie, holding young Jim's hand on the wharf at Recherche, dispelling all those fears of not seeing all of them again and as the ship's boat bumped against the wharf, both he and Domingo leapt from the whale boat onto the wharf and into their arms.

That night, William told Sarah, Rosie and Domingo of the day he was black birded from Navigator's Island, at just eleven years of age. The Tedman's and Mister and Mrs. Domeney listened attentively as William related his tale of abduction and abuse at the hands of his captors. When he finished, he was at once inundated with questions about his family. Who were they? Where were they? Even Sarah, who was a little more that miffed William hadn't told her of his past in detail, shook her head and rested her hand on his arm. 'You should have told me,' She said sadly and he dropped his head and whispered, 'There was no point.' He looked up at the rest of the people gathered around the table. 'I was too young, and there was no way of going back.'

Domingo broke in. 'Well, you're not too young now.' He added, 'And you're the captain of the ship, now.' He pointed at William's chest. 'You can decide where we go.'

'I was hoping one of you would say that.' William answered, and the rest of the table voiced their encouragement at a return to Navigator's Island, in search of William's family.

It was decided, Sarah, James and the baby would sail on the next voyage to the western grounds in the hope of a profitable voyage, thus saving money in rent to the Domeney's and in the hope of paying a builder to build two new homes. One for William and Sarah and one for Domingo and Rosie. Rosie would stay with her parents, for the same reason, and Mister Domeney would arrange a builder and materials to be paid for, in advance, at a very reasonable price while they were away on the second voyage, and hopefully, after meeting his parents and his two brothers, they could each return to brand new homes in just a couple of years. Each person in the room agreed that if they did not take this step now, then William would never see his family again, so, with a thump of Domingo's fist on the table, it was decided!

The Marie Laure left for the next voyage to the western grounds on May 17th, 1879. Sarah stood and waved to her parents and her sister from the stern of the ship until the headland of Fisher's point blocked her view of Recherche Bay and home. Then she turned and hustled James past the hurricane house where William sat with the baby on his knee, left forearm around her and one hand resting on the spokes of the large ship's wheel, smiling contentedly, now he had his family with him on the sea, where he needed to be.

After four months at sea the Marie Laure sailed back into Port Davey with just nine and a half tuns of sperm oil in her hold. She had seen quite a few humpbacks and black whales but William, much to the crew's chagrin, resisted the taking of them in favour of the more valuable sperm whales. It took some cajoling and promises of a better payday for the crew who didn't understand that whales 'weren't whales.' William argued that a hold full of sperm oil was worth ten times as much as a hold full of black oil, and with humpback whale oil prices dropping, the only one's worth taking these days, were sperm whales.

Sarah busied herself with the baby in between kitchen duties and running after young Jim, who sought every chance he could to escape his mother's clutches and tear off across the deck to be caught in the arms of some ever watchful seaman. Both Sarah and Jim had suffered badly from seasickness for the first four days, such so, that William began to fear for their health, especially the little ones, and thought he would need to turn the ship around, luckily, by lunchtime of the fourth day, both Sarah and Jim were eating and drinking the somewhat unappetizing cook's food as well as any man on deck and Sarah's breast feeding of Mary Ann had not lessened.

Back on her feet, Sarah took over the galley and the men's appetite improved significantly, as did their demeanor, even so there were some grumblings about being an 'unlucky hen ship'.

Back and forth the Marie Laure crisscrossed the vast expanse of the bight with little success, until, after three months of sailing, and after turning for home, they chanced upon a pod of sperm whales heading in their direction, just before dark. William wanted to wait until dawn but Domingo urged him to go after the whales now before they lost them, he reminded William the Marie Laure was now a 'Hen Frigate', and it wouldn't do to raise what might be construed as bad luck among the crew for having a woman aboard. After a minute's thought, William agreed and the chase was on. From a quiet, almost lazy afternoon with crewmen sitting about idling the day away, Sarah was amazed as the Marie Laure came alive at Domingo's call.

There would be only one chance to get one whale before dark. The captain and crew knew the dangers of a single boat harpooning a whale and being dragged off into the night, never to be seen again. William ordered two boats swung out and the lookout to keep any eye for the direction the pod might take. He knew they only had enough daylight to secure one whale and the rest of the pod would get away, but hopefully they might turn and head in their home direction and they would catch up with them on the morrow.

With the boats down William had the ship hove to and they waited. Sarah had put Mary Ann to bed and young Jim in his pen below deck. She had never seen a whale chase before and stood at the rail, near the stern, excitement building as the ship hove to, bows to the wind and directly in front of the pod of whales, heading in their direction.

She could see the whale spouts in the distance, gouts of misty spray blown on the wind, as first one, then two, then more, broke the surface intermittently as they drew closer and closer. Then they were among them, Sarah couldn't believe the speed of their approach as the pod turned away to the east, from the ship, straight into the path of the two waiting whale boats. The boatsteerers had anticipated the whale's movements and had already singled out a medium sized bull. She watched in awe, and more than a little fear as both boats approached the whale as it veered past, almost touching its side as the harpooner threw the first harpoon. The startled whale thrashed about and flung its tail high, before putting on a turn of speed that had Sarah lifting her hand to her mouth in fear for those in the boat. Now it was Domingo's turn. With the whale hamstrung by the drag of the first boat, Domingo had time to maneuver his boat directly in the path of the monster and his crew only just had time to turn out of the leviathan's path to avoid being crushed by its powerful jaw. Seeing them, the whale turned away and this was Domingo's chance, he flung his harpoon, the lance biting deep into the whales jaw and lodging tight, but instead of the lance coming free of its iron head in order for him to replace it, the lance came free and locked around the first rope, the weight of two boats tearing the first harpoon free of the whales flesh and leaving the first boat wallowing in the wake of the whale as the giant cetacean added a burst of speed and tore off into the twilight, taking Domingo's boat and crew with it.

William immediately ordered the ship under sail, cursing himself for allowing Domingo to talk him into this foolish venture. He knew they would have a head wind that would slow the ship considerably, the whale would have a turn of speed that the Marie Laure couldn't hope to match and for all he knew, the whale would have sounded by now and his brother and the boat's crew would be halfway to Davey Jones's locker, and all in front of his wife's terrified eyes.

The first boat had headed back to the ship post haste, her crew were aware they could never match the speed of the whale and they needed to get aboard the ship and try to hunt down Domingo's whale boat in the dark.

The whale had put on a turn of speed that had the men fearing it would sound and drag them under, but the monster had no idea the boat was the cause of its problem and was too consumed with the pain in its jaw and desperately tried to shake the harpoon free. For three long hours, the men in the boat locked their oars in the down position and laid out as much rope as both tubs would allow, creating as much drag as possible in the hope the whale would tire and stop, or at least slow. It was now dark and the Marie Laure was nowhere in sight, still the whale pushed north into the inky blackness, although Domingo thought he could feel the whale beginning to slow. He looked over their stern, already the stars were twinkling overhead, but there was no sign of the Marie Laure anywhere on the sea. Two of the men offered up the option of cutting the line to the whale and rowing back to the ship but Domingo mentioned that the sea was calm and if they could get alongside the monster again, he could climb onto it's back and kill it. Had they not seen it happen before, the men would have written his offer off as preposterous, but they had seen the negro in action and had no doubt what he was capable of. They weighed up the blame of the loss of the whale as their fault for cutting it free, as opposed to being heroes for capturing the whale and surviving the chase, *IF* they survived the chase.

William had the fires in the tryworks uncovered, to give a beacon to the ships boat or any sailors that may be still afloat on the flotsam of the smashed whale boat. As well, he had lanterns hung on the yardarms and even carried to the lookout, in the hope of the men sighting it and somehow signaling their position. All hands, including Sarah, were lined along the rail and the bow, keeping their backs to the flames of the tryworks so as not to blind their vision of the darkness outside the ship's gunwales.

The ship had to beat up slowly into the headwind and William was careful not to sail too far outside the line he reckoned the whale would travel and thus cross over the path the boat should have taken, missing them altogether, and condemning his crew and his brother to a lingering death on the sea, that is, if they weren't already dead.

The whale was tiring, even the men could notice how the consistent plunging was taking longer and longer, the time between rasping sound of the air from the whale's blowhole becoming shorter and shorter. Domingo knew it was now or never. He gave the command to release the oars and row for all they were worth. He knew that once the whale realised it was free of the drag of the boat, it would sound and they would all be dragged to their doom. He had to act fast. Both he and the steersman pulled in the line as fast as the oarsmen could row, keeping a constant pressure on the line lest the whale sense the drag lessening, as the boat approached the tiring whale, he knew he would only have one shot at this and he had to be quick. He picked up the harpoon and leapt from the gunwale straight onto the back of the whale. As he did, the extra weight of the man on the tired whale's back caused the beast to sound, amid cries of dismay and fear from the men, the whale began its plunge to the briny depths. The men watched in terror as Domingo drove the lance deep into the fleshy softness about five feet back from its blow hole and then disappeared into the sea as the whale sounded. Already the steersman was throwing line out as fast as he could to give them time to cut the line before it went taut and pulled them under as well. Then a miracle happened, as fast as it had dived, the whale rose again, with the figure of Jose kneeling on its back, hanging onto the last two foot of the lance for dear life as the whale's life blood, free of the water that covered its wound, began spouting into the air. The men covered their faces and turned their heads down towards the deck of the boat. In the darkness, they couldn't see what was happening, only the gushing blood that covered them and threatened to choke them, until Domingo and the steersman pulled the rope in close enough for him to jump back into the boat.

It took a while for the men to realise the whale was dead, and their immediate problems were solved but it soon dawned on them, they were still in a world of trouble. They were cold, exhausted, covered in blood, on a moonless night in the middle of the Southern Ocean and a dead whale in tow. And just where were they going to tow the whale?

Domingo rummaged around in the survivor pack stowed under the steersman's thwart, and produced a tiny lantern and matches. After lighting the lantern, the men lifted the mast into place and lashed it upright. Making the whale fast to boat, they unfurled the tiny sail and felt relieved as the breeze took hold and began to slowly push the boat, with its precious cargo in tow, southwards, from whence they had come. They had washed what they could of the blood and salt water from their eyes and faces but some still complained of the salt from both still stinging their eyes and Domingo knew that if the Marie Laure didn't sight them during the night, they were going to have a very rough day of it tomorrow.

The Marie Laure looked for all the world like a floating carnival. She was lit up from stem to stern and from yards to tops, still there was no sign of the lost whale boat. Both William and Sarah looked to the heavens in awe of the millions of stars that seemed to rise infinitely slowly from the eastern horizon to the centre of the sky, then cascade towards the western horizon in a slow moving river of twinkling lights. There was no moon, and William was thankful for that. It meant that if the boat had survived the whale hunt. There was much more of a chance for the lookout to see a light on the water. As if he had mentioned this out loud, they both looked to the tops for a sound, any sound, but none was forthcoming. Except for the creaking of the masts and the sounds of waves on the hull, as the ship pushed its way against the waves, the ship was quiet, deathly quiet.

William was about to give the call to heave to, he didn't want to overrun the search area, but decided to give it ten more minutes on the starboard tack.

'Light midships to port, on the water.' The call came from the tops. William couldn't believe it! He had all but given up hope. It had to be the boat, there would be no light on the water unless it was a whale boat, and they were crossing directly in front of it. Had he switched on to the other port tack just a few minutes earlier, they would have missed them. He held Sarah in his arms as she burst into tears with relief and a cheer of relief came up from the ship, but nowhere near the relief of those in the little whale boat who had seen the Marie Laure's lanterns and watched as the lanterns hanging from the yards swung away, until they could see both ends of the yardarms and the myriad of lights that were strung from them. She had seen them, and was heading towards them!

There was a festive air aboard the Marie Laure that night, William ordered a beer keg opened and the crew that had remained on board ship toasted and retoasted the miraculous return of their shipmates. The keg remained open until it was empty, and whilst the flensers and specktioneers began their work, the whale boats crew sat singing and drinking the health to the hero of the hour, Domingo Evorall. Sarah joined in the singing and was welcomed with open arms as the captain's wife who was indeed a good luck charm on the good ship Marie Laure.

On September 8th, 1879, the Marie Laure reported from Port Davey that she had nine and a half tuns stowed and nothing untoward had occurred so far during the voyage, and after taking on board fresh water and some basic supplies from the Huon piner's gardens at Port Davey, Sarah had the opportunity of meeting some of the ladies from the settlement. With arms full of vegetables and some much needed fresh milk and butter, as well as fresh fish, Agnes Dougherty and Mrs. Heather, wives of local pine cutters and boat builders, well known to William and Domingo, came aboard to meet Sarah and her little ones. With the weather clearing and spring in the air, the ladies chatted aboard the ship while they watched the kids play on the deck, Agnes Dougherty recalled the bravery of William and Domingo in the shipwrecks of the Flying Childers and the Maid of Erin. As they watched the kids playing on the deck, on September, 10th 1879, they could never have known that one day, Agnes' two year old, Henry, and little Mary Ann Smith would someday wed and begin the story that otherwise would never have been told.

The Marie Laure set sail once again and would plow the same area of the Southern Ocean, returning twice to Recherche Bay to resupply. Sarah lived up to her name of lucky charm with the ship returning with eighteen tuns of sperm oil, which was transshipped from Recherche to Hobart aboard the Zephyr, a schooner, also owned by Mister Sherwin.

On her second return to Recherche, on 10th August, 1880, Sarah surprised everyone except the crew, by giving birth to a son, Thomas Alexander Smith. Sarah and the three children would stay with the Tedman's, whilst the Marie Laure went out for the last leg of her Voyage. The Marie Laure finally returned from the western whaling grounds to her home port of Recherche Bay, on Thursday, 7th of January, 1881 with a total whale oil catch of fifty five tuns, worth three thousand eight hundred and fifty English pounds. In 2024 that sum would be worth $252,350.50. Williams share of the 'lay' would be two hundred and twenty six pounds, worth sixty six thousand dollars and Domingo's share was one hundred and seventy five pounds, worth 51,000 dollars.

On 5th of august, 1881, at two years and five months old, Mary Ann Smith set foot on land for the first time in her life! Her audience laughing as she lifted first one foot high, then the other, to counter the rolling and pitching motion of the of the deck. It would take three weeks before she become accustomed to solid ground without falling. In march, she went to sea again, this time for grounds much farther afield, and it wasn't long before she gained her 'sea legs' again, and as the story goes, she walked with a rolling motion for the rest of her life!

With the money received from this last voyage, both William and Domingo contracted mister Domeney to supply the timber and build two homes for them, one near the mouth of Cockle Creek on the land Sarah had purchased and one on Evorall's point across the Bay. Once this was done, it was time to put their plan into action.

Chapter 33

River Derwent, Hobart
1st march 1881

William and Domingo watched as the ropes lifted and rose out of the water, ripples springing out from the cables like giant butterfly wings as they cleared the water and bounced up and down on the surface with each pull of the waterman's boats oars. For a while it seemed as if the oarsmen were wasting their time, simply beating the water with their oars, then slowly, ever so slowly, the oarsmen's long bladed oars began to overcome the press of the water against the side of the ship, and like a scene from Gulliver's travels, the many thin ropes attached from the Marie Laure to the tiny lilliputian waterman's boats inched the Marie Laure's bows away from the wharf and began swinging her clear of the whalers Helen and the Lufra, toward mid stream. Once the ship became side on to the current, the bow of the ship began to move downstream and the coxswains in all of the eight boats began urging their crews onwards, the wash from the little boats becoming less as the boats began to make way and the cables from the giant ship tightened and began pulling the Marie Laurie from the new wharf out towards mid stream.

The ship came clear of the dock and the last ropes on the stern were lifted from the curved iron bollards on the wharf and let fall into the water, to be heaved aboard by the straining crewmen on the deck. At the same time both the fore and mizzen sails were unfurled, the slight south west breeze coming down off mount Wellington, pushing her even further away from the dock and allowing the helmsman to have at least a modicum of steering, much to the relief of the oarsmen in the waterman's boats.

It was still going to be a slow haul out to her usual mooring and the two men moved their eyes from the waterman's boats to landward. The sandstone buildings of offices and warehouses along Salamanca Place took central place in one's vision until the ship moved further away from the dock and beyond the easternmost three and four storied sandstone buildings, they could see, quite clearly Captain McGregor's house, Lenna, atop the hill overlooking the river. This fine, two storied, Italian renaissance grand home was built by captain Alexander McGregor, from a cottage of the same name. McGregor, who had become prosperous in the whaling trade and who owned the largest slipway on the domain as well as a fleet of whaling and trading ships, had commenced building in the eighteen seventies and Lenna hadn't long been completed. With no expense spared, Lenna was a tribute to the success of the whaling industry in Tasmania, a success that sadly, was waning, with the scarcity of the whale population. Captain McGregor had installed a clerestory atop the building between the dormers, with views taking in the whole of the dock district, as well as the river in front of Sullivan's Cove, and crews, especially from his own ship's, quietly joked about the 'spying eyes of mister McGregor' while they readied his ships for their long voyages.

The McGregor's owned the Waterwitch, Helen, Harriet McGregor, Lufra, and the Ethel as well as numerous smaller craft that were moored ahead and aft of the Marie Laure.

As the Marie Laure began moving out into the river, the brothers could see the brig Zephyr, moving slowly up stream to rendezvous with her. William had arranged through the ship's agent and owner, Mister Sherwin, to have the Zephyr come alongside and off load two tons of potatoes, one ton of onions and numerous other vegetables. William had also arranged with the skipper of the Zephyr to have a dozen chickens, four small pigs, two sheep, four goats and a woman and two children, who they would pick up in Recherche Bay.

Those crew who were not concerned with getting the ship out into the river, lined the railings and watched the people of Hobart docks go about their business. They could see all the way to McGregor's slipway on the domain, men climbing on ladders and scaffolding as they careened and readied the ships for their next two years at sea. The watermen had begun casting off their tow cables and heading back to waterman's dock where rows of boats were lined up ready for the next arrival or departure, of these cumbersome workhorses of the sea.

Hobart was a typical busy seaport with drays lined up on the docks, readying to bring provisions to the ships, or alternatively, move the myriad of barrels of cargo, be it whale oil from the south seas or coal from the mines of New South Wales, it all had to be taxed, moved and stored, creating further industry for the colony. Down river, to the south, they could see the new flagstaff tower on Mount Nelson, the old semaphore tower being only recently taken down with the advent of the newly invented telegraph.

The Zephyr had moved alongside and fenders were dropped to prevent the ships timbers chafing against each other. William and the captain of the brig chatted amiably whilst Domingo organised the stowing of the stores. This done, the crew took to the more menial tasks of shipboard life, or simply sat back and enjoyed the view of Hobart from the river as the ship dropped anchor and waited to leave at dawn.

A thick mist covered the glassy surface of the Derwent at dawn of the next day, the light of the new day had not yet reached into the river and the tall masts of the Lufra and other ships moored alongside the new wharf were yet to distinguish themselves from the misty backdrop of the foothills of Mount Wellington. Even the lapping of the waters around the shore, a constant near the river's edge, was absent. In the distance, somewhere within the dark mist that completely obliterated the township beyond the docks, the clip clopping of a single, unseen horse, could be heard heading for waterman's dock, the sound of its hooves striking the cobbles echoed down Hunter Street and out across the water. Even the gas street lights were completely obliterated from sight. The Marie Laure was nonexistent, not even a shadowy outline belied her existence on the water, save for a tiny pin point of light, a firefly floating twenty feet above the water, in reality, a lantern sitting on a ditty box under the hurricane house at her stern.

The two men sat in silence, staring into the darkness, waiting for the view to unfold before them. Domingo knew there was something on his brother's mind but just what, he wasn't sure. In typical Domingo fashion, he didn't press, William would tell him in his own time.

Since he had arrived, William had witnessed Hobart Town, a dilapidated and out dated convict settlement, grow into the boom town of Hobarton on the back of the whaling industry, and now, just two months ago, the new city of Hobart had been pronounced and the city fathers had declared a transition from whaling to a trading centre, even the colony of Van Dieman's Land had changed its name to Tasmania, and was in the throes of becoming a state in its own right. William knew it was now or never, with whales becoming more scarce every voyage and never knowing whether he would ever get another chance, he knew had to go back.

William and Domingo sat drinking from the pannikins of tea the cook's boys had brought them, quiet whispers between the watery slurps had them planning their next voyage and William whispered his intentions of heading deep into the south pacific, though what exactly for he didn't say, and Domingo didn't ask. He would tell him in his own good time.

William loved this time of morning, the cool, crisp sting of the frosty air against his face, but he was concerned there was no wind and repeatedly craned his neck to look at the surface of the water, and catch the tiny ripples that would signal a lifting breeze.

There was no sound from below but the two men knew the first shift would be awake and quietly eating their breakfast while the captain was on deck, waiting for dawn. Then, as if on cue, like a giant ethereal curtain rising from a watery stage, the mist began to dissipate, drawing back towards the mountain, revealing one by one, the other ships in the bay, their white topgallant poles glinting through the fog, as the first rays of dawn struck.

Both William and Domingo smiled at the scene and watched speechless, as first, the ships on the water subtly appeared as if from nowhere, ghostly apparitions becoming tangible. Then, the mist on shore faded to reveal first, the Waterwitch, then Lufra, and last, the Helen, riding stately against the new wharf as they appeared out of the mist. The previously unseen horse and dray had ridden on to waterman's dock, and although the men could no longer hear the hoof falls of the horse, they could plainly see the driver moving about and two other drays crossing Davey Street to fall in alongside the first. Domingo pointed without speaking, lest his voice destroy the magic of the moment, and the two men watched as the square sandstone shape of the much loved Nautilus Hotel on the corner of Salamanca and Montpelier, bared its façade through the fading mist, and William grinned. The pub was a favourite haunt for whalers, originally being called the Whalers Return and had they not already gotten the crew aboard the previous day, there was a very likely chance the majority of the crew would still be carousing within its walls.

As the fog dissipated the men knew they had just witnessed a show befitting any of the great theatres in Europe, something showgoers of the cities would never hope to see, but for William the show was over. He leaned over the stern of the ship and smiled at the tiny wisps of breeze skittering in all directions across the surface of the water, like the wings of a thousand invisible mosquitoes, signaled the wind about to arrive and the captain lifted his leg and stamped his right foot hard on the deck.

Immediately the rumble of rousing men and clinking of tin on tin as their pannikins were placed, no, almost hurled, into the large tin basin that served as the washing up receptacle, amongst other things, for the men were well used to this morning ritual, and played to it as if were a rehearsal for a theatre play.

By the time the sun's rays struck the deck of the Marie Laure, both anchors had cleared the muddy bottom and all sails bar the topgallants had set and even those had snapped to their full as the anchors came up to the bits. With a light south west breeze, she made a proud sight under full sail as she cleared between Tinderbox and Dennes Point and shaped a course for Recherche.

There was the usual excitement in Recherche Bay as the Marie Laurie hove in to view off the Acteaons and turned into the bay proper. Sarah and Rosie were already at the wharf, as was Mister Domeney and dray. He had arranged for the Marie Laurie to carry a load of vegetables and hardware from Hobart in an effort to cut transport costs and in light of family friendship, William and Domingo were happy to oblige, and laughed when they saw Mister Domeney's questioning look at the other tarpaulin covered stack on the deck.

The girls squealed with delight as the tarpaulin's were thrown back, revealing the household goods and furniture that lay beneath. William and Domingo explained that mister Domeney would store their furniture and goods at his place so that they might be ready when the houses were finished, but this wasn't good enough for the girls and they pored over the furniture even as it was being loaded aboard the dray and the tarpaulins were not replaced until it was time for tea at the Domeney's. After tea, the dray was used once again to convey them to the wharf where Sarah cried and hugged young Jim, who would be staying with her parents as would

Rosie. Both Rosie and her mother assured her he would be alright and Rosie promised to take good care of him. Goodbyes were said among tears and laughter, before the whaleboat finally pulled away and headed out to where their home for the next twenty months was moored in the bay.

The deck of the Marie Laure looked for all the world like a farm yard. There were goats bleating, chickens squawking, pigs grunting and squealing, and even pigeons cooing. Mary Ann loved it. She rolled in the hay and petted the piglets, much to the annoyance of the sow, who did her best to herd her charges into the makeshift pens near the foc'sle bulkhead, away from these interfering humans. It was summertime and the ship had an air of a picnic trip about her, men were singing as they walked out under the yards, both feet balancing on the ropes that hung underneath, as they leant over the yards to unleash the sails from their clews. Then, leaning back and hanging on tight, as the giant sails dropped heavily through the air. The deck crew releasing the sheets from the belaying pins on the rails and hauling them through their blocks until the sails snapped tight, then quickly securing the sheets once again. As each sail filled, the ship surged ahead, both the children and Sarah feeling the deck roll and lift beneath their feet as the wind took hold and both sailors and captain alike, laughing as Mary Ann fell on the bed of straw with each surge of speed, then struggling to her feet, only to fall again as another sail caught the wind.

Sarah was in charge of the animals and with the baby in his crib she got to work, reinforcing their pens as soon as the ship got under way. It was hard work, as William had demanded the animals be secure in all weathers, it wouldn't do for goats and pigs to be washing around the deck in a blow, injuring themselves and putting crewmen's safety at risk. By the time the ship had cleared the steep, sheer cliffs of Cape Pillar, daylight was waning and Sarah was satisfied the animals were secure. She called to William, and the captain walked down the deck from the hurricane house to the cramped area aft of the foc'sle. Sarah had housed the pigeons and chickens in battery boxes, formed into walls and pens and nailed together to house the pigs. Goats were hobbled to restrict their movements but otherwise they shared the pig pens. William and Domingo strode to the foremast at Sarah's call, expecting to have to shower accolades on the work she had done, but as they approached the foremast, they saw what she was directing their attention to, and there, in the centre of the pen, cuddled up to two young kids was Mary Ann, fast asleep, the nanny standing guard over the three of them. Both William and Domingo laughed as they stepped over the wall of boxes and were then forced back as the nanny advanced on them, angrily. 'So that's what you called us down here for!' Exclaimed William as he leapt back over the pens. Domingo and William were at a loss until a seaman stepped past them and lassoed the goat before running the rope around the foremast and heaving on it, dragging the nanny on to her knees and holding her there whilst William and Domingo climbed into the pen and retrieved the sleeping child, amid jeers and laughter from the rest of the crew.

There followed the same ritual each morning, around daylight each day, the goat would start bleating for her lost child until Sarah arrived to milk her, and whilst she nuzzled her new found 'kid', Sarah would collect the chicken and pigeon eggs and feed the pigs with the swill from last evenings meal. Thereafter, the nanny would have to be lassoed and tied, until Mary Ann could be rescued by their new mum. Sometimes, Sarah would leave Mary Ann in the charge of her new babysitter all day, the nanny having no problems with Sarah 'helping' to feed and change them, and Sarah was grateful to her surrogate 'mum', enabling her to help with the cooking and washing of baby Tom, and the mate's clothes.

With fair weather and a southwest breeze behind her, The Marie Laure made Maria Island by the end of the third day and turned east. She had gone but one hundred miles east of Maria Island, when she spied her first whale. This was a good sign William had made the right choice. A large sperm whale, possibly a fifteen tunner, and two boats were swung out with William trying his luck as a harpooner and Domingo manning the helm of the ship. The whale was heading northeast, the same direction as the Marie Laure, so Domingo held back the whale boats until the ship was almost on the unsuspecting whale. The ship lost ground on the whale after Domingo gave the order to back sails, stopping the ship in its track, and when the boats hit the water, each of them raised the small sail kept inboard for this very purpose and set out after their quarry. The whale boats were light compared to most boats. Made from the much sought after Huon pine, from deep within Tasmania's rain forests, the creamy yellow planks were light and curved upwards to allow minimum depth of keel, yet allowing for fantastic maneuverability and strength to weight capability. With the added sail, these lightly made, but strong, craft could skip lightly and quickly across the water, easily and silently overtaking an unsuspecting whale.

Both boats made contact at the same time and the taking of the whale went without a hitch. Still, Sarah was nervous. She had become adept at tying the nanny to the foremast and after taking Mary Ann from the goat pen to the cabin, and making sure the baby was comfortable, she fell to her duties of helping the ship's boy to ready the tryworks and trying to stay out of the way of the crewmen as they readied the ship for flensing and trying out the whale.

With the episode in the bight, where the boat and crew were almost lost, still fresh in her mind, Sarah was still very nervous and kept moving to the rail to watch the two tiny sails bucking and rocking as the whale boats fought the giant sea monster to a standstill. The ship was only about half mile west of the battle and at any time she expected to see the tail of the leviathan come crashing down on her husband's boat, dashing the lives out of all aboard and as if to justify her fears, the masts of the little boats begun rocking violently, almost crashing into each other as the whale began thrashing its tail violently and swimming around in circles. As she lifted her hand to her mouth in fear, a crewman came to her side at the rail and reassured her that this was the whale 'flurrying' a characteristic of dying whales and as if to prove his words, the activity in the distance, stopped and the masts of the little boats were still. Immediately, the sailors began hauling on the sheet attached to the yards and the sails of the ship once again turned to catch the wind. With her skirts and petticoats tucked into her stockings, Sarah came away from the rail and ran to where the cook and the ship's boy were readying the hearths for boiling the blubber. She fell in beside the cook, whilst the ships boy grabbed up the tin of molten pitch from the hearth and ran to where the cooper was busy at the mizzen mast, fitting staves into the groves of the barrel ends and lashing them loosely together, the boy would then tar the joins between the staves as the iron hoops were beaten over the ends to tighten up the perfectly fitting staves, rendering the tuns water tight.

The boats had dropped their sails and tied off to the whale as they waited for the Marie Laure to come to them. The men stood at the rail whilst William caught the leather bucket and climbed onto the back of the whale. He cut the usual hole in the head of the whale and began climbing into the hole the flensing axe had made. Sarah grimaced in disgust, as her husband began clambering head first into the hole to bail out the spermaceti and hand the bucket to the line of men leading up to the deck. Only when the bucket got to her, did she realise that she was part of the crew, and as such, she was expected to take part in the process, like everyone else on board. Inquisitively, she lifted the bucket to her nose and was surprised at the clean smell of the clear, almost rose tinted, liquid inside. The seaman next to her held his hand out impatiently, explaining that the spermaceti would harden and crystalise in the bucket, unless it was fed to the trypot immediately, they had to work quickly. He also explained that spermaceti also made the highest quality candles and was used in taking photometric measurements, something neither of them knew anything about but were grateful for the high price it commanded. She passed the bucket on quickly lest she fall behind in the parade of buckets that carried the precious oil up to the steaming cauldrons of the tryworks as fast as William, who was completely inside the whale by this time, could scoop, only his hand and the leather bucket visible, as he bailed the head cavity dry. Then, as William declared the spermaceti chamber empty, like ants on a carcass of a cicada, the flensers and specktioneers clambered down the sides of the ship onto the platform and began attaching the chains to the head of the whale for lifting onto the deck. The smell wasn't that noticeable at first, more of a not so unpleasant, scent on the wind, becoming heavier as the whale was broken down, gradually increasing to a cloying stench as the heavier oils were rendered down and the amount of blood and oily flesh coming over the rail with the long strips of blubber, increased to an inch deep layer of filthy stinking cess, that coupled with the smell of boiling blubber, had Sarah running to the stern of the ship just to get a few breaths of fresh air, or into the captain's cabin, ostensibly to 'check on the children.'

The smell permeated everything, even the children's clothes, which Sarah tried so hard to keep clean, avoiding the touch of anything related to the rank smell of whale flesh. Everything on board ship would be subject to the erratic gusts of wind that occasionally picked up the smoke and steam from the trypots and circulated it across the ship and through the jalousies, into the bowels of the Marie Laure.

With the whale shipped, stripped, rendered down and stowed in the tuns below deck, the cleanup began. The crew were divided into three teams, the first team would haul water in buckets from the sea and pelt it across the deck whilst the second team would man the scrubbers, a three foot wide broom with hard, wire like bristles, and run the length, as well as every nook and cranny, of the deck, whilst a third team spread boiling water from the trypots mixed with lye and carbolic to break up the greasy mix of blood and whale detritus. Sarah was impressed that a deck she thought would never be clean of the stinking blubber and blood that rose up her boots and soaked the folds of her dress as she traipsed back and forth from the trypots to the helm, could come so clean in such a short time. The constant flow of water from the bucket brigade flowing across the deck, carried the muck and waste out through the scuppers in the rail and the lye and carbolic gave a white, clean smell to the deck and rails, which would look even cleaner as the sun and salt water began bleaching the timbers of the deck.

The smell seemed to disappear as well, although Sarah suspected it was more her olfactory senses getting used to the smells of a whaling ship and she vowed to keep up her meticulous regime of washing both her and the children's clothes and bedding.

The whale yielded sixteen tuns of oil, worth more than eleven hundred pounds, and as they finished their meal and scrubbed up, all looking forward to a full night's sleep, pandemonium reigned when the call came down from the top's once again, 'WHALE HO! Thar She Blows!'

All eyes looked to the tops and followed the lookout's arm. This time it was Domingo's turn and he was already at the port whale boat swinging the davits out as the dog tired second watch clambered aboard. The whale was about a mile to the south and moving to cross the ship's path about two miles ahead. William ordered on all sail and signaled Domingo to hold off on the whale boat. Sarah felt the surge of the ship as she gathered way and ran to her station at the tryworks. The cook held his arm up to stop her, 'Beggin' pardon, Missus,' He grinned widely, 'The fires are already hot, and with everyone already on deck there is really no need for your help up here.' He nodded towards the door of the captain's cabin. 'Best you check on the bairn, and probably get some sleep. You've earned it.'

Sarah was so relieved, 'Thank you, Jonesy,' she nodded and looked to William, who, although he couldn't hear above the noise of the deck, got the gist of what Jonesy was saying and nodded. What Sarah didn't know, and was probably too tired to care, was that it was very rare for a captain's wife to take part in the ship's activities, especially the trying out of a whale, and her efforts of late had gotten the respect and admiration of the crew to a man.

Sarah went to her cabin, followed by the ship's boy and another deckhand, with two large basins of hot water. She was so weary, she could barely lift her head, and after checking on the children, she washed the sweat and grime from her body and collapsed onto her bunk.

It was just after dawn when she woke. She could sense from the warmth of the timbers of her cabin and the thin streams of bright light that filtered through the slats in the jalousie, it was a sunny day. The thumping, banging and men calling to each other on the deck had ceased and from the smell of lye and carbolic that filtered down to the cabin, she could tell that the cleanup was well under way. A knock on her cabin door, and the cabin boy called to her that her eggs and bacon, with the ubiquitous ship's biscuits and huge pannikin of tea, were on a tray on the captain's table.

Assuring her the bacon was from the ship's stores, and not from one of her pet piglets, the boy left the room and Sarah dressed and had breakfast.

On deck, everything had returned to normal, and the mood was a happy one indeed. A gentle westerly breeze had cast away the sights and smells of the trying out and already the salty air was bleaching the deck and sails of the Marie Laure.

There was an air of confidence among the crew and although most were still below deck in the cramped, airless foc'sle, some had opted to come out on deck and slumber in the warm morning sunshine. With twenty seven tuns stowed, and a happy ship, the Marie Laure sailed east.

Sarah was playing with the babies in the goat pen, she had made friends with the nanny by now and was free to come and go as she and the babies pleased. In the afternoon, the lookout sighted a sail, and called to the deck below. Sarah looked up and climbing over the boxes of the pen, ran to the rail. She stared towards the sail on the horizon and felt the loneliness of the wide expanse of ocean and realised how homesick she was for her family. The ketch 'Dauntless' changed direction and began heading in their direction, curving in a wide arc, coming around the Marie Laure's stern to draw up on the ship's port side. Domingo had the Marie Laure's mains and fore tops turned, spilling the wind out of one set of sails, against the others, and the ship was barely making way.

Sarah stood at the rail near the helm, Mary Ann in her arms with Thomas sleeping to the gentle rocking of the boat and waved a welcome to Mrs. Boucher, the captain of the 'Dauntless' wife whilst William and Captain Boucher reported information to each other to be entered into their ships logs and relayed to the respective owners and agents. This would be the only method of keeping track of a ship's movements until they reached port.

Both Sarah and Mrs. Boucher made conversation by using hand signals and gesticulations, moving their hand to their mouths indicating drinking of tea and taking the bonnets off their babies to proudly show the colour of their hair and curls, fingers indicating the number of children and their ages. With the captain's conversations finished all too soon, the Marie Laure turned her sails and picked up speed. The Dauntless slowed for a bit and then began to draw away to the south, under the Marie Laure's stern, continuing her arc and heading towards Hobart and civilisation, whilst Sarah could only look to the vast expanse of ocean before her and wonder what was in store, as she and Mary Ann swayed across the stern of the ship to the starboard rail to watch the Dauntless disappear towards the south west, she had, in her stilted gesticulations with Mrs. Boucher, been made aware of her own daughter's age. Mary Ann would be three years old in July, and where would they be? She voiced her concerns over the evening meal, how would they celebrate, their little girl had not celebrated a birthday in her life and although her first two years would not be remembered, she had fully intended her third birthday to be something to be remembered. William had thought for a moment, before simply saying, leave it with me. She did.

William conferred with Domingo on the following day, and both men were aware the ship would not land for at least six months, until they reached Navigator's Island. William considered a seal skin, but discarded the idea as not suitable for a baby. Domingo offered to get the carpenter to make a baby's toy. That was fine, but then that present would be from uncle Domingo not from her dad. No, it needed to be something special, something that would last her all her life. He rubbed the caul between thumb and forefinger and even considered giving her the caul, but a piece of leathery human skin, burnt brown with his sweat, was no present for a little girl. The men walked towards the carpenter's workshop and store, and on entering the dark shadowy realm of the wood working genius, watched as Josiah Innes, the ship's carpenter, was in the process of removing the teeth from the lower jaws of the two sperm whales.

First, Innes made three cuts down the gums of each tooth, to the bottom of the root. He then pushed a thin bladed knife down between the gums and tooth and worked the knife in under the bottom of the tooth, to cut the sinews that attached the serrated and lumpy ends of the tooth to the boney jaw. Once he was satisfied the bottom of the tooth was free of the mighty jawbone, he took a wooden mallet from the tool rack and stood back, smiling as he gave the side of the gums a good hard whack, and cheered as the tooth literally flew out of its socket and landed in Williams hands.

William laughed and rolled the tooth around in his hands. He had never seen this done before and was amazed at the shape of the tooth. Unlike the roots of a human tooth, this pure white, halfmoon shaped root was about four and a half inches long and in perfect symmetry with the upper four and a half inches of the tooth, and apart from the broken tips of the exposed section which had undoubtedly done battle with many a giant sea creature, the tooth was perfect in every way. He had seen the scrimshaw on many teeth and bones of seals and whales and knew they had value. If he could get a pair of teeth scrimshawed and polished with resin, they would make an ideal present for his daughter. William and Domingo waited for Innes to extract another tooth, identical to that in his hands and then took them to where the crew were lounging underneath the foc'sle awning.

A seaman named Dinny owned up to being the best scrimshaw carver on the ship and what's more he had travelled to Vladivostok and the Bering Sea, in his earlier trips on American whaling ships and he promised he would have no problem carving the fashions of the day, including fur coats on beautiful princesses, a perfect and long lasting present fit for the captain's princess.

On the morning of the 8th July, 1881, the Marie Laure had reached the tropic of Capricorn, just five hundred miles south of the Fiji Islands when a sperm whale was sighted just off the starboard bow and the chase was on! William ordered the ship clap on all sail, and three boats swung out. He had an idea, and wasn't taking any chances on missing out.

With less than three hundred yards out from the young whale, he ordered the ship hove to and the three boats set off in pursuit of the birthday present for his daughter.

Sarah became caught up in the excitement of the chase and even thought about accompanying them in the third boat but William shook his head. 'Far too dangerous.' He said, as he climbed down to the boat and took the position of harpooner in the first whale boat. It was a text book kill, the young juvenile had never seen a ship before and didn't 'gally' even as William drove his lance into its side. With three harpoons anchored to its head, the whale was dispatched in record time and the three boats had no trouble towing its carcass back to the ship. With the whale securely fastened to the side of the ship by cables and chains, William and Domingo led Sarah down the ladder to stand on the back of the dead whale and even though it was only a juvenile, at about twenty feet in length and in comparison, to the hull of the Marie Laure was very tiny, to Sarah it was the largest animal she had ever seen, the action of the waves causing the body of the whale to roll and move as if it were still alive. Domingo and another crewman drove a lance into the back of the whale, near its blowhole and Sarah steadied herself by holding onto the lance, while two other members of the crew passed down the gurgling and laughing Mary Ann. The atmosphere became sombre, as William then took delivery of the Ditty Box and knelt down in front of his daughter. It was all Sarah could do to stay on her feet as the whale carcass slowly swelled and rolled up and down on the current and she reached out and held her daughter steady as William presented her with the Ditty Box. As he did so he opened it, and Sarah saw the two beautifully scrimshawed whale's teeth inside and smiled, then, to Sarah's horror, William passed the box to Mary Ann to hold, her tiny arms barely reaching the edges of the box and the weight of it threatening to overbalance her. Sarah grabbed the box out of Mary Ann's arms and quickly passed it to Domingo, she quickly declared it the best birthday present ever as Mary Ann fought to break free of her mother's grip and run along the back of the whale. William saw the panic on Sarah's face at the thought of her daughter slipping from the whale's back and falling into the sea. He stepped forward and swept his daughter up into his arms, Mary Ann screaming with delight, while Sarah, surrounded by applauding whaler men, was led to the ladder and began climbing to the deck above.

With Mary Ann safely aboard and the excitement dying down the crew were about to begin their work when Sarah called out to the cook and the ship's boy, Isaac. The men stood quietly while the cake, or cakes, were brought on deck. Sarah explained they didn't have enough room in the ovens for one large cake and even though they were running low on luxuries, she and the cook managed to squirrel away enough ingredients for cake for the whole crew!

The cakes were cut and pannikins of beer were handed round and the birthday song was sung to both Mary Ann and Thomas, who by this time had woken for his feed, so 'the little fella wouldn't feel left out' as cook put it, then it was back to work before the sharks became aware of the free feed they had tied alongside.

Chapter 34

Suva Harbour, Fiji,
August 10, 1881

The Marie Laure stood off the outer reef of Suva Harbour, careful not to be enticed too close to the treacherous reefs that encircled the island. A call from Domingo in the tops, had the helmsmen following his direction and she sailed cleanly through the perfect natural gateway, into Suva Harbour. Sarah was beside herself. She just couldn't believe the beauty of this place. The ship had been moving in and around the myriad of islands that made up the Fiji group and every time the ship slowed, Sarah would anticipate that this was the island where they would stop to resupply. They had lost two pigs, five chickens and all of their pigeons to the meal table and their goats, apart from the nanny, which had gone dry after her kids had grown, were getting to be a nuisance by escaping and running the deck at all hours. At first, the idea of killing the animals was abhorrent to Sarah, but as the weeks of the monotonous ship board diet took its toll, she finally agreed with the cook, that the animals were their only source of decent food, and after having to choose between bacon and eggs or weevil filled, hard tack biscuits and muddy coffee, she willingly accepted the killing of the animals. She even chopped the heads off the chickens that were not laying herself, with Jonesy the cook and Isaac the ships boy looking on and cheering as the poor old headless hens leapt around the chopping block, Sarah catching them in mid air before hanging them on the rail to bleed out.

They were down to just two chickens, a couple of pigs and four goats that were all too big to keep on board, so it was either slaughter day on the Marie Laure, or the islands market for them.

Suva Harbour was beautiful, Sarah had the children, and herself, scrubbed and dressed and was ready to go ashore until William ordered her and the children under the hurricane shed at the helm where they had a good view of the deck, and just as well. At least a dozen canoes pulled alongside the ship just as soon as the anchors touched bottom and half of the natives aboard the canoes, were grabbing at the railing and pulling themselves up and aboard the Marie Laure.

Since 1874, the Fijian Islands had been a colony of Great Britain, as such, the threat of attack from the natives was almost negligible, but not the threat of thievery. William had all the jalousies closed and locked and anything that wasn't bolted down, removed to the store room. Moreover, every man aboard was warned not to trade or fraternise with the natives until a deal could be struck with the chief.

Sarah watched as the calabashes of pork and fish, vegetables and fruit, the like of which she had never seen before, was laid out on the deck. The carpenter and blacksmith were ready with trade goods, such as nails, iron and anything that could be wrought into a hook or weapon but they refused to trade until the chief came.

The chief climbed over the rail and was most surprised and pleased to see a black islander in charge of the ship. He gave the customary 'Bula' greeting and accorded Sarah the utmost respect by bowing slightly when he noticed that Sarah had removed her bonnet in respect of his presence. The chief then blessed the presentations of food and sat in the shade of the hurricane house, with William and Domingo, whilst Sarah haggled with the island women to swap her animals for fresh food and fruits. Much to her annoyance and the laughter of the women, she had to forcibly hold Mary Ann back from attacking and destroying the fruits that lay on the calabashes of palm leaves on the deck, but in truth she was overjoyed to see women of her own age, and be able to converse with them, even if the language barrier did produce some difficulty.

After the women completed their bartering, it was the men's turn and following that, it was time to go ashore.

The sights and sounds of Suva were wonderful to Sarah, a native girl volunteered to look after Thomas as she and Mary Ann played in the shallows of the bay, reveling in the feel of the land beneath their feet. They wandered through the markets and villages, trying the exotic fruits and flavours of the honey covered treats the women of Fiji offered. Never having experienced sandy beaches before, Mary Ann was constantly picking up handfuls of sand and running it through her fingers, much to the native ladies amusement.

Sarah had managed to replenish their supplies with more chickens and pigs by swapping the old ones and the rest of the pigeons at a much reduced rate, and another two nanny goats, one with kids and one still heavily pregnant, to ensure a longer supply of milk. She was even offered a cow, which she did consider, until William informed her that a cow would probably die from the cold in the Aleutians.

William had also told her that, in order to catch the tail end of the whale season in the Bering Sea, they would have to head north immediately after leaving Fiji and bypass Samoa until they came back from the Bering sea. Sarah knew he was disappointed in not being able to see his family, but his obligation to the ship and its owners came first.

The Marie Laure stayed just two days in Suva Harbour before the large sheets of canvas rolled down from her yards and she made her way back through the channel in the reef and north towards the Aleutian Islands.

For days, the Marie Laure wended her way through the countless islands of the Fijian group, traveling across the antemeridian near Somosomo, before swinging back east to pick up the line again and then moving north along the antemeridian towards the whaling grounds of the Bering sea. The imaginary lines of the Equator and the Tropic of Cancer were crossed before the temperature began to get cooler. From eighty degrees at the equator, the temperature was now less than sixty and still dropping, although Sarah was far more comfortable in these climes than the stifling heat of the tropics.

Two whales were caught on the way north, one near Howland Island and another near Midway Atoll, breaking the drudgery of the long voyage north. Perhaps it was the endless miles of empty ocean or the fact that they had just left the idyllic isles of Fiji to sail into the open wastelands of the north pacific that brought about a solemn atmosphere aboard the ship that never lifted until the lookout called to the deck below, 'Land Ho!' that had the whole crew out at the rail, staring into the distance for a glimpse of somewhere they had never seen before, that is, all but two of them.

Dinny the flenser, had sailed into the chain of islands known as the Aleutians before and, unknown to anyone on board, the Marie Laure was no stranger to the Bering Sea herself. When she was British owned, the Marie Laure had transported seal oil, whale oil and sea otter pelts from Alaska to England during the fur trade boom of the eighteen fifties.

With the sea otter trade decimated by over exploitation, Russia determined she had no further use for Alaska and in an effort to halt her arch enemy, the British, from taking control, she sold the colony to America for just seven and a half million dollars only fourteen years ago.

With the trade in furs and oil from Alaska finished, except for the poaching of seals around the islands, most ships were either hulked, or, like the Marie Laure, sold off to the southern seas whaling industry.

William had plotted a course along the antemeridian line, that imaginary line that cuts the globe in half, the prime meridian cutting through Greenwich on the Atlantic side of the earth, and the antemeridian on the pacific, or opposite side of the globe.

Sarah and the rest of the crew stared from both rails of the ship as the Marie Laure approached the chain of islands to both port and starboard. Neither William nor Domingo, had been in this part of the world before and they were pleased when Dinny, the scrimshaw, man explained that the island on port bow was Semisopochnoi, or seven hills island, and the closest island to the 180 degree antemeridian which was the longitude they were following. With the low archipelago beginning to grow larger across the ship's bows, William called the crew to the deck. Explaining to them that the Bering Sea was much farther north, than Tasmania was south, subsequently, everything was on a much larger scale. Larger islands, larger expanses of seas, larger storms and hopefully, to the laughter of the crew, much larger whales!

He would follow the antemeridian past Semisopochnoi Island and along the northern coast of the Aleutians towards Dutch Harbour. There would be no shore leave or visits and as soon as the ship was resupplied with the few things they needed, they would be off to hunt whales, before returning to Samoa, his home island.

Even though the weather was clear, with a light southerly breeze barely raising the wave height above three feet, the sky was not blue, more an opaque light grey, blending the horizon with the hills of the island chain they were approaching. Giving this world a somewhat gloomy, forbidding appearance, and this feeling seemed to be transmitted to the crew who stood at the rail, the usual excitement of visiting new shores not evident in their demeanor at all, and Sarah shivered. Her thoughts went back to Fiji and the beautiful white, sandy beaches and crystal clear waters of the lagoons inside the reef.

As they passed through the Aleutian Island chain, the steep, grey, craggy cliffs of each island, each with thousands of seabirds wheeling and diving about their shores, did nothing to dispel the lonely atmosphere that pervaded the ship, even Dutch Harbour, the main fishing station and harbour, could not compare with their own Recherche Bay, or Hobart. A large Russian orthodox church stood out on a promontory in the centre of the bay, a neat scattering of stone buildings and animal pens spread out along the grass covered rolling hills that stretched from the shore to the steep, snow capped hills beyond. There was no wharf in the harbour and the Marie Laure anchored close off shore to allow the whale boat the shortest trip possible to land and within two hours, Domingo had replenished their supplies, and they set off to skirt the Bering Sea back to the antemeridian as fast as possible south, towards the sun.

The Marie Laure tacked back and forth in a seemingly haphazard manner. Taking advantage of the wind to sail east, wherever possible and even Domingo had begun to question Williams reasoning as the food larders began to empty and as yet no whales were in sight. Even so, when both Sarah and Domingo questioned him, he only raised his finger to his mouth, grinned, and shook his head.

It was on the extreme western end of the Aleutian chain, under bare poles and with a calm sea and no one but the lookout and the helm awake, Sarah smelled it! A pungent musky smell that permeated the ship throughout, and had William leaping out of his bunk at the commotion on deck.

Sarah and most of the crew tumbled out of their bunks, wondering what the hell was going on, the lookout had not called a warning, nor had the helmsman who had tied the helm off and been lightly dreaming of warmer climes as the Marie Laure took her first hit!

Thud, thud, flop, the birds hit first the rigging and then the deck, their numbers growing from just a few, until the whole ship was covered in the them, and still they came on. The lookout was being battered by fast moving wings and bodies and was hanging on to the iron hoops of his post for dear life as the birds came out of the twilight, and mistaking the dark shadow of the ship for the water, proceeded to attempt to land on the sea, smacking in to the invisible rigging and masts. William called him down before he was belted to death by the erratically flying birds. He called for lanterns and the hearths to be lit so the birds could make out the shape of the ship and avoid the collision that must occur when hundreds of thousands of sooty shearwaters make their annual migration from Tasmania and New Zealand to the Aleutians and California at this time of year.

'They're here! William yelled excitedly, as Sarah held her hand to her face in an effort to filter the pungent odour of the birds from her nostrils. She now recognised the smell. She had smelled it every April in Recherche when her father had brought home dozens of mutton birds from the islands around the coast of Tasmania. The pungent smell was the signal they would be eating off the fatty juvenile birds her mother would cook in the camp oven outside, for at least a month, and she loved it, but here on the ocean among thousands of them, the smell was simply too much.

William explained that this was what he was waiting for. The birds flew across the Pacific Ocean in a figure eight pattern. From Tasmania and its tiny islands, to Japan, then across the pacific to the Aleutians and California, to return to their home burrows in Tasmania and the Bass Strait islands in the following March.

Sperm whales follow the pelagic fish columns through the ocean, smashing the squid and smaller fish to pieces in the deeper water and swimming back to the surface to shit. Whales can shit a huge amount, creating columns of food for krill, or 'Brit'. The Brit is in turn sought after by Mutton birds, or Sooty Shearwaters. 'So,' William said, looking at the clouds of birds heading east, along the Aleutian archipelago and out into the Bering Sea, 'Find the Brit, find the mutton birds, find the mutton birds, find the whales!'

At daylight, the Marie Laure set full sail and began following the birds. It seemed to Sarah, an impossible task as the birds simply seemed to wheel and dive in all directions, with little or no sense of direction, until William pointed out a dark cloud ahead of them towards the horizon. The birds had centered around a large column of Brit that had spread across the surface of the sea and no sooner had Sarah and William noticed it than the call came once again from the lookout. 'Thar, she Blows!'

The first group of whales were humpbacks, but beyond them, the lookout could see the solitary puffs of salty air rising from the waves and called down to the deck, 'We've got spermaceti!'

William halted the men at the davits and chose to sail through the pod of humpbacks towards the sperm whales in the distance. Most of the crew, including Sarah, were engaged in grabbing up those mutton birds that had landed, voluntary or otherwise, on the ship. Pandemonium reigned as the birds flew into the animal pens, terrifying the pigs and chickens, who mistook them for hawks. The goats, flustered at the wings beating on their faces, tried to attack the birds and pushed the wall of the pens over, allowing the chickens and pigs to run riot over the deck, adding to the chaos that threatened to overtake the ship. Sarah looked to William and Domingo for help, but the two men had whales to catch and could not be bothered with rounding up Sarah's farmyard. With the help of the cook, Sarah had gotten Mary Ann out of danger of both the riotous animals and the dangerous flapping and pecking of the birds, and with the help of the cook, the blacksmith and the ship's boy, she turned her attention to the birds. At first the trio tried to grab the birds with both hands around their body but the birds were too strong and beat, no, bashed them, with their wings and pecked viciously at their heads and faces, causing them to let the bird go and defend their eyes. The ship's boy finally found a way of disposing of the unwanted avians, when he lost control of a bird and only managed to hold on to one wing as he slipped on the rolling deck. His falling action cartwheeled the bird up into the air and over the side of the ship. As soon as the bird found air under its wings, it was away, and flying towards the brit patches. There was still some way to go until the ship reached the pod of sperm whales and everyone fell to by roughly grabbing each bird by one wing and heaving it over their head, making sure it's beak and the other wing was well away from their faces, and towards the rail.

The antics of the crew over the next hour was the subject of hilarity for many weeks to come. Some managed to grab a bird securely and begin to fling it over the side, only to be knocked off their feet by a panicking pig. Some men jeered at the poor efforts of the cook and joined in the fray, only to find it was much harder to corral a piglet on a rolling deck whilst being attacked by terrified chickens and mutton birds, than they imagined.

William, Domingo, and the second mate, sat at the hurricane house and roared with laughter at the mostly failed, antics of the rest of the crew, and Sarah, even though she was angry at first, at the men's refusal to help her, couldn't help but laugh at these big strong men who would do battle with one of the largest animals on earth, but were being totally outclassed by a few tiny piglets.

By lunch time they had corralled most of the animals and disposed of the majority of the birds over the side. Sarah had intended to keep and cook some of the mutton birds as a treat for the crew, but the over powering musty stench of the birds turned her off ever eating mutton birds again. Besides, more than one member of the crew had told her that the birds were only edible until they could fly, after they reached adulthood, they became rank and tasted very much like whale shit.

They began swinging the boats out about two o'clock that afternoon and by dark had two whales alongside and the hearths were billowing their inky black smoke through the rigging, although the danger of being struck by an errant mutton bird continued throughout the night.

By first light they were off again, and from then on for the next month or so it was almost a ritual, two or three days, looking for main body of the birds, then whale chasing was the order of the day, until they caught up with their quarry and perhaps a full day killing, and some time three days and nights trying out, then they were off on the hunt again.

For more than two months, the weather gods were kind to the Marie Laure. In November that began to change, the cool dry weather turned to hot and wet and most days were spent slipping and sliding on the deck as the ship moved along the island chain. It was decided it was time to sail through one of the many gaps between the islands, to the calmer waters to the south of the island chain, and not a moment too soon.

The darkening thunderheads in the northern sky had convinced William they needed to be on the southern side of the Aleutian chain lest heavy weather caught them on a lee shore, and in these latitudes, there would be no help forthcoming should one's ship be driven on to the craggy islands of the Bering Sea.

The Marie Laure had chosen to sail through the wide channel to the east of Adak Island and with the winds now turning northerly she easily negotiated the wide channel, with the intention of turning west once again to fish, as she made her way towards the antemeridian. On clearing the channel, William was surprised when the call from the tops came down, 'Sail Ho!' thinking she might once again have company, Sarah ran to the rail, only to see that it was not another friendly whale ship coming up on her starboard quarter, but a gun ship, flying a flag with not horizontal stripes, but vertical ones, and the American eagle in the upper right corner.

'American.' William said bluntly, as he put down the eyeglass Sarah had passed to him. 'I hope we're not at war with them!' The flag was of the newly formed united states coast guard service and in flying the flag, she was signaling others that she had the right to order them to heave to in order to board, and that is what she was doing!

William had the ship hove to, which was not an easy task in the building sea off Adak Island. The ships stood side by side, only a hundred yards separating them, the American ship at two hundred feet, was much larger and higher than the Marie Laure and the bearded men at the rail above the line of gunports beneath their feet were very imposing and intimidating. At first the party of smartly dressed sailors coming aboard the Marie Laure were indifferent, almost hostile, to those on the whale ship. The officer in charge asked to see the ships manifest and when William showed him the logs and he noted that the Marie Laure was a whaler and not a seal poacher, as evidenced by the fifty tuns of sperm oil aboard, his demeanor changed dramatically. He apologised for the inconvenience and advised William that an arctic storm was on its way and he would do well to make haste for calmer waters south. When William told him it was their intention to sail for Samoa, the commander grinned and said, 'Good decision, in light of the weather we are forced to ride out over the next couple of weeks, I wish I was coming with you.' They bid the commander and his crew adieu and once they well clear of each other, the Marie Laure changed course to the southwest, to intersect the antemeridian at a lower latitude and hopefully avoid the storm. But it wasn't to be.

Chapter 35

Somewhere south of the Aleutians,
12th December, 1881

The storm struck at about 2am of the Twelfth. Sarah felt her bunk lift before dropping away from her body causing her to jolt awake and feel as if she was falling through space, as indeed, the Marie Laure was. She felt for William in the dark, but he and most of the crew were already on deck. The Marie Laure had been under bare poles and William had ordered a drogue over the bows to act as a sea anchor, keeping the ship's head into the waves, as well as a solitary steering sail to help the helmsman control the ship.

Sarah dared not leave the cabin, instead she climbed out of her bunk and groped around for anything she could find to steady herself to get to the children and carry them to her bunk and climb in beside them. It felt like she was living a nightmare inside the blackness of the cabin, she could hear the gimballed lamps swinging wildly in the dark but dare not light a lamp, even if she could find one, lest it be torn from her grip in the bouncing cabin. She carried first Thomas, then Mary Ann, to her bunk and climbed in with them. The children were unusually quiet and held tightly to her, as if sensing all was not well. She could hear the ships timbers creaking in protest above the noise of the shrieking arctic wind, one minute her body felt heavy and pressed into the bunk as the ship rose high on the thirty foot waves, then, after halting at the apex of the wave and throwing tons of water across her decks and out through her scuppers, the sensation of falling, caused Sarah to hang on to the children and brace herself against the sides of the bunk. Occasionally, she could feel the drips of water landing on the bed as the ship mistimed a wave and the scuppers were hard pressed to rid the deck of the many tons of sea water that crashed green over her rail as she dipped her gunwales under. Sarah closed her eyes and prayed.

If it felt like living a night mare below deck, on deck was surely the real thing. With only a skeleton crew huddled under the hurricane house and under the foc'sle awning, there was no lookout, for any man foolhardy enough to be in the tops on this night, would surely have met his maker by now, and the storm was only just beginning.

Daylight came a dark twilight, that only served to dampen their spirits even more as they looked out on a sea of sweeping waves tearing past the ship, the occasional one crashing against her bows and lifting her stern high, causing her to broach into the next one and dip one of her gunnels under. As she did, tons upon tons, of grey, foamy, water poured over her gunwale and threatened to rip the side clean out of the plucky ship. But the Marie Laure was made of stern stuff, she had been here before and with a thousand miles of ocean over her stern she had plenty of sea room to do battle in.

There would be no breakfast this morning, most of the bricks from the trywork hearths had been scattered about the deck, as were the chicken pens, some of them had split open and dead chickens floated about the deck until the storm picked them up and cast them over the side to join the streaks of foam that stretched for miles north and south of the ship.

Goats and pigs were huddled in the awning with the deck crew, safe, until one inquisitive piglet moved from the protection of its mother as the boat rolled and was instantly washed along the deck, towards the stern, the sow, seeing her baby in danger, tried to follow and was bowled over by the rushing water and hurtled along the deck to crash heavily against the bulwark, squealing in frustration as her baby hit the edge of the scupper, breaking two of its legs before being washed out through the hole to its doom. The boat heeled again and with a supreme effort, the sow found her legs and scuttled back to her remaining charges. Only the goats seemed unmoved by the commotion surrounding them. The two mothers and kids braced themselves against the bulkhead of the foc'sle and each other, chewing idly whilst staring at the chaos on the deck.

William and Domingo's only thought was for the safety of the ship, and all things considered she was holding up pretty well. The drogue was keeping her head to the weather and even though she had many tuns of oil stowed, she was riding high in the water. There was nothing anybody could do in these trying conditions, but keep watch for anything that might break and be prepared to fix it.

For Sarah it was a living hell, the only things stopping her from climbing out of the bunk and going out on deck were her children's safety and the fact it was far worse outside than it was in the cabin. In the dim light that finally permeated the cabin, she managed to light one of the gimballed lamps and crushed a couple of ships biscuits with a heavy spoon and mixed it with yesterday's goat's milk. Sharing it with Mary Ann whilst Thomas was content with her breast milk, she wondered how the animals were faring. *'Not well, I'll bet.'* She said to herself as she felt the ship lift again under the power of the storm. William had only poked his head through the jalousie a few times to see if she and the children were alright and to tell her there was no point coming on deck, as if she didn't know that already.

The storm raged for three days and finally pushed the Marie Laure far to the south and out of the path of the centre of the storm, into to relative calmer waters on the perimeter, William ordered the mizzen and a storm jib up and the drogue cut loose, enabling the ship to turn and run before the wind, and although the sailing was far from comfortable, the sea was no longer coming aboard and work could be carried out to get the Marie Laure ship shape. Moreover, the hearths could be lit with what scraps of shavings from the carpenters shed that were still dry and it wasn't too long before the hearths were blazing and food was cooking. Bleary eyed sailors crept out of the foc'sle, hungry, thirsty and their clothes wet through underneath their oilskins, the result of the endless drips that managed to find their way through the deck timbers as the ship flexed under the stress of the storm.

The cook brought Sarah and Mary Ann hot tea and johnny cake, which they scoffed hungrily. When Sarah enquired as to the condition of the animals, he sadly told her there would be no eggs for the rest of the trip, but on the bright side, there would be plenty of chicken broth over the next few days.

The ship was making a good nine knots before the wind and by noon of the following day was out of the storm and heading for the antemeridian line. The mood aboard had lifted considerably as the incessant rain the storm brought, passed away to the east, and the sun spread its warmth over the ship and its compliment once again. Hearths flamed hot, clothes dried and conversation became cheerful over a steaming mug of chicken broth. Sarah was surprised to see the majority of the animals survived and with the help of Jonesy and a few crewmen had them penned up and bedded down on fresh straw as if nothing had happened.

William's talent for navigation had the Marie Laure encountering the antemeridian at the forty degree north latitude, before proceeding due south for almost two months, then south east, towards Samoa.

The trip south was uneventful, but with fifty tuns stowed and the trip far from over, the crew were happy to be resting in the pacific sun once again. It took almost two months to reach Samoa and food supplies were running dangerously low, with most of the flour and tea mouldy due to the storm. One of the nanny goats had given birth which ensured a supply of milk for Mary Ann and Sarah. Pigs were killed at least once a week for cold meat and lines were strung from the deck in the hope of catching some fresh fish but to no avail. Christmas day 1881, saw them crossing the tropic of Cancer along the antemeridian. The last of the chickens were gone, cook killed a pig and two goats and made sea pies, a concoction of flour dumplings and ground bone, as well as lobscouse, a stew of salted goat's meat and onions, pepper and duff in the hope no one would know the difference, they didn't, until Sarah noticed two of the goats were gone. Johnny cakes covered in jam or golden syrup were a favorite for dessert and a tankard of beer always went down well. There were discussions as to whether they should keep going ahead to Fiji for resupply, but Sarah argued that William had been desperate to find his family and she knew that any one incident on these voyages could send them back to Tasmania without even seeing Samoa, and she urged him to keep going. It was decided they should push on to Samoa.

Chapter 36

Apia Bay, Samoa,

January, 1882

It was raining heavily as the Marie Laure entered Apia Bay and William was disappointed, he could not recognise any landmarks. Sarah reminded him that he had been just eleven years old, and really had no memory of this part of Samoa anyway.

The Marie Laure was the only whale ship in the harbour, although there were many smaller craft settled around the shores of the bay and as soon as the rain stopped, the shore came alive with people of all shapes and sizes, in boats of all shapes and sizes, that left the shore to paddle out and trade with the newcomer.

Within a short time of the first skiff reaching the ship, the deck of the Marie Laure was transformed into that of a street bazaar. Sarah ordered the ship's boy to keep charge of the children as she tried to barter with no less than three natives at a time. A white man, accompanied by a native boy, was selling vegetables and toys made from coconut husks. He approached her and asked if she was English. Surprised at the man's impeccable English, Sarah replied she was and pointed to William. Surprised at an English woman being married to a Samoan man, it usually being the opposite, he nodded and went over to where William and Domingo stood, overseeing the deck market. In conversation with William, he couldn't recall any specific white man, island girl, among the many liaisons throughout the islands, and he advised William to go to the British Consul, a mister William Churchward at the new British consulate, on the northern shore of the harbour.

The following day William strode up the steps with Sarah on his arm and their two children in tow. The consul welcomed them warmly, especially as British citizens. He warned that things were 'very difficult' between the English and the islanders and not being helped by interference from the Americans.

They spent two hours talking with the consul before leaving empty handed. It seems there was no record of William, or his family, mainly due to the fact the British consulate had only been officially proclaimed in march of this year, prior to that, with the islands in an almost constant state of war, no records had been made, or kept.

Mister Churchward also warned William of the falling price of whale oil. Since the Marie Laure had been at sea, the price of their commodity had fallen by almost half. With the discovery of oil at Titusville, Pennsylvania, in 1857, the oil industry was beginning to make inroads into the whaling industry, and coupled with the scarcity of whales, it seemed the industry William loved and dedicated his life to, was doomed.

William and Sarah walked slowly down the steps of the consulate, at a loss what to do next, when a voice called out to them a name William had not heard for thirty years, 'Villiamu! Villiamu'. They looked up, Sarah half expecting to be attacked by the men running towards them, after the warnings given them by the Consul, but William recognised the men, even after all these years, he knew his brothers.

The brothers hugged each other, both Louis and James, not being able to believe their brother was alive after all these years. The foursome sat on the bench outside the consulate and talked for at least two hours, and William was devastated to learn his parents had died years earlier, their father from sepsis, contracted after a cut from a jagged piece of iron he was working, and their mother had contracted a severe strain of influenza from a European trading vessel and died a couple of years later. Both their parents had been cremated and their ashes scattered among the gardens of the church at Leulumoega, near reverend John Williams remains. Since then, the brothers had eked out an existence clearing bush for gardens or fishing. Both William and Sarah were devastated there was not even any headstone, or remains, for William or Sarah to relate to, and Sarah reached out and held William's hand as the foursome sat quietly for a few minutes. A call from the babysitter brought them back to reality, calling to Mary Ann as the latter began to run towards the beach.

William ran after his daughter and scooped her up into his arms. He knew that from now on, this is what he had to live for, this was his future, and there was no past, it was all gone, such as it had been.

Over the evening meal on the deck of the Marie Laure, the brother's reiterated the story the consul had told them, it was clear there was going to be another war and this time the Americans and the British could be involved. They advised not to go to Leulumoaga as the fighting seems always to begin there and it was not a safe place to be.

They talked long into the night, before Domingo ventured that the two brothers' come with them to Tasmania, the same as he did, when William saved him from the cannibals on Lord Howe Island. William interjected. 'I didn't see any cannibals.' He laughed, as Domingo countered, 'Neither did I, but I assure you there was someone in that forest,' he went on, 'And whoever, or whatever they were, I wasn't sticking around to see if they were friendly or not.'

Both louis and James had seen their fair share of violence and heard the stories of cannibalism, and they tended to believe Domingo's version of events and readily accepted William's offer to take them to Tasmania. So, it was decided, the Marie Laure would add two more brothers to her manifest, and set sail on the morrow.

The Marie Laure didn't retrace her path from Fiji, instead, William had her sail north to the antemeridian near the island of Tuvalu to once again pick up the mutton bird's path and follow them home to Tasmania. Unlike the mutton birds, which would cover twelve thousand miles in less than three weeks, the Marie Laure would take until July, 1882, before she would once again, round south east cape in Tasmania and head into her home port of Recherche Bay. She would capture two more whales as they followed the smell of the birds, taking her total catch to sixty one tuns, the highest tally William ever caught as a captain, and apart from a few hours on the beach in Fiji, Mary Ann would have known no other world than the inside of the Marie Laure's gunwales for the first four years of her life!

On a rainy 5th of July, just three days before her fourth birthday, William lifted her out of the whale boat and into her grandmother's arms as the people of Recherche, Catamaran, Leprena, and Cockle creek, gathered around to welcome them home. As luck would have it, Mister Sherwin was there on his ketch, Zephyr, and was most pleased when he received the tally of sixty one tuns and called for the crew to make haste to transfer the oil for transshipping to Hobart. He claimed he could get better than the going price for spermaceti and was pleased William had opted to go for sperm whales instead of humpback, as the price for black oil was less than a quarter of sperm.

Whilst the girls hurried off to get reacquainted with their families, the crew were reminded they had still two more weeks until their contract ran out, so, it was a quick resupply and out to sea again. The Marie Laure would finish her cruise on the 14th of August, 1882, giving William and Domingo time to inspect their new homes, get used their 'land legs' and be off on one last voyage.

Both William and Domingo could see Lemuel Domeney had done good job and their faith in him had been well placed. The two men resisted the demands of their wives to come inside and see the well appointed kitchens and although the houses were on opposite sides of the bay from each other, they were built to identical plans to save on costs.

The fences were yet to be erected but Sarah had already ordered the climbing roses from Mrs. Domeney that she was intending to plant over the gate, once it was erected, and that would be Williams first order of business.

Not the slab clapboard walls and split shingle King Billy pine roof of the pioneer houses, these were built of mill cut weatherboards and painted brown, with green trim around the architraves. What's more, Lemuel Domeney pointed out, the house had a brand new corrugated iron roof, good for sixty years in this climate.

Bill Tedman, who had made his living by slitting shingles for houses ever since he was released on ticket of leave, didn't agree, and was still arguing the merits of shingles as the party made its way into the wash house skillion at the rear of the house. Both Sarah and Rosie squealed with delight at the sight of the huge wooden stave water tank, fed from the spouting's that edged the roof, with two outlets, one directly into a timber wash basin near the kitchen door and one feeding into a wooden bath just inside the wall of the bathroom, each with its very own brass tap.

The sides, ends and bottom of the bath was made of single Huon Pine slabs, sanded glass smooth with carved scrolls on each end, curtesy of Risby Brothers, in Hobart. But the piece de resistance was undoubtedly the cast iron wood stove that graced the large brick inglenook in the kitchen. Complete with oven and hot plates for cooking and keeping water hot, its large brick surround studded with hooks built in, would ensure dry clothes every day. To Sarah and Rosie, this meant they would have an endless supply of water, to carry just ten steps, to cook and clean with. Bill Tedman shook his head at these newfangled inventions and was about to expound the merits of three hooks in the chimney and a cast iron cauldron, when a stern look from his wife had him dropping his head and staying silent.

A passage from the kitchen led into the house proper, past the first bedroom on the left and sitting room on the right, and two large bedrooms graced the front of the house, accessed from the same passage, each with its own double bed and crib for the babies. The walls of all four front rooms of the house, including the passage, were lath timber, covered in scrim, a type of hessian, and wallpaper. The floral design of the wallpaper had all the women sighing with envy at the luxury these girls were living in, even Mrs. Domeney commented that this younger generation were so lucky to have all the conveniences that her generation never had. For the men, they were just happy their wives were happy, and after giving their wives enough of their time to satisfy them that they too were impressed, they retired to the wood heap, also curtesy of Lemuel Domeney, each man selecting a block of wood to sit on, and plan their next voyage.

Just one month later, after settling their families into their respective homes, The Marie Laure set off on another voyage, this time to the middle grounds, between New Zealand and Lord Howe Island and around the south coast of Tasmania into the Great Australian Bight, she would call in to either Port Davey, on the west coast, or Recherche for resupply on at least four occasions, and although she would manage to stow sixty tuns of sperm oil in her hold, the price of oil continued to drop until in May, 1884, the sails of the Marie Laure cleared Acteon island for the last time and it was with a heavy heart William and his brothers, Domingo, Louis and Jim walked off the ship they had grown to love, for the last time. The Marie Laure would do one more whaling voyage under another master, before ending her days as a hulk in the Yarra River in Melbourne, Victoria.

An article in the Melbourne newspaper Argus, on Tuesday, 21st of September, 1937 reads: 'The former Hobart whaler Marie Laure, now a hulk in Melbourne, the oldest vessel afloat in the Southern Hemisphere, built of teak in the Seychelles in 1840, this bluff bowed old hooker, of a design all her own these days, arrived in Hobart Town with sugar from Mauritius in April 1849. Fitted out there as a whaling barque for her Tasmanian owners, she cruised the waters of the Pacific for the next 44 years, lowering her boats as far north as the Bering Sea and south, amid the staggering gusts of the Antarctic. For some years her skipper was a Cape Verdean Islands black.' An obvious, but common, mistake regarding William as he had been described throughout his lifetime, as Aboriginal, Cape Verdean, Tongan, as well as Samoan, but for most of the time William, like all other people of colour in Tasmania, were either described by officialdom as 'Various', half caste or black.

Chapter 37

Recherche Bay,

Tasmania, 1885

In the year 1880, Recherche Bay was growing into the 'hub of the south' with a thriving timber industry that reached all the way around the west coast to Strahan, mineral exploration for coal and tin, whale ships continued to sail in and out of the port to resupply and it was not uncommon for visitors to travel down the D'entrecasteaux channel from Hobart one day, take a day trip around the bay on a fishing yawl, overnight at Captain and Mrs. Domeney's Ramsgate Inn, and return to Hobart the following day having still not seen all the sights of the south coast.

After William and Sarah, Domingo and Rosie, settled into their newly built homes, William and his brother continued to take voyages on whaling ships out of Recherche, mostly as first and second mate, whilst Louis and Jim, referred to locally as 'Black Louis the Portuguese,' and James was referred to simply as 'Black Jim' his brother, took work wherever they could find it, be it piece work at the local sawmill or hitching a ride to Port Davey with Tom Dougherty and Harry Longley, there to camp on the beach in make shift huts whilst they worked in the saw pits, or snagged logs out of the Davey river for the river piners that lived in Port Davey.

Life was hard but the couples took it in their stride, with Sarah taking her total of children to four with the birth of William Domingo in February of 1883, but life for Sarah and William was about to take a disastrous turn.

Once again, William had missed out on the birth of his fourth child, by just hours. The Marie Laure had rounded Fishers point on the 16th of February, 1883, only to be told of the arrival just yesterday morning of their newest addition to their family. Leaving Louis and Jim to look after the ship, William and Domingo, now locally called James, leapt aboard Lemuel Domeney's gig and raced to his house.

'Just in time to name him.' Sarah smiled. William could see she had had a hard time of it with this one and searched his mind for a name, before Mrs. Tedman ushered them from the house. 'It must be William,' Sarah winced, 'but what for a second name?'

William looked to Rosie and James, he knew he had to name the baby before he left, otherwise he would be four or five months without a name and said without faltering. 'Domingo, let's call him, William Domingo Smith.'

He looked at the proud smile on his brother's face and knew he had made the right call. After all, Domingo Jose Evorall, or 'James', as he liked to anglicise himself, had been with him through good times and bad, and was the only person in the world he felt he could, and did, place his life in his hands.

Sarah Tedman, his mother in law, explained both mother and baby had a hard birth but the doctor was coming to check on him later, and he should be 'as fit as a fiddle' by the time the Marie Laure returned in four month's time. Seeing no point in staying home with Sarah in good hands, William and Domingo returned to the Marie Laure and the ship got under way.

William got to spend just six days in total with his son before the Marie Laure returned to her home port with sixty tuns of sperm oil stowed. The price of oil was falling but mister Sherwin managed to get almost sixty dollars a tun for the barrels in the Marie Laure's hold, worth almost three thousand, six hundred dollars before expenses. William's share of the lay on his final voyage of the Marie Laure would be one hundred and fifty three pounds and James's share would be one hundred and eighteen pounds, having the purchasing power of almost twenty five thousand pounds in 2024.

On the 19th May, Eighteen eighty four, with a full complement of crew and well wishers, including Lemuel Domeney and his wife, as well as the Tedman's, the Marie Laurie set sail for Hobart. With a festive air tinged with sadness of sailing the ship for the last time, the Marie Laure sailed up the channel into the river Derwent for the final voyage under captain William Smith. Mary Ann was almost six years old and treated the ship as if it was her own, asking her father where all the animals had gone and demanding he bring her goats and piglets back. Everyone laughed at her demands as she ran across the deck with that peculiar rolling gait William and Sarah were so used to. She had never known a life outside of deck of the Marie Laure for the first four years of her life and though other memories would fade, to her it was a beautiful name she would remember for the rest of her life.

Sarah stood at the rail with her new baby, William Domingo, in her arms. She felt sad they were parting ways with the Marie Laure, but was happy to have a home and a future at Recherche. William's money from whaling was still good, even though he was away for months at a time. Besides, she had told Rosie, with Recherche thriving as an industrial and fishing port, both William and James could find work anywhere they pleased, and listening to Mrs. Domeney, even the newspapers were commenting that Recherche was on its way to a bright and happy future.

The picnic party had a wonderful time in Hobart, high tea was the order of the day for the ladies, the girls filled up with fashionable clothes at the stores, much to mister Domeney's chagrin, and the kids filled up with sweets and treats following little William Domingo's christening at the same congregational church the two couples were married in, on the corner of Burnett and Argyll Street.

Following their wages being paid into their accounts at the Bank of Van Dieman's Land, the party had dinner at their hotel before enjoying an evening at the theatre royal, William and Sarah taking a buggy ride around the park before taking the children back to their hotel rooms for a well earned rest. The party stayed two nights in Hobart before saying a final farewell to the Marie Laure. William stepped up from his cabin and leaned across the rail of the ship to place his now revered Ditty Box in his daughter's arms in an effort to console her for not being able to return home on 'her ship', and catching one of the many ketches bound for Recherche and home after a trip to the city that they all hoped would be one of many they would share in the bright future they believed was theirs.

But it was not to be.

Slowly, but inexorably, Recherche began to slow. With each whaling ship that sailed past the bay on its way to Hobart, never to return, the business of the once thriving port began to dry up.

William and Domingo got work as first and second mate on the Othello and after a seven month stint at sea, on September 17th, 1885 both William and his brother stood at the rail and stared at the sole figure on the wharf. No welcoming wave, no children to greet them, just the lone figure of Rosie in the misty rain that swept in from the south.

The whaleboat bumped against the wharf and the two men could see the grief on her face, she stared at William, 'Oh William, its Domingo.' Was all she could get out before collapsing into the arms of her husband.

William ran. He ran as fast a she could, towards home, not even knowing why he was running. Rosie hadn't told him just what was wrong with his son, perhaps he'd only had an accident, or was ill, but nothing could have prepared him for the tragedy that awaited him. his worst fears were realised, when he came through the gateposts that Sarah had entwined the climbing roses around just last year.

The doctor's buggy was parked outside, as was constable Driscoll's horse and Lemuel Domeney's dray, and he could hear Sarah sobbing hysterically, as he ran down the side path.

He burst through the door and Sarah came out of her mother's arms and ran to him. She tried to explain what happened, but she was so distraught William couldn't make out what she was saying. The doctor spoke up and explained that just a week ago, Thomas had developed a slight cough that, by nightfall on Tuesday, had developed into scarlet fever, Constable Driscoll had ridden to Southport for the doctor but it was to no avail, by the time the doctor arrived in Recherche, Thomas had died. The doctor then turned his attention to the baby, but despite every effort he made to get the fever that racked his little body, to ease, it was too late, young William Domingo too, had passed away during last night.

The doctor ordered everyone outside into the skillion woodshed, even the policeman, constable Driscoll. Apologising to everyone, he recommended that water be boiled and all furniture and bedding be brought outside into the fresh air and all clothes and bedclothes be boiled. Neither William or Domingo was allowed into the room where the children's bodies were. Sarah and Rosie had changed their clothes and washed their hand and faces, both staring dumbly at the beautiful bath they were so excited to see, just a few short months ago. Helpful neighbor's poured hot water into the timber bath, and Sarah Tedman and Rosie, stripped the other children down and scrubbed them, before dumping their clothes into another tub for washing. The doctor had attempted to check the baby, Robert, for signs of the disease, but Sarah would not let him, fearing he too, was afflicted. After a few moments gentle coaxing by her mother, the doctor checked his mouth and tiny throat, pronouncing him okay, for the moment, anyway. It was likely, the doctor said, young Thomas had picked up the disease from the yard and transferred it to the baby by sneezing or even just touching him. Robert, who was in a separate room and had no contact with his brother's, was also clear of the disease, and Mary Ann had been at her aunt Rosie's, a visit that probably saved her life!

William and Sarah stood in the wood shed holding each other and sobbing unashamedly, as the bodies of their two children were carried out by constable Driscoll, tears streaming down his own face, as he apologised to everyone, and no one, in particular. William wanted to intervene and keep the baby's home for just a little while, but he knew it was against the law. Both typhoid and scarlet fever were highly contagious, and the community could not afford to let such a deadly disease loose beyond the wall of this house. No one knew what caused the disease, or where it came from. They only knew it could strike without warning and could kill within hours, especially in children. Some children would go to bed, seemingly healthy and happy, only to be dead before morning, such was the devastating effects of these evil diseases.

William and Sarah just stood and stared as their little one's bodies were taken away, the reasons, they didn't care about, they just felt numb, like there was nothing left to live for. Sarah's mother offered to take James and Mary Ann home with them and Sarah never spoke, she just nodded her head as it was buried into William's chest. Rosie and Domingo stood alone in the kitchen as William and Sarah went into the children's bedroom and closed the door behind them. Then it was all over. The Tedman's left with the two older children, James and Mary Ann. Lemuel Domeney and the constable took the boys bodies to the hospital mortuary in Esperance, whilst the Doctor and Mrs. Domeney followed in his gig. Domingo and Rosie stood watching as the procession moved slowly up the rain soaked, sandy track, and across the wooden bridge, Rosie's sobs still racking her body, while Louis and Jim stood in the shelter of the skillion and listened to the soft rain beat upon the iron roof on that sad day in September, 1885.

Domingo, Louis and Jim all noticed a change in William after the death of his two sons. Death was no stranger to these pioneers of the area, but the death of their two sons hit William and Sarah particularly hard. William swore off going to sea again, and just seven months later, when his fifth son, Alexander, was born, William was working as a labourer for McDougall's sawmill, pulling logs from the dank forests by bullock team, treading the same muddy track each day, back and forth to the forest, a far cry from being the captain of a whaling ship on the ocean, choosing what path his ship would take across the four corners of the world.

William never forgave himself for not being there to protect his sons and would stay close to home in an effort to ensure the safety of his family, but even his physical strength, nor strength of prayer, could prevail against the unknown organisms that threaten the lives of mere mortals.

In 1886, another son, Alexander, was born, and with Rosie giving birth to her first, Joseph William Evorall, it seemed the spell of bad luck had left them and the lucky caul and coin had triumphed, a tentative happiness again reigned supreme in the little settlement. Still, William and his daughter, Mary Ann, could often be found sitting on one of the many wharfs around the bay, some getting quite dilapidated, but still managing to support the odd fishing boat or ketch that would come from around Fisher's Point, that to this old man and his daughter, was the gateway to the world.

In 1886, only four whalers operated out of Hobart and in 1900, Tasmania's last whaler, the Helen, lowered her boats for the last time and so ended the last chapter of the whaling industry of Tasmania.

With whaling in decline and with only sporadic voyages available to them, the men were forced to take work where they could get it, and with their families continuing to grow, both William and Domingo, now commonly called James, took work at McDougall's sawmill, as did Louis and Jim and the world, although much slower than it was once expected to be, still provided a happy existence, even blessing the couple with another daughter, Sarah Ann Jane, on 29th June, 1889.

William was nearly fifty years of age and resigned to the fact he would never captain a whaling ship again and much was his surprise when Sarah informed him, she might be pregnant once again. Mary Ann, now eleven years old, was excited she would have a baby sister in Sarah Jane and couldn't wait for her to grow up. Sadly, Sarah Jane would never grow up, and after suffering breathing difficulties one night in January, 1890, at just eight months of age, little Sarah Jane, too, succumbed to the ravages of some unknown fever.

Once again, the little settlement was thrown into sorrow, unable to contain her grief, and suffering morning sickness as well, Sarah was inconsolable. Sarah Tedman, her mother, took the children in and cared for them once again, until Sarah gave birth to Amelia Rosetta Violet on October 31, 1890, barely nine months after her sister had tragically passed away.

Both Sarah and William busied themselves with the new baby, but William knew Sarah was never the same after the loss of her daughter. Three tragedies in a row were just too much and Sarah's mental health, as well as her physical health, was starting to fail.

Chapter 38

Port Davey,

January, 1891

The three black men stood on the sandy beach and watched as the barque made her way into bramble cove.

Louis and Jim had begged William to come with them to Port Davey in the hope of finding work among the piners, after work at the mill became sporadic, but William had refused. After he and Sarah had lost three of their children to scarlet fever, neither one of them ever fully recovered from their grief and William was loathe to leave Sarah and the kids with her newborn barely three months old. But money was tight, and his mother in law, Sarah Tedman, convinced him he should go and she would shift in and help Sarah with the baby. Still William refused, and it was only when Sarah intervened that he finally conceded he had to earn some money somehow.

William could see by the awkward way the old whaler was moving, she had a whale in tow alongside. 'That's my old ship, Waterwitch.' William told his brothers. 'I served on her in the Seventies.' He stood watching, imagining the movements that were being carried out on deck, trying to remember the exact year and places he had sailed in her as the ship moved closer and anchored just off shore from them.

They had been seen from the lookout and a boat was put down to make contact. The Waterwitch had smashed a boat and needed to repair two spars. Years of neglect and patch up jobs had taken their toll on the old ship and she seemed a little worse for wear to William, 'Just like me.' He mumbled under his breath. As the whale boat drew closer, the first mate recognised William, and he was welcomed aboard as an old friend and fellow captain.

The men stood at the rail of the ship, William running his hands back and forth on the smooth timber of the rail, captain Harrison remarked, 'Just like patting a faithful old dog, eh, William.' William smiled, he was glad he came to Davey now, even just to stand on the deck of one of these trusty workhorses of the sea, and feel her deck move under him, was worth it. They watched as the flensers carried out their work and the long strips of blubber were winched up and over the rail. Both Louis and Jim were skilled in trying out, and fell in besides the crew to give them a hand.

When they were finished, Captain Harrison offered the men a portion of the lay but, instead of accepting a pay that may take all of three months to finally receive, once the ship finished her voyage and cleared into her home port, Louis spoke up. 'How about giving us the rest of that there, sardine?' He asked.

The captain laughed and lifted his arms, resignedly. 'Might as well.' He answered. 'It's only shark feed now, and we've no further use for it.'

After bidding the Waterwitch and her crew goodbye, the men hooked a long rope onto the carcass of the whale, and began blocking it into the shallows. This done, William took his knife and passed it to Louis, smiling. 'Now then brother, it's your sardine, you can have the honour of the first cut.'

Louis took the knife and climbed into the now stinking, cage of whale ribs. Blow flies covered his face and head each time he stuck his head out for a breath of fresh air. Using the bailing bucket from the whaleboat, William and Jim sloshed buckets of water onto louis' head each time he came out for air. Blood, flies and blubber mixing with the sweat and sand as he laboured away, carving a cavern into the sperm whale's gut, trying to find that forward cavity in the whale's stomach, the 'first stomach,' as it was often referred to, where the hundreds of beaks of giant squid, cuttlefish and seabird's beaks had accumulated over the years and congealed into a single spongy mass.

'Aha!' Signaled Louis had found the cavity and the other two men braved the flies and stench to see what he had found inside. He had his whole head and shoulders inside the whale's stomach and the giant sea monster's stomach acids were beginning to peel his skin away from his flesh. Still, even after his brother's urgings, he refused to give up his task until he lurched backwards, falling against the wall of ribs and sliding down to the sand. William and Jim stared at the large lump of ambergris in their brother's lap. They couldn't believe their eyes! They were staring at a fortune! Literally, a stinking fortune! The sweet, almost sickly smell was somewhat of an offset to the putrid malodorous stench of the whales rotting flesh. Ignoring the familiar smell, the brothers grabbed a small tarpaulin they used for shelter and bundled the smelly mass on to it and dragged it up the beach to safety.

After scrubbing themselves clean, they loaded their precious cargo into the whaleboat and set off across the Harbour to the almost abandoned pining settlement on the banks of the Davey River. Once there, they waited for a boat that would take them first to Recherche, then Hobart.

In 1891, Black Billy the Samoan, and his brothers, Black Louis, the Portuguese, and Black Jim, sat in the antechamber of the Commercial Bank of Hobart, waiting to talk to the bank manager, David Barclay.

When they were finally admitted to his office and announced their discovery, Barclay was astounded. He recognised their discovery for what it was, the most valuable commodity known to mankind, ambergris. At eleven English pounds per ounce, ambergris was more valuable than gold, the 1801lb. of ambergris was sought the world over by fashion houses, commodity dealers and perfume makers alike, but there was a catch. The men would have to travel to London, England, if they wanted to get the best price for their find and William, with Sarah grieving and not at all well, would not be going.

For months, the find was kept secret and Louis spent the whole time in England as the ambergris was doled out to prospective buyers over time, even so, the price of the unusual commodity dropped from eleven pounds per ounce, to just over four pounds per ounce and the two brothers received a grand total of ten thousand pounds, which would be worth 1.5 million pounds value in 2024.

For his efforts, Louis took the lion's share of about six thousand pounds and the two other brothers and their representatives, received about three hundred pounds each, a veritable fortune for William and Sarah and most sorely needed.

In 1892, a horse called Glenloth won the Melbourne Cup, and being a follower of the sport of kings, from his share of three hundred pounds apiece, Jim had a forty foot cutter built, under his anglicised name, George Smith, and called it Glenloth. The Glenloth was instrumental in saving the crew of the Lowrah, off Port Davey on 15th January, 1900, but was lost herself when caught in a storm off Maria Island, the following year, in 1901. 'Black Harry', aka 'Black Jim' aka George Smith as he was also known, died when he fell overboard from the ss Breone in August, 1924.

Louis Smith, aka Black louis the Portuguese, died the following year, leaving a six thousand pound fortune to David Barclay's two daughters. The will was contested by his own daughter, Mrs. Mary Selina Tye, claiming racism due to the fact Louis had disowned her because she had married a Chinese man. David Barclay contested Mrs. Tye's claim, arguing that he was 'well off' and didn't need the money, he was only contesting on behalf of his daughter and her sister 'as a matter of principle.' David Barclay was a wealthy, well known businessman and benefactor, and had great influence in Hobart business and political circles. It is not known just what influence he had on Louis Smith, or on this case, but the court ruled in David Barclay's daughter's favour.

William and Sarah must have thought well of louis, as they named their next child after him, Charles Ernest louis was born in 1894, and Arthur Frederick, was born in 1899.

Following the rape of her daughter, Mary Ann, in 1898, and the authorities being unable to charge the perpetrator, Harry Glover, due to the fact she was 'of colour' and had no witnesses, closely followed by the birth of Frederick, Sarah suffered a breakdown, and at the age of forty three, she was diagnosed with 'Dropsy' a condition once related to kidney failure, and was admitted to New Norfolk mental institution. Sarah's mother, Mary Tedman, an ex convict, from Maidstone, Kent, once arrested for the common crime of prostitution, theft and alcohol addiction, and sentenced to Van Dieman's Land for seven years. Whilst there, she was given one month's hard labour for threatening the life of another woman. She was pardoned in 1854 following her release from hard labour, and released into the custody of William Tedman, who later became her husband. Thereafter, she became a loving wife, mother and grandmother, who cared for her family and others, until her death in Recherche in 1899. With her daughter being interned at the New Norfolk mental institution, Sarah Tedman took her daughter's children in and with William's help, looked after them until they were grown. On his one appearance at the hospital, to visit his wife, William was mistaken for a black beggar and turned away. William and Sarah never saw each other again, although the elder children visited her when they could.

Sarah died at New Norfolk in 1902 aged just 45.

Chapter 39

Recherche Bay,

Tasmania, 1913

The old man tottered through the rose covered archway over his gate for his usual morning walk along the foreshore. He stopped in the gateway, as he did, every morning, and asked himself the same question, as he did, every morning. What year did Sarah plant these roses? Was it '84 or '85? No matter, he picked a rose and smelled it. 'Even better than last year, my darling.' He whispered aloud, as he put the rose in his lapel. He didn't notice the fading paint, nor the weatherboards splitting, the dusty window panes, and the spouting hanging from the verandah as he turned and looked back at his and Sarah's home. He saw what he wanted to see, a home where their children had grown up, a home where they had said goodbye to their babies, and a home where they had said goodbye to each other. This was the pathway where Sarah ran to meet him as the Marie Laure sailed up the bay, and this was the archway of roses that she had planted.

The old man walked along the dusty track until he reached the entrance to the wharf where he and his daughter would sit for hours, talking about whales and ships, and the sea. A commotion brought him out of his reverie and he looked to where two young boys were struggling to pull a huge stripey trumpeter up onto the wharf. Succeeding in their task, the elder boy sent his brother to bring his father, so the fish wouldn't get away. As he looked up, he saw the old man, and his face broke into a proud grin. He held up the fish, half the length of the creature still on the line and too heavy to lift clear of the deck, and called to the old man, 'I bet you've never seen a fish this big, mister,' and was surprised at the old man's blank expression as he stared at the fish, visions of whales and sea creatures playing through his mind, before he smiled broadly at the boy. 'No, son.' He shook his head slowly. 'Not for a very long time.'

The boy saw his dad coming, and called for him to hurry up, the old man forgotten, until his dad had the fish in the basket. He looked again in the direction where the old man went, and could see him tottering into a rose covered gateway, stopping to pick one of the roses, before he disappeared behind the house.

In his lifetime, William Henry Smith had experienced cannibalism go from commonplace to nonexistent, he had seen the advent and demise of indentured labour, he had witnessed the indifference to the dying out of a race of people that were a family to him, saw the creation of a Tasmanian state from a colony of convicts, and was present as that convict settlement evolved through a town to become a thriving city. He watched as his beloved whaling, the richest industry the world, rose and fell, to become as extinct as his aboriginal family, both the ships and the people, simply fading away. He would witness methods of transportation go from walking, to horses, to motor cars and buses. From the beautiful timber ships, their white sails gleaming in the sun, to grimy steel monsters, belching their smokey fumes across the Derwent. And sadly, witness his home town of Recherche, boom, decay and die just like he would.

He hadn't been feeling well for a few days now, and readied himself for bed, he instinctively reached over and tapped the Ditty Box, only to find for the umpteenth time, it wasn't there. Then he remembered, he had given it to his eldest daughter Mary Ann, and she had taken it to Strahan when she married young Harry Doherty. He felt cold and clammy and struggled to sleep.

William Smith was taken from his home at Recherche Bay, on 25th October, 1913 to the Hobart General Hospital where he died from diphtheria, on 27th of October, 1913.

He is buried in Cornelian Bay Cemetery, alongside his wife, Sarah Ann Smith. A ground penetrating radar device played over the grave, showed the remains of a man and a child in his grave.

Mary Ann married Henry Doherty, of Port Davey and they went to live in Strahan, Tasmania. In 1951, on a visit to her granddaughter,

Wacky, in Rosebery, she fell and broke her hip. She was taken to the Zeehan Hospital where she later died on May 2nd, 1951.

Corner Andrew and Henry streets
Strahan, Tasmania.
June, 1951
Where the story first began.

Wacky stared through the railway carriage window at the old house between the pine trees, as the train from Zeehan rocked and rattled past on its way to the Strahan Railway Station. 'Typical of this bloody government railway,' her mother Phyllis, said, as she looked over Wacky's shoulder. 'Now we have to travel all the bloody way into town, and then walk all the way back here.' Wacky smiled. It was good to be home, even if it meant putting up with her mother's nagging. She had left Granna and grandfather's house after she married her husband Charlie McDermott last year. They had shifted to Rosebery when Charlie teamed up with her uncle Arthur Doherty's timber cutting team and saw little of Granna, the woman who had brought her up as her own daughter, since then. Now the woman she loved with all her heart, had died and she and her mother had travelled to Strahan to check on her grandfather.

Her mother was right, it took almost as long for the train to travel the mile and a half from Granna's house to the station as it did to walk it. Luckily, the taxi station was just across the road, next to the Bay View Hotel and the two women walked across the graveled road to the solitary grey taxi that was parked outside the corrugated iron building.

Arriving at Granna's house, Wacky smiled to herself again. She just couldn't stop calling it that, to her, it had always been Granna's house, not grandfathers, and she supposed it always would be.

They could smell the smoke from the incinerator as they alighted from the taxi. Wacky was looking around her, nothing had changed over the past thirty years, only the buildings looked a little more dilapidated than she recalled. Her mother called, 'Come on Wacky, hurry up.' She waved her hand for her daughter to catch up. 'He's burning her things, I know he is.'

Wacky waited until the taxi drove away, and stepped across the road to catch up with her mother. She knew her grandfather, as did her mum, Harry Doherty was not one for keeping things, his motto was 'anything not of immediate use, needed to be disposed of,' and that usually meant being burned.

Harry was standing, one hand on hip, the other holding a long pole. He was stirring up the papers and other paraphernalia, as the flames licked around the pile of household goods.

He turned around, a look of surprise and 'hand in the cookie jar,' frown on his long, bewhiskered face.

'Oh,' he said. 'It's you, Phyll,' he said, acknowledging his daughter. Then his expression changed from surprise, to happy surprise, as he saw Wacky. 'Hello darling, how've you been?' Wacky walked over and gave him a big hug. She could see the tears welling in his eyes, but she knew he would never cry, this was as sad as he ever let anybody see.

'What are you doing, dad?' his daughter, Phyllis asked, and the old man turned his face back to the burning pile of furniture and papers, stoking them as he did so with the pole. 'Oh, nothing, just getting rid of things your mother kept, for no apparent reason.'

'Dad,' Phyllis' voice lifted a few octaves and the old man dropped his head, ready for the admonition, as she went on. 'Mum cared about these things, these things were part of who she was, part of our history!'

The old man shook his head, 'No history there, darlin,' just a lot of old papers.'

Harry Doherty was illiterate, and as such could see no value in the written word. To him, the personal letters and historical items were just dust collectors to be disposed of as rubbish. He began to stir the corner of the pile that had yet to catch fire and Wacky almost fainted with fright as she caught the corner of something very familiar, something she hadn't seen for a long time. There, hidden under a pile of newspapers, one corner of dark, brown wood just inches away from the hungrily licking flames, was the Ditty Box,

Granna's pride and joy, her only connection to the past, and here was her grandfather, burning it!

Ignoring her grandfather and mother's pleas, Wacky began kicking the burning paper's away from the box. She was relieved to see the flames hadn't quite reached the box, but it was obvious the whale's teeth were in the flames and lost forever. Harry had stepped around the fire, put his pole under the Ditty Box and deftly flicked it out and away from the flames, as he did, the box flew open and its contents spilled out onto the grass. The two women stared at the contents as Harry Doherty turned to go inside to put the kettle on, he just couldn't see what all the fuss was about. Wacky lifted the lid of the ditty box, its hinges now broken away from the main body of the box, revealing the two whale's teeth lying unharmed on the grass, the two scrimshawed ladies of fashion, carved so diligently by a forgotten whaleman in the middle of the Pacific Ocean all those years ago, staring up at her. She grabbed them up and held them to her chest, just as she did all those years ago when Granna told her the stories of her father, the Samoan whaling ships captain, and in that moment, she vowed to relate all of those stories she remembered, to her children in the hope one of them would finally tell the story.

Copyright Kim McDermott, 2024

More Books from Kim McDermott

Last of The Wildcats – Join three generations of prospectors as they battle hardship and the elements of Tasmania's west coast.

Where they make the Wind. – First printed as Dougherty's Way. - The story of Thomas Patrick Dougherty and the piner's of Port Davey.

Trilogy of the Sea – A trilogy of children's adventures as they battle sea monsters and wizards in the Southern Ocean.

The Legend of Timbs Reef – A Tasmanian story of greed, deceit, murder and bush justice.

www.ingramcontent.com/pod-product-compliance
Lightning Source LLC
Chambersburg PA
CBHW011147290426
44109CB00023B/2516